Business Studies

FOR

DUMMIES

A Wiley Brand

by Richard Pettinger, MBA

Business Studies For Dummies®

Published by: **John Wiley & Sons, Ltd,** The Atrium, Southern Gate, Chichester, www.wiley.com

This edition first published 2013

© 2014 John Wiley & Sons, Ltd, Chichester, West Sussex.

Registered Office

John Wiley & Sons Ltd, The Atrium, Southern Gate, Chichester, West Sussex, PO19 8SQ, United Kingdom

For general information on our other products and services, please contact our Customer Care Department within the U.S. at 877-762-2974, outside the U.S. at (001) 317-572-3993, or fax 317-572-4002. For technical support, please visit www.wiley.com/techsupport.

A catalogue record for this book is available from the British Library.

ISBN 978-1-118-34811-6 (pbk); ISBN 978-1-118-34814-7 (ebk); ISBN 978-1-118-34817-8 (ebk)

10 9 8 7 6 5 4 3

Contents at a Glance

Table of Contents

Introduction

There's never been a more important, exciting or vital time to be studying business. So much has happened in the past: achievements and successes, but also mistakes and business conduct that, excellent though it may have been then, is no longer suitable or effective. And so much is going to change in the years to come, such as increased competition in a world that's electronically charged and linked; industrial and commercial revolutions in countries such as Brazil, Russia, India and China; and the commercialisation of public services like health, education and security.

So it's clearly time to take a step back and think about just what business is, how it's conducted and how it should be conducted, and the benefits that it should be delivering for society at large, as well as for companies and organisations. And that's where *Business Studies For Dummies* comes in: it's a concise point of reference for everyone who wants to know and understand what business is and what it ought to be, and how to succeed in business now and in the future.

About This Book

This book provides the basis for acquiring and developing the substantial body of knowledge, skills and understanding that's required of anyone who comes to study business. This knowledge forms the base upon which you can build practical excellence and expertise, and relate the lessons learned to what goes on in the world.

This book is full of vital and useful information. Everything included in the book is tried and tested. Of course, I introduce organisation and management theories, and I also introduce the distinctive disciplines of business – marketing, finance, numeracy and the understanding of people and their behaviour. I concentrate on what's useful and valuable. All these aspects give you a firm foundation on which to build your professional knowledge, understanding and expertise.

I also include lots of real-world examples that I hope inspire you to understand the expertise and principles on which they're based, and learn from the failures also, so that you can make sure you never make these mistakes yourself.

I also place an emphasis on providing practical information – so you'll find lots of tips and guidance you can apply to your own career in business. Becoming fully professional and expert in business is terrifically rewarding and fulfilling, whatever sector you go on to work in.

Always put in your best effort! Remember that the best directors and managers in the world have reached their positions because of their personal and professional commitment, as well as their expertise. In addition to working very hard, they have read books like this and many others so that they know as much as they possibly can about everything to do with business.

Foolish Assumptions

In my line of work, everyone I meet has an active interest in business, companies and organisations, how they work, and what causes some of them to be profitable and effective, while others fail. In this book, therefore, I assume that you're studying business on a course, or else actively interested and/or involved in business – what it is, how it works and how it can be improved.

I assume that you need and want comprehensive basic information about every aspect of what business is and the different elements – organisation, people, marketing, sales, accounts and finance – that together make up the whole.

I also assume that, whatever your occupation, rank or level of qualification, you can get something out of this book – just a few insights, or a pearl of wisdom, or a different approach to reviewing those things with which you're familiar. As you work your way through this book, you're able to access both the whole of what business is, and also those specific parts that are of greatest value to you (feel free to browse the table of contents if you're looking for a particular topic to dive into).

Icons Used in This Book

We use icons next to blocks of text to draw your attention to particular nuggets of information throughout the book.

The bull's-eye highlights a good idea or shortcut that can save you time or trouble.

This icon draws your attention to a piece of information about business that you shouldn't forget.

This icon indicates information that can help you to avoid disasters.

The world of business is full of inspirational stories of business successes and failures, and this icon highlights them.

This icon shows vital lessons to learn, based on the experiences of others.

This icon draws your attention to the main things that you'll likely learn and apply as you study business and develop your knowledge and expertise.

Everyone in business has their own point of view on all aspects of what is good and best practice, and this icon highlights the best of these.

Beyond The Book

As you make your journey into the world of business studies, you can supplement what you discover in this book by checking out some of the bonus content available to you at Dummies.com.

You can locate the book's e-cheat sheet at www.dummies.com/cheat sheet/businessstudies. Here you can find handy hints about the importance of people in everyday business, identifying and assessing risk, and relating your studies to real-life business.

Be sure to visit the book's extras page at www.dummies.com/extras/ businessstudies for an extra Part of Tens chapter and many other interesting articles.

Where to Go from Here

The beauty of a book broken up into easily identifiable and manageable chunks is that you can start anywhere in your reading. Being new to business studies, you may want to start at the beginning and work your way through to the end. Then, later on, you can delve into the book, finding topics that are useful at different stages. A wealth of information and practical advice is waiting for you. Simply turn the page and begin!

Part I

What Is Business?

In this part . . .

✔ Get to grips with business. Identify whether studying business is for you and get advice on exactly how to go about doing this.

✔ Apply a business-like approach to all business activity in order to improve the running of your commercial, public sector or not-for-profit business.

✔ Acclimatize yourself to your business's environment by learning about the internal and external influences on your business.

✔ Optimize your business analyses skills to evaluate opportunities, constraints, drives and pressures from all parts of your business environment.

Chapter 1

Understanding Business and Business Studies

*W*elcome to the world of business and business studies!

The world of business is truly exciting. It provides everything that you need, want, consume and use in every part of your life. But the world of business can also be a scary one – times are uncertain, and this uncertainty is causing great changes in how companies and organisations conduct their affairs, how people organise their working and domestic lives, and how essential services (such as housing, energy and transport) are provided, delivered and paid for.

So, people knowing as much as possible about business is vital – how business is organised and structured, and how it goes about delivering what it's supposed to produce.

That's where you come in! Whether you're studying business in order to get qualifications, or whether you're doing so purely out of interest, you will acquire much greater knowledge, insight, understanding – and, ultimately, expertise – in everything to do with business and how business is conducted by reading this book!

In this chapter, I start you off on your business studies path by laying down the basics of this field of study, from defining business and understanding why people study it and how, to looking at the role of businesses, risks, the business environment, beneficiaries and stakeholders and, finally, the pressures that businesses face.

Defining Business

Business students must know the answers to two key questions:

- ✓ **What is *business*?** Answer: the provision of products and services for consumption, in return for an agreed-upon price, charge or fee, or for having paid taxes and charges at some point (usually for public services – this also applies to direct debit payments for electricity, gas and water).

- ✓ **What is *a* business?** Answer: an entity – an organisation – that conducts a particular set of activities, the purpose of which is to provide something – products, services or both – that's of value to all or part of the community.

Ultimately, think of all organisations as businesses, whether they work on purely commercial lines, or whether they're government departments, public service providers or charities. This makes studying business much more straightforward. Besides, all public service and charitable organisations are now run very much on 'business lines', with the kinds of pressures on their resources that have always occurred in commercial activities.

Why Study Business?

Business provides a fundamental structure for every part of society, affecting every walk of life and part of life. Most of what you do relates to businesses of one sort or another.

Obviously, businesses provide work, but they also provide plenty of other things that people need, such as holidays, cars, clothes, food and furniture. If you need healthcare, or want an education, or even water, gas or electricity, then schools and hospitals and the utility companies – *businesses* by any other name – exist to provide these services. And, of course, you expect businesses to be business-like – professional and expert. For example, you want healthcare or education to be delivered by experts, not just by people who fancy the job.

So you have an immediate rationale for studying business – without business, you'd have a hugely different life. People depend on businesses of all kinds for every part of their daily lives. Business delivers work, income, energy, transport, communications, food and drink, leisure activities and more. Organisations run along business lines deliver healthcare, education, security and defence. So business really is at the core of everything people do and are.

You study business, then, because you need to understand the following:

✔ How everything about the world that you live in operates and the position business has in making sure that the world works as well as possible

✔ How organisations can be improved for the benefit of everyone, and how those improvements can best be made

✔ Whether people are getting the best possible services from public businesses like utility companies, and the best possible value from the taxes and charges that they pay to support the public businesses

You also study business because businesses directly affect your quality of life and your ability to do the things that you need and want to do. For example, think of your reaction

✔ To increases in car parking charges.

✔ When you read of waste in government circles – for example, when it overspends by £40 billion on defence contracts, or writes off £14 billion on computer projects for the UK National Health Service (NHS).

Happy? No! It is, after all, your money that's been increased or written off, so you have a vested interest in how businesses operate.

Business studies is about:

✔ Looking after money

✔ Making progress as an individual and for everyone

✔ Organisations, and creating the conditions in which you can be business-like

✔ People – in their roles as workers, customers and clients, and as they go about their daily lives

✔ Products, services and service

✔ Resources and their usage

✔ The law

Knowing How to Study Business

If you want to study medicine, you go to medical school. And so the superficial answer to the question 'How to study business?' is 'Go to business school.'

Well, business school can teach you a lot, but to really find out about business, you need to take a wider view. Business is all-pervasive (much more so than medicine, which, although critical, is only one part of life and, therefore, only one part of business life). You observe business all the time, and so you have the opportunity to make up your own mind and begin to form your own opinions, whether you go to business school or not. And as with the study of medicine, studying in a school, college or university isn't enough! How you *apply* your knowledge and, therefore, build your expertise, is crucial.

Tom Peters, one of the great business gurus, said in a televised lecture on Channel 4:

> *'The number of business school graduates has been rising at exactly the same time that the country's real-world share of goods and services has been falling. So something is going wrong at business school. You need practical experience as well as theoretical knowledge, and the two have to go together.'*

Thinking for yourself

You need to study and observe how organisations conduct themselves. In doing so, you form your own opinions that you apply in all your business dealings. So, you ask:

- ✔ Why is company X so successful, but company Y isn't?
- ✔ Why do I always use one supermarket but not the others?
- ✔ Why do I like (or hate) working here?

. . . and so on. In this way, you begin to develop an enquiring mind. You build knowledge and understanding of your own behaviour, attitudes, values, prejudices and preconceptions that you have about businesses overall, how they conduct themselves and what you expect from them. And you then use this knowledge, understanding and insight to form the basis of your own expertise.

Putting theory into practice

The study of business is full of theories – this book contains plenty of theories – and the test of theories is what they contribute to practice.

Heathrow Terminal 5 in practice

When Heathrow Airport's Terminal 5 opened in 2007, it was equipped with technology that could handle 250,000 passengers and one million pieces of luggage per day (in theory). Nothing could go wrong (in theory). In practice, the outcome has been different. The technology can't handle what actually happens:

✔ People arrive in parties and groups, and then the system faces a huge demand.

✔ Quiet periods occur.

✔ Luggage is loaded and unloaded according to what the actual demands are.

✔ Some planes are late, others are early and others still are diverted or re-routed.

✔ Some passengers have connections to and from the airport.

Under perfect conditions, everything was fine with the systems; in practice, it wasn't. And effective practice is what lies at the core of all successful business. This is the same for all businesses – everything you try to implement has to work in as many sets of practical circumstances as possible.

When it comes to theories, you need to bear in mind two key points:

✔ **A theory doesn't work in every single set of circumstances.** If something works well in most sets of circumstances, you've a clear guide, of course. However, always be aware that a theory may not work, or work fully, all the time.

✔ **If something isn't working, you should probably change the theory, not the practice.** For example, if you've bet everything on an Internet marketing campaign for your new product because you can theoretically reach half the world's population, and yet the campaign has no effect on sales, you should probably try (or at least consider) something else. After all, you don't want to reach half the world's population; you want to reach that (probably tiny) part of the world's population that will buy and consume your products.

Theory never makes life predictable or certain. People have never before had greater access to information and data, and so, theoretically, creating business and businesses with a great deal more certainty of success than in previous times should be possible. But the international, economic, political, financial and business crises of the early part of the 21st century show clearly that success isn't assured, whatever the availability of data.

When studying business – theory and practice – remember that business is:

✔ A huge and complex subject, consisting of many different subjects and facets, and with an awful lot of information on which to base your knowledge and understanding

✔ Ever-changing, as people come up with new ideas and inventions, and new ways of doing things

✔ Unpredictable – you can't always state that something in business is going to work perfectly in all circumstances

✔ Bounded by people and how they behave, and needs to recognise that their behaviour (collective and individual) changes according to whether they're being customers, staff, tradespeople, managers, car drivers, public transport passengers or clients of healthcare and other public services

Keep these four bullet points in mind when reading all the books, papers, news media, journals and website articles that come your way. And if you're studying at business school, approach the syllabus armed with this knowledge and it will help you get the most from your education.

Considering the Role of Business

To study business, you have to form your own opinion of what business and businesses are for. In the earlier section 'Why Study Business?', I indicate just how big a part of daily life businesses are. You can split their role into two key areas: economic and social.

Seeing the economic side of business

The economic role of business and businesses reflects the fact that everything that people do has a cost, price or value. However, these economic aspects sit in a wider context:

✔ **Costs:** The costs incurred relate to everything that any business has to pay in order to be able to operate. Costs exist to the environment in terms of energy and other resources used and consumed. *Opportunity costs* also come into play – if you choose to do one thing, you forego the opportunity to do something else (at the same time at least). Finally, a business has direct or indirect costs to do with waste and effluent management and disposal, a necessary consequence of being in business.

✔ **Prices and charges:** Companies and organisations place prices and charges on all goods and services, and these prices reflect the value (see the following bullet point) that they're deemed to carry. Some companies and organisations are able to charge high prices because of the value that they deliver; others charge high prices because they have captive markets. Customers have to pay for most products and services at the point of order or delivery, but some (especially those provided by public services) are free at the point of order or delivery. (These kinds of products or services are usually paid for through taxation.)

✔ **Value:** A reflection of the utility that particular products and services have. Note the following two extremes:

- If something has no usefulness or value at all, there won't be a price low enough that you can sell it for.

- Nothing is absolutely perfect, which means that, ultimately, everything has its price – a price above which people aren't willing to pay.

The following examples are worth noting in support of understanding the economic point of view:

✔ A huge demand for housing – bought and rented – exists in the UK at present, but not at the prices, charges and rents currently on offer.

✔ The success of Ryanair and easyJet proved that huge demand (and, therefore, value) exists for air travel, but not at the prices that were being charged before these companies started up.

Understanding the social perspective

The economic perspective that I explain in the previous section also indicates the social side to business. In particular, the prices paid and the value ascribed to business, products and services are matters of collective and individual (that is, social) choice. No linear or one-dimensional economic rule or theory exists that states 'Because product X or service Y is only price £Z, I will buy it', and works in every set of circumstances.

Prices charged and paid also reflect personal and collective value. For example:

✔ If you're offered a Rolls-Royce for £3,000, you'll probably turn it down because you think something must be wrong with it (a social, not economic judgement).

✔ If a company is offering consultancy services for £10,000 a day, clients have absolute faith (a social judgement) that the services are excellent because of the high prices charged (a social judgement). If the services were no good, the consultancy couldn't charge these prices (also a social judgement).

Council taxes

Not long ago, one of the larger UK local government authorities paid a consultancy firm £2.5 million. The local government authority had decided that it needed to restructure itself as an organisation and also the ways in which it delivered its services. When the news broke of this exercise and the huge fees attached, a public outcry occurred. The local government authority defended its position by stating that because it was responsible for 2.5 million people, the cost was only £1 per person.

And the lesson? The economic is nearly always justified by the social. You can make up your own mind whether the consultancy was genuine value for money!

Understanding Business Risks

Nothing in business is certain, and risk exists when you can't know everything about a situation. In business, things go wrong:

✔ You lose money.

✔ Your products, services and customer service lose their competitive edge.

✔ Your technology crashes.

✔ You're attacked and/or defrauded.

✔ Your costs rise and/or your income falls.

The above are all risks that businesses face. Businesses have to recognise the risks and be prepared to deal with them.

When it comes to identifying risks, businesses need to understand:

✔ The ins and outs of the business

  • The company's products and services, the service that's delivered and the risks of product and service faults and shortcomings

  • How reliable their suppliers and supplies are, and the risks of the loss of a key supplier or supply

  • The loyalty of customers, and the risks of losing a particular customer base or group

  • The loyalty, expertise and conduct of staff and their collective and individual attitudes, values and behaviour, and the risks to your performance of the loss of key staff or the inability to source good staff for the future

✔ What can possibly go wrong and why, and what the possible consequences are

✔ Some of the behavioural aspects of risk, including complacency, denial and an unwillingness to address the less certain parts of business activities

When a business is aware of a risk, it can mitigate the risk by taking steps to ensure that the bad things don't happen or, if they do, that plans are in place to deal with consequences.

Two areas of business in particular require risk management:

✔ **Accidents at work:** Accident prevention is often common sense – you need to keep the workplace clean and tidy, and train people to use equipment correctly. If you do this, you're certain to cut out about 90 per cent of the accidents that can potentially happen at work.

✔ **Crime:** You need to be aware of the crimes that can occur at work, including:

- Financial crimes, such as fraud, theft and cheating

- Vandalism, including sabotage of production equipment and information technology

- Violence, especially of staff toward each other

- Bullying, victimisation, discrimination and harassment

- Corporate crime, including insider dealing in shares and commodities

- Infiltrating the security of databases and information systems for criminal gain

- Drug dealing, and drug and alcohol misuse

Risk management can be a negative approach to understanding business – you're always looking out for things that can conceivably go wrong. Nevertheless, if you study business from this point of view, you get an excellent insight into how companies and organisations behave, and how they should behave. You also take a realistic view at all times, giving yourself the discipline of looking at all the constraints, as well as the opportunities.

Situating the Business in Its Environment

The *business environment* is the part of the world in which business takes place. If you're to understand business, you have to recognise that a business doesn't operate in isolation. Instead, business activities are set in the context of how things are in the world, the state of markets, the ability and willingness of customers to spend money on products and services, and the wider state of local, national and international economies (turn to Chapter 2 for more on external influences).

All businesses have to be capable of operating successfully and profitably within their environment. Your knowledge of the environment – its pressures and opportunities – is absolutely critical.

You get your immediate knowledge of the business environment from news and current affairs media, company and organisation websites, and knowing about the nature of activities going on and the pressures being faced.

Thinking about Beneficiaries and Stakeholders

The *beneficiaries* of a business are those people for whom the business is especially important, or for whom the business was constituted. Table 1-1 outlines types of business and their beneficiaries.

Table 1-1	Business Beneficiaries
Type of Business	**Beneficiaries**
Business organisations	Shareholders, staff, customers and clients
Utilities, including gas, electricity, water, transport, post and tele-communications organisations	Society at large – everyone needs the services provided
Public service organisations (for example, health, education, social care and welfare)	Client groups needing the particular service
Cooperatives	Staff, customers and clients
Convenience organisations (for example, food stores, libraries, local amenities and sports centres)	Those who find the organisation convenient for whatever reason
Mutual benefit associations (including trade unions, churches, political parties, clubs and also cooperatives as above)	Members
Regulatory bodies constituted by government	Society at large – these bodies ensure that the sectors they regulate conduct themselves to legal and ethical standards
Government at all levels	Society at large – in the provision of essential services, for example health and education; also infrastructure, security, law and enforcement

In addition to beneficiaries, businesses have *stakeholders*: people who have an interest in the business.

Look at stakeholders from the point of view of:

- ✔ Who benefits from the business?
- ✔ Who takes advantage of the business?
- ✔ Who's disadvantaged by the business?

Identify the stakeholders involved as follows:

- ✔ **Staff:** They depend on the organisation for salaries, wages and security.
- ✔ **Customers and clients:** They depend on the organisation for products, services and service.
- ✔ **Suppliers:** They depend on the organisation for their own regularity and assuredness of business.
- ✔ **The media:** They have a legitimate interest in covering every aspect of business – successes, failures and scandals.
- ✔ **The community at large:** They're affected by the contribution that business and businesses make.
- ✔ **Legal and regulatory authorities:** Their job is to make sure that work is carried out to the highest possible standards.
- ✔ **Shareholders:** If the business is a public company, shareholders (or stockholders) are the investors who may expect a financial return on their investment.

When you look at business in this way, you get a clear idea of who the companies and organisations are supposed to exist for and who they actually do exist for.

Of course, who businesses are supposed to exist for and who they do exist for ought to be the same! Unfortunately, that isn't the case in practice:

- ✔ Over the period 2010–2012 in the UK, the average salary of commercial company directors rose by 49 per cent; at the same time, the average wage of middle and junior management, supervisors and operational staff rose by 6 per cent.
- ✔ The directors of Lloyd's Banking Group and RBS received average bonuses in 2013 of £330,000, despite the fact that the performance of both organisations continued to decline.

When assessing the actual beneficiaries and stakeholders of business, take the broadest possible view.

Recognising Present Business Pressures

No introduction to business is complete without understanding the pressures that the business is facing at the moment and is likely to have to face in the future. Clearly, pressures and their effects vary among organisations and business sectors. However, some common pressures exist that every business is certain to face at one point or another:

- **Shortage of money and declining revenues:** Shortage of money is invariably the result of not having enough capital to support present and future developments. Declining takings and revenues are caused by falling sales. Whatever the cause, the critical pressure is that all companies and organisations have to know the worst set of circumstances in which they can possibly survive, and what actions they need to take in order to survive.

- **Rising costs, especially those that the business can't control:** These costs include, above all, energy, fuel, transport and waste, effluent management and taxes.

- **Declining business volumes:** Customers and clients seek ever-greater value for their money and change their spending habits in response to their own environmental pressures.

- **Increased competition:** The overall expansion and globalisation of trade and trading practices means that other companies and organisations have easier access to markets, customers and clients.

- **Making the most of your staff:** This pressure arises from the fact that people and wages are the largest single expense that business has to carry. The consequence is that in many cases everyone is going to be asked to do more and more in return for their wages and salaries.

- Additionally, in uncertain times, upward pressures exist on wages and salaries from staff. This is because employees would rather have a big pay increase now than the same rise phased in over two or three years. This, in turn, is because they want to secure their own immediate future and because the company for which they work may not exist in two or three years.

- **Declining property values:** The pressure that arises from declining property values means that premises have to be seen by managers primarily as a place to do work rather than an asset that has value in itself.

- **Competition for critical supplies and resources:** The pressure to secure all supplies at a cost and price that's more or less assured, at least for the immediate future.

> ✔ **Outsourcing:** The pressure to outsource comes from shareholders and backers above all. The advantage of outsourcing is that you know how much a certain service or activity is going to cost you, and so can plan with a degree of certainty.

 I return to outsourcing at regular intervals throughout the book. (Turn to Chapter 5 especially for different aspects of outsourcing.) Outsourcing is a major aspect of current business practice, and if carried out with integrity, it makes a great and enduring contribution to business viability.

Chapter 2

Identifying the Internal and External Influences on Business

In This Chapter

▶ Recognising internal influences on your business

▶ Preparing for external influences

*Y*ou can sum up what affects business with a few words from the Greek philosopher Heraclitus: 'Change is the only constant.' Directors and top managers come and go. Businesses start, grow and flourish (and sometimes collapse and die). New products and services come onto the market; old ones fail and fall by the wayside. Customer behaviour and demands evolve.

Some of these changes are internal; others are external. But businesses have to be capable of accommodating them all. Some changes you influence and control, while with others you've little, if any, control. Others still are evolving all the time – your ethics and standards, and your managerial expertise. Whichever they are, you just have to work with them and accept the constraints.

In this chapter, I walk you through the major internal and external influences that your business faces.

Considering Internal Influences: An Inside Job

Internal influences on a business come from within the organisation. These influences include the directors and top managers, the technology you use and the expertise of your staff, the organisation's ethics and employees' work ethic, the factors driving and pressuring your business, and crises and emergencies caused by the business itself. In this section, I cover each of these categories of internal influence.

Directors and top managers

The directors and top managers are the ones leading the business – they're the ones telling people what to do. So, the key questions are:

✔ What are they telling their people to do and why?

✔ What are the intended outcomes and results that the top managers have to deliver?

✔ What's supposed to happen next and why, and how does this serve the interests of the whole business?

Seems pretty simple and straightforward, doesn't it? But an awful lot can and does go wrong if directors and top managers exert their influence in the wrong way or if their judgements are faulty.

Here are some examples of situations in which top managers led their companies astray:

✔ The top managers of Lehmann Brothers failed to recognise the pressures in the financial services sector, and then simply assumed that they were too big to fail.

✔ The top managers of Comet, the UK white goods retailer, failed to respond to online competition and alternatives provided by other electrical goods providers, and assumed that they were too much of a national establishment to fail.

✔ The top managers of HMV assumed that customers would continue to use them, despite online competition for music and video products from Amazon.com and YouTube.

Because of the influence that directors and top managers wield, they need the fullest possible understanding of the whole business environment so that they can make accurate and informed judgements in support of the entire organisation.

Technology and expertise

The technology that an organisation uses and the expertise it has available are critical to the organisation's success and effectiveness. All business is driven by the available technology and expertise, but that technology and expertise has to be harnessed profitably and effectively. You can think of the ways in which an organisation commissions, designs, implements and integrates technology with expertise as the organisation's engine.

Technology is only as good as the people who use it. It doesn't replace human beings, nor does it always faithfully execute what humans want it to do. Technology only does as it's told.

When they're fully integrated, technology and expertise revolutionise individual activities as well as the overall structure of the business. Here are a few examples of ways in which organisations have used technology and expertise effectively:

- ✔ Primark, the good-value clothing retailer, was able to revolutionise how it got high-fashion clothing into its stores in short periods of time. The company developed a scanner that scanned the designs of high-fashion clothes from photographs and videos taken at fashion shows. The scans were accurate, which meant that instead of waiting for designs to be released, the company could commission its own versions of those runway designs the minute the models strutted out onto the catwalk.

- ✔ Harvard University has a huge online presence. Since 2011, anyone anywhere in the world has been able to study at Harvard online, provided that they meet specific admissions criteria. Today Harvard has more online students than they have had on-campus students throughout their entire history.

- ✔ Apple uses technology-driven social media and viral marketing to gain an identity for each of its new products in advance of its launch. Doing so has meant that, for example, by the time the iPhone 4 and iPhone 5 came to market, they were already highly desired and sought-after products.

As an organisation, you need to recognise where technology and expertise *are* serving and complementing each other, and where they *should be* serving and complementing each other. In particular:

- ✔ Pay attention to where and how you can develop and transform all organisational activities by harmonising the capabilities and potential of technology with your own business expertise.

- ✔ Regularly explore and evaluate the technology that is available, and examine it for its actual and potential benefits.

As with all influences on your organisation, you want as much stability as possible. Occasionally, technology and expertise have to be replaced. Make sure that when you replace technology or expertise, you do so for carefully evaluated or operational reasons. Do as much pre-planning as possible so that you don't disrupt the environment and those who work there. Also, be sure to communicate to employees why the shift in technology or expertise is happening, in order to get their buy-in and support – people are a lot more likely to get behind a change if they see the benefits it brings.

Ethics and the work ethic

An organisation's ethics and the work ethic of its employees are major internal influences on the business. Although they're related, I cover the two issues one at a time.

An organisation's ethics

Given all the stories in the news about corruption in business, it's no wonder that some people don't believe they can have ethics and be in business! Here are just a few examples from recent years that understandably reinforce this pessimistic outlook:

✔ Goldman Sachs paid out over £6 billion in staff bonuses the year before the company collapsed with debts of £4 billion.

✔ RBS continued to pay record staff bonuses even though the company had lost £4.4 billion.

✔ Three MPs were jailed in the period 2009–12 for presenting fraudulent expenses claims to Parliament.

✔ Microsoft agreed to a $10 million one-off charge against the European Union for engaging in anti-competitive practices.

Here's what all these examples (and many more like them) have in common: they're all failures. When you're thinking about business and ethics, and whether you think that the two can mix, ask yourself the following questions:

✔ Would you prefer to do business with organisations that are honest and wholesome or organisations that are dishonest and unfit?

✔ Would you prefer to work for a company that respects and values you or one that disrespects and undervalues you?

The answer is clear – just as you would prefer to do business with (and work for) honest, wholesome, ethical organisations, customers do too. Being ethical isn't always so simple, however. Sometimes, complicated decisions have to be made and the options and answers aren't so black and white. However, the questions above highlight the importance of ethics in business. They also give you a starting point for understanding them better.

Provided your overall business is sound, if your company has ethical standards it abides by then you're much less likely to have organisational, behavioural and operational problems. If the organisational structures and collective and individual behaviour have a fundamental honesty, then problems and issues get raised early and dealt with quickly and openly.

Just as you can't be 'a little bit pregnant', you can't be 'a little bit honest'. You *are* honest or you aren't. If you can't tell the whole truth, at least don't tell lies.

Collective and individual work ethic

The overall ethics of an organisation provide the basis for the collective and individual work ethic. The work ethic reflects the standards of conduct, behaviour and performance that individuals set for themselves and that organisations establish overall.

Businesses have to establish their own code of ethics. Codes of ethics state clearly how people are required to behave, and what the business will and will not tolerate.

Be sure to include the following in your code of ethics:

✔ How people must conduct themselves in all their dealings with customers, suppliers, the public and each other

✔ How people must go about their work and achieve their performance targets and objectives

✔ How the business addresses issues such as bullying, victimisation and discrimination

✔ How the business tackles all forms of dishonesty when they become known and apparent

Top and senior management set the overall standards, and they're enforced throughout the organisation. You can't have double or multiple standards. Everyone has to know what's right and wrong. They need to know how the organisation expects (and demands) that its people conduct themselves.

Fixing the world, one label at a time

Going about his weekly shopping, an employee of the Colman's mustard factory in Norwich, UK, was horrified to find a batch of his company's own products stacked on the shelves – with the labels badly stuck on. Some of the labels were askew, others had been crunched up and weren't quite legible.

So the Colman's employee bought all the products off the supermarket shelf and took them back to the factory, where he told the factory manager what he had done. The factory manager thanked him for his efforts – and reimbursed the employee for the money he had spent.

The employee's commitment to his company and his own high standards meant he couldn't bear to see its products being so badly presented. Colman's commitment to its own absolute standards meant that when the employee solved the problem, the company supported him fully.

Drives and pressures

Drives and pressures relate to nearly every aspect of business activity: product and service delivery, customer service, quality and quantity of activities, and the use of resources. Each organisation has its own specific drives and pressures, but every organisation is sure to face drives and pressures surrounding the following:

- ✔ **Cost effectiveness:** Working to the financial standards set by top and senior management.

- ✔ **Health and safety (not only of the workplace itself, but of staff, products, services and activities):** Ensuring that everything is as safe and healthy as possible, and that product and service faults are kept to an absolute minimum and rectified as soon as they become known.

- ✔ **Maximising resources and minimising waste:** Using finance and resources so that as little is wasted as possible.

- ✔ **Resource effectiveness:** Using staff, expertise, technology and raw materials in ways that support the business activities to best advantage.

- ✔ **Securing the distribution effort (including web services, as well as physical transport and the provision of outlets for products and services):** Ensuring that all forms of delivery are reliable and conform to the company's own stated standards.

- ✔ **Securing the supply side (including the supply of technology, expertise and energy, as well as the inputs for products and services):** Ensuring that everything is available as and when the company's operations demand.

- ✔ **Style and effectiveness of leadership, management and supervision:** Ensuring that the chosen leadership and management style works effectively in terms of staff, company operations, and financial needs and wants.

The problems that arise from all these drives and pressures vary from one organisation to the next. But in order for your organisation to become and remain effective, you have to identify, understand and tackle the drives and pressures that are unique to your organisation. To work out the drives and pressures, ask the following questions:

- ✔ How often are there product recalls or service complaints? How are these issues resolved? What are the consequences for the company and its reputation?

- ✔ How much waste is generated by product and service activities? What, if anything, can be done about this waste? How much waste is generated by laziness and sloppiness, such as leaving the lights on?

✔ How much waste is generated by bad supplier management, leading to overstocking or to production being halted while you wait for supplies? What, if anything, can be done about this problem?

✔ How much time is spent on needless staff disputes resulting from bad or inappropriate leadership? How much do these kinds of disputes cost?

Addressing each of these questions in detail gives you a starting point for working out where the business can make improvements in activities and performance, whatever pressures are present.

Crises and emergencies

Uncertainty (like the kind that can result from not evolving – see the nearby sidebar 'Give 'em what they want') can quickly change to a full-blown business crisis and emergency if not tackled or if the effects of uncertainty aren't addressed and managed. The result? Brand-new crises, like the following:

✔ Crises of confidence on the part of investors, staff and customers

✔ Suppliers requiring payments to be made upfront

✔ Wider economic crises as people rein in their spending habits

---

Give 'em what they want

Organisations have to progress and advance over time. If you stop moving, you become stagnant. Here are just some of the ways that people expect your organisation to evolve:

✔ Staff expect increased wages, salaries and standards of living. They also expect to be given new opportunities, challenges and promotions.

✔ Customers and clients expect a greater range and better quality of products and services.

✔ Suppliers expect as much assurance as possible that they're going to be able to profit from steady and known volumes of business and be able to develop their business with you.

✔ Financial backers expect assured and, ideally, improving levels of return on their investment.

Remember: If you're not progressing as an organisation, it leads to anxiety and worry. Staff become anxious about their jobs, customers rein in their spending habits, suppliers look elsewhere for steady and assured business, and financial backers look to speed up their returns or cancel their investments. Uncertainty is a major drive and pressure with which all organisations have to be able to cope.

If you're fully knowledgeable about your business environment (the markets, and trading and operating conditions), you should be able to see the possibility of crises and emergencies on the horizon. You should be able to identify where they may come from and then take steps to keep their impact to a minimum or prevent them altogether.

The biggest causes of crises and emergencies – indeed, the biggest sources of risk for any organisation – are the following:

- ✔ Not quite getting around to doing things
- ✔ Not being bothered about doing things
- ✔ Avoiding things because you don't like to do them
- ✔ Refusing to believe the evidence before your own eyes when faced with problems
- ✔ Complacency

Seldom do you find these issues in a risk management plan, but they're pervasive in every aspect of human activity.

Remember the story of the *Titanic* – the ship that supposedly couldn't sink? All the factors I mention in this section were present aboard that ship. Nobody got around to recognising the conditions under which the ship could, and would, sink. People just accepted as fact the idea that the ship was unsinkable, so a collective complacency fell into place. Nobody wanted to address the possibility that the *Titanic* could sink, so nobody did. The rest is history: the ship came across the wrong set of conditions, in the wrong place, at the wrong time – and it sank! If your organisation becomes complacent, you may face a similar fate.

Exploring External Influences: Looking Beyond Your Walls

The internal influences on your organisation are tough enough to recognise, address and manage, but the external influences are even tougher. Why? Because you've little or no control over them. At least you can get your arms around the internal pressures on your organisation – for example, you can establish a code of ethics or plan for potential emergencies. But with external influences, you can end up feeling like you're being buffeted about like a toy boat in the ocean.

Here's the good news: even though you may have little or no control over the external influences on your organisation, you do have control over how you respond to them. You can maintain and develop confidence in your business through marketing, building relationships and delivering excellent products or services.

The main external influences any organisation faces are trade and the trading environment, and environmental issues. In this section, I tackle both of these big topics so you can start looking at how they influence your organisation and how you can respond in turn.

Trade and the trading environment

The *trading environment* consists of everything that affects your ability to deliver enough products and services to be profitable. Of particular importance are the following:

- ✔ Globalisation
- ✔ Competition and collaboration
- ✔ Trading conditions
- ✔ Local, national and international markets

The state of the trading environment as a whole, and the parts of the trading environment that concern your particular market and customers, are critically important external influences. You have to know all those factors that are driving and restraining business activities, and how they're affecting your part of the world in particular. You have to recognise the critical factors of the availability of finance, the propensity of consumers to spend and the volumes of business necessary to ensure that the business survives and prospers. And you have to be able to relate these factors to the trading conditions that exist.

Globalisation

The whole trading environment has been, and continues to be, revolutionised by the globalisation of business. Opportunities exist all over the world for organisations. And competitive pressures come from every corner of the world, in every market, sector and location.

If you don't conduct business as effectively as possible, another organisation will be ready to take your place. In addition, customers today don't just look to domestic markets and suppliers for excellent products and services – if they can't find what they want at home, they look online. The World Wide Web has put the world at customers' fingertips.

BMW

For many years, BMW remained viable only because of the volumes of business generated by its motorcycle and aero engine sales. They did so not because BMW couldn't sell cars – cars were being snapped up as fast as they came off the production line. However, the sheer volume of cars being sold wasn't enough to support the overall profitability of the company. It wasn't until BMW diversified into smaller cars that it was able to make the car part of the business viable. Luxury car sales didn't deliver the volumes necessary to support the cost base that a car manufacturer has to carry. In spite of the successes, BMW needed the small car business to ensure its enduring viability.

However buoyant the trading environment, and however well received your goods and services may be, you must be able to produce and deliver in the volumes necessary for your company, as well as the markets. You may need to diversify and develop even when you're already successful.

People have been trading around the world for hundreds of years. But years ago, international trade was not only slow but also restricted by what could be moved around by land and sea. The Japanese manufacturing revolution of the 1960s and 1970s should have been the early warning that woke the world up to the possibility that they could lose their markets to newcomers. This possibility was reinforced by the services revolutions of the 1980s and 1990s, especially with the arrival of McDonald's and Starbucks. Today, driven by a combination of Internet presence, e-commerce and mobile technology, anything can be bought and sold from anywhere. Companies that don't recognise this fact are up against those that do. So, your organisation must recognise where competitive pressures come from – and where they can conceivably come from in the future.

Competition and collaboration

A key part of the trading environment is the extent and nature of the competition that exists within it. Competition exists on several levels:

- **Macro competition:** Competition that exists among the major companies in a given market. For example, McDonald's competes with Burger King and KFC, and Boeing competes with Airbus.

- **Local competition:** Competition that exists among specific branches of large providers, and with any local or independent companies, organisations or traders. For example, individual McDonald's restaurants within a city may compete with each other, and they may also compete with pizza houses, cafés, pubs and sandwich bars.

- **Online competition:** Competition that exists between a retail outlet and an online storefront, or between two online storefronts. E-commerce is driven by convenience (you don't even have to leave your office or home to shop). The main points of competition are quality of service and security of financial transactions.

One bad apple

A party of school teachers was visiting a large fruit farm in Kent in southeast England. For over a hundred years, this fruit farm had prospered, selling its produce to all the local markets and shops in the region and becoming a preferred supplier of two of the larger supermarket chains.

The farm manager was particularly pleased with the quality of the product and the volume of business done, and he announced to the party that he had plans to expand. A member of the party piped up: 'What happens if the supermarkets cancel their contracts with you?'

The farm manager said: 'This can never happen. We're right on the doorstep. Anyone else would have to come in from elsewhere.'

Two years later, the farm had to close. Its contracts with the supermarkets in the region had been cancelled, and they were replaced by (perceived) better-quality products at lower prices coming from the European mainland.

The lesson? Never ever think 'This can never happen'! No matter how good you are (or think you are), you can bet the competition is waiting to snap up your customers. And if you have a profitable market, others always look for a way in so that they too can profit.

Sometimes no direct competition exists, but a viable and recognised alternative does. For example, Ryanair competes directly with no other airlines and on few routes; its strength is that it provides an alternative (for example, instead of flying from Heathrow to Barcelona Reus, it flies from Stansted to Gerona) that is made attractive by its unique selling proposition (its low fares).

You also have to look at competition from the point of view of the customer's spending power and/or propensity to spend. So, for example, if a customer has £10 in her pocket, she can have a meal out and walk home or skip the meal and take a taxi home (with a growling stomach). The taxi and the food outlet are in competition for that customer's money. Similarly, if a customer has £10,000 to spend, she can spend it on a new car, substantial home improvements or a luxury holiday. In this context, the car, home improvement and luxury holiday companies are all in competition for that £10,000.

As you can see, competition isn't as straightforward as it appears at first, and is made even more complex by the areas where companies and organisations operating in the same market agree *not* to compete. So, they collaborate! For example:

  ✔ Petrol retailers agree to charge the same price (or more or less the same price) in a particular locality.

- Burger bars agree not to sell fish, if fish and chip shops agree not to sell burgers.

- Builders agree not to tender for work in one area, if others agree not to tender in their areas.

Trading conditions

Trading conditions are a combination of the market and financial pressures, opportunities and constraints under which you have to work and be effective in business. They exist in every location and market sector, and you need to know and understand what they are, no matter which sector you're working in. Trading conditions are bounded and influenced by the amount of money that's available in particular markets and locations, along with people's propensity to spend. These facts apply across all sectors and aren't just related to consumer behaviour.

For example, if spending on major capital projects *increases*, jobs are created, so people typically have a greater propensity to spend. In addition, some of this money goes to businesses working on those projects, which, in turn, leads to businesses having money that they can spend themselves. On the other hand, if spending on capital projects *decreases*, less money is available for fewer activities. In times of extreme difficulty, business activities reduce and companies shut down. The result: fewer companies exist to compete for a declining or reduced market.

You need also to understand the effects of the law and consumer behaviour on trading conditions and business activities.

The law

All trading conditions are bound by laws. Organisations must be aware of these laws and work within their constraints. For example, you need to know and understand the following:

- Advertising and marketing laws and regulations

- Company and organisation law

- Employment law

- Internet usage regulations

- Product and service regulations

- Taxation and financial laws and regulations

Specifically, you need to know how these laws affect your sector, and how you need to respond to your obligations and duties.

If you break or ignore the law, count on being held responsible sooner or later.

Here are some examples of companies that eventually had to face the music:

✔ In 2012, Glasgow Rangers FC called in administrators as the result of debts that had accrued. These debts were primarily taxes that should have been paid over the previous ten years.

✔ In 2011, Microsoft settled a patent case relating to the possible plagiarism and adaptation of the search capacity of other companies; the case dragged on for 11 years before it was finally settled.

✔ In 2011, NewsCorp was forced to close *News of the World* following allegations of phone hacking and irregular payments for stories. To date, the legal issues around the story have run on for over seven years, and are likely to go on for much longer before everything is settled.

If you get involved in legal proceedings for any reason, the process takes a long time. You'll also find it really expensive in terms of costs, energy and damage to reputation. So you're always better off staying out of legal trouble in the first place. Take the time to find out the laws and regulations that apply to your company, and then follow them closely.

Customer behaviour

Customer behaviour is a major influence on trading conditions, and trading conditions are a major influence on customer behaviour. You need to understand how your customers behave, because they have a huge influence on your business. So, you need to know and understand the following:

✔ **Customer attitudes:** By 'attitudes' I'm referring to how much money customers have and where your particular line of business exists in their order of priorities.

✔ **Customer confidence:** This confidence affects the wider environment, as well as the trading conditions of particular sectors.

In many cases, confidence in one sector feeds confidence in others. For example, a large sales volume of holidays benefits the food and drink industry as well. Similarly, activity in the furniture sector likely benefits the painting and decorating industry as well.

Customer behaviour is managed and influenced by things like government policy, using interest rates and the availability of credit and loans to boost or reduce spending. Above all, however, customer behaviour is founded on collective and individual attitudes, behaviours and perceptions about how much money customers have, how much of it they think they should be spending and what they should be spending it on.

These same rules apply to businesses in their role as customers and consumers. If organisations believe that hard times are on the horizon, they hold off on building new warehouses, implementing new technology and opening new ventures until they're confident that they can sustain and gain the returns they seek.

Local, national and international markets

Organisations are always seeking ways of improving – if they aren't, they can easily be replaced by the competition! Obviously, they try to improve everything they can internally. And as they grow and become successful, they also seek new markets for their products and services away from what they're familiar with.

If you want your business to grow, you have to understand your local markets, as well as the national and international markets that you may want to enter. In particular, you need to know:

- ✔ What has made you successful in your existing locations and markets

- ✔ The places that you want to expand into and whether they're right for you

- ✔ How much you need to invest in order to get a foothold in those new places and then grow viable business volumes there

- ✔ Whether what you're doing successfully now can translate into the new locations

Everyone who's successful is under pressure to expand. When you've achieved a certain level of success, everyone around you (especially your backers) begins to see the possibility of what may happen if you can only double your business volumes or get into new markets and locations.

Like everything else, new markets and their prospects are a major external influence on businesses. If you get it right, you can build a business empire like Virgin, which has managed to expand from being a magazine and music publisher, into airlines, railways, fashion, finance and holiday resorts. Get it wrong, and going into new markets can kill or seriously injure your business.

Here are a few examples of expansion gone wrong:

- ✔ The highly successful UK Sock Shop business lost everything when it tried to conduct business in the USA.

- ✔ Marks & Spencer had to close its French and American operations because it couldn't sustain the volumes of business needed.

- ✔ Leeds United FC lost £90 million trying to become a major European football club rather than sticking to what it was good at (providing twice-weekly football entertainment locally).

I told you so

When Arnold Weinstock was chief executive of GEC, the UK electronics and defence organisation, he made it into the most profitable company in the country. Then he came under enormous pressure to use the profits to fund expansion to generate ever-increasing profits from a greater diversity of markets and activities. Weinstock refused, concentrating instead on improving the range of products and services that the company produced for its existing customers.

Eventually, Weinstock was ousted. The financial interest looked to spend everything that he had so carefully built up. GEC went on a major expansion plan and acquired telecommunications and media entertainment companies. However, the business volumes generated by these acquisitions weren't enough to sustain or produce returns on the money invested. Five years after Weinstock had been ousted, the company went bankrupt and was forced to close.

GEC had been a profitable and highly regarded company. However, those who ousted Weinstock failed to recognise the company's core strengths in the defence and electronics industry. They saw only the huge pile of cash – and they squandered it on ventures that they knew nothing about and that had no affinity with GEC or its activities.

Remember: If your organisation is going to expand, you need to do your homework first! Make sure that you fully understand the markets you want to expand into, the reasons those markets will start to do business with you and the reasons they'll stop using the existing providers after you move in. GEC did none of these things – it simply assumed that it would be successful in the new activities because it had been successful in the old.

Environmental issues

Every organisation produces waste, and managing that waste is a key responsibility. The external influence comes from:

- Having to deal with a universal business problem
- Having to manage what is produced so that it causes as little damage to the environment as possible
- Using resources to their optimum capacity and minimising waste

Organisations have to recognise and pay for the pollution and damage that they cause. They do this by accepting direct responsibility for it themselves or by offloading their waste management to companies that specialise in these activities.

As the business world expands, environmental issues and waste management are becoming increasingly important. National governments are now beginning to take a much firmer line in terms of laws and regulations governing the disposal of waste. International trading agreements often require that participating organisations make it clear how they're going to manage their waste.

With the rising cost of energy, companies are increasingly looking to utilities such as gas, electricity and water as key areas in which they can reduce expenditures. New sources of energy are constantly being sought, and if these new energy sources are fully exploited, organisations will be able to reduce their energy bills, as well as the amount of waste they produce.

Political and environmental lobbies are increasingly looking at the amount of greenhouse gases produced by companies. Companies' *carbon footprint* (the amount of carbon dioxide generated through their use of energy) is being much more closely monitored, and failure to tackle this part of environmental management can lead to loss of reputation and negative media coverage, not to mention the cost of the energy itself.

Chapter 3

Using Business Analyses

In This Chapter

▶ Understanding the importance of business analysis

▶ Analysing the organisation and the business environment

▶ Evaluating data and information produced by the analyses

▶ Analysing every aspect of business and businesses, from value to risk

A *business analysis* is an analysis conducted by taking one part of the business and its activities, or the whole, or both so as to gain as much information as possible. You then use the information to support your decisions and understanding of what you're doing or what you propose or intend to do.

To know and understand the detail of every aspect of business, you need to be able to carry out certain analyses. In this chapter, I cover who analyses what, when and for how long; the benefits for the organisation; and then how exactly you analyse organisations, the environment, products and services, competitors and risks.

Starting with the Basics of Analyses

To get you started on analyses, I answer some basic questions:

✔ **Who conducts business analyses?** Anyone can conduct business analyses for any reason. Everyone needs to be able to conduct business analyses effectively. You never know when someone will ask for your opinion on something, and you need to be able to answer fully and effectively when asked.

For the business world of today and tomorrow, you have to know what you're doing and talking about. You can't rely on standard business knowledge – you have to be able to figure things out for yourself. And getting your own expertise in carrying out business analyses is essential for this.

✔ **What do business analyses consist of?** To be expert in business analyses, you set out everything that you know about your business, company or organisation, and then address each of the points in turn. I set out in this chapter all the main ways of doing this. You've a choice of different analyses depending on whether you want to study and evaluate:

• The strengths and weaknesses of your own company and position

• Your competitors

• The environment and location (or locations) in which you work

• Risks

You need to be able to do all of these things. You therefore need to practise and become fully knowledgeable and expert in every part of your organisation's activities and the places in which these activities are conducted.

✔ **How long do business analyses take?** That depends on how much you practise! You have to start by doing them in full, and doing them in full takes time. You also have to make sure that you attend to the details in everything that you look at.

For example, those who manage and work in town and city centre shops always study roadworks and other transport bottlenecks and their effects on access and egress to their premises. They then start to see:

• **The opportunities that exist:** For example, having deliveries during the night; making sure that they're open when the maximum numbers of people are going by.

• **The risks that exist:** Not being able to take deliveries during the day; having to engage deliveries for the night-time – and having to pay higher charges as a result.

You then go on and build your knowledge up from this kind of attention to detail. Note also from the example that the same thing is given as both strength and risk; this example shows that there are always at least two sides to all parts of business and the ways in which you think of them.

✔ **How often do you do business analyses?** Up to you! You need to analyse on a regular basis so that you always remain fully informed about what's going on in and around your company. It's hard at first, but gets easier as you practise and become more and more expert. As you develop this capability, you then start to build your knowledge and understanding about everything else that's going on. You find out which sources of information you trust. You form a basis for your own decision-making processes. You test your own analyses and the judgements that you formed against what happened in practice.

The result is that you start to build up a sound and expert basis for arriving at judgements, conclusions and decisions. You need to make sure that you analyse often enough so that the results are fully current and reflect the state of the company and its environment as it is today – and not as it was last week, even!

Figuring Out Three Principles of Business

Analysing organisations, the environment, products and services, competitors and risks is based on three fundamental principles of business:

- ✔ **You have to know what you've got.** The results of your analyses show the detail of what you've got. They show the position you're in from the widest possible perspective. They force you to consider everything – your strategy, operations, products, services, customers and backers.

- ✔ **You have to be able and willing to work with what you've got.** When you know what you've got, you need to work with that, and within the market and trading conditions present. In summary: you have to be able to be effective and profitable within your environment.

- ✔ **You have to know that what you do isn't nearly as important as why you do it.** This means that you need to be able to support, justify and where necessary defend the views that you hold, and the courses of action that you have chosen. And you can only do this if your judgements and decisions are supported by the fullest possible organisational, business and environment knowledge.

If you conduct your analyses effectively and fully and then classify and prioritise the results in full, you've a wealth of data and information available. You can then use this information to support and justify the decisions you take across the whole business.

 If you've a wealth of data from all your analyses at your fingertips and you use it fully and effectively, you'll nearly always be able to know and understand why things succeed or fail. Without this information, you're simply guessing at what's right and wrong in any given set of circumstances. If you have the data and use it in full, you can review your actions and activities and see where your lines of reasoning went well when you succeeded and where they went wrong when you failed.

Analyses only retain their full usefulness and value if you do them continually. The fact that you analysed risks three years ago and found that everything was under control doesn't mean that things are the same now. For your own benefit, at least, you need to make sure that you update everything in your own mind. That's why many organisations require detailed analyses to be carried out formally at regular intervals. As you get all of the information in front of you, you're able to see what's important and what's not, where the big influences lie and what to do about them.

Analyses are essential because they:

- ✔ Give you data on which to base your judgements and decisions

- ✔ Inform the business of what it should be doing and why

- ✔ Make sure that everyone concerned gains the widest possible knowledge and understanding about the business

- ✔ Allow you to speak with authority on the different aspects of the business, company, organisation or environment that you've analysed

Knowing and understanding what you're talking about and making decisions means that you've a basis for everything that you say or do. And if someone does point out to you the fact that you've made a mistake, then you've enough knowledge and understanding to know what they're talking about too – and then, if necessary, you can admit your mistake and move on. If you had less knowledge and understanding, you would probably dig your heels in!

Analysing the Environment

All business takes place in its environment. By *environment* I mean the combination of location – physical and online – and markets, customers and suppliers, together with the legal and social constraints that exist. For example, the environment of Tesco consists of:

- ✔ The places where the company has its stores (including the Internet)

- ✔ The markets that it serves: groceries, and also clothes, gifts, some furnishings, cards and newspapers

- ✔ The volumes of customers that it serves and their demands

- ✔ Its relations with suppliers and making sure that supplies can get to all of its stores when required

- ✔ The laws and regulations that it has to abide by in terms of food and trading standards, employment law, security management and financial reporting

Several types of environmental analyses are available:

- ✔ **PESTEL:** PESTEL stands for political, economic, social, technological, environmental and legal, and refers to the factors affecting your business.

✔ **Five Forces:** These forces are the power of buyers, the power of suppliers, the threat of entry, the threat of substitution and competitive rivalry.

✔ **Competitor analysis:** Competitor analysis involves an assessment and evaluation of the other players in the field.

The following sections explore each environmental analysis type in turn.

In all these analyses, you're studying and evaluating the environment from the point of view of the:

✔ Political, economic and social forces present

✔ Competitive forces present

✔ Strengths and weaknesses of others who work in the same area

PESTEL analysis

In a PESTEL analysis, you analyse factors within and around the company or business that you are studying by evaluating the following:

✔ **Political:** Internal political systems, sources of power and influence, key groups of workers, key departments, and key managers and executives. You also are looking for possible future trends and pressures that may come about in the long term (this applies to all of the PESTEL factors).

✔ **Economic:** Financial structure, objectives and constraints in the place of work.

✔ **Social:** Social systems in the workplace, departmental and functional structures, and work organisation and methods.

✔ **Technological:** The effects of the organisation's technology, the uses to which you put the technology and the technology that may become available in the future.

✔ **Environmental:** The effects of the organisation's activities on staff behaviour and activities, including waste disposal, health and safety management, specific training and development needs, specialist equipment and technology.

✔ **Legal:** The law's effects on your activities and any regulatory or statutory demands that you have to comply with, including employment law, product and service regulations, advertising and marketing compliance – and, of course, presenting your accounts when required!

Next, you consider forces outside the control of the organisation, or of particular managers. Although outside your control, the following factors nevertheless constitute the boundaries within which your business operates, and you need to understand them in full:

✔ **Political:** Potential legal and statutory changes, such as legislation that limits the ways in which companies can provide advice, or legal changes to maximum and minimum work hours.

✔ **Economic:** The effects that prosperity and hardship have on your activities.

✔ **Social:** How people's habits and customs change and how these changes may affect your business or your ability to employ staff.

✔ **Technological:** Technological changes and advances that are being developed, whether your company needs them and the effects of other companies acquiring and using them.

✔ **Environmental:** How the activities and operations of the company affect the 'green' environment, both in the short and longer term, and how changes in environmental attitudes change prevailing business practices.

✔ **Legal:** The fundamental shifts in the legal sphere as these shifts affect businesses. They include new and more stringent provisions against price collusion and bribery, and new corporate governance statutes and regulations introduced in the UK, EU and USA over the past few years.

To conduct a PESTEL analysis, follow these steps:

1. **Gather together your team or department.**

2. **Brainstorm a list of all the factors that you recognise under each of the PESTEL headings, from both inside and outside the organisation.**

3. **Use your findings to start a discussion about how each force may affect your company.**

4. **Work out ways in which to deal with, influence or work around each factor to the benefit of your organisation.**

When you've gathered all the information, you need to evaluate each aspect of it for likely and possible impact on your business. For example, if you recognise reductions in consumer spending as an economic factor, you can investigate ways to make your product appealing to people on a limited budget. Or if you spot that a new technological innovation will make your own equipment obsolete, you can plan how to budget for new machinery over the next couple of years.

Five Forces analysis

You need to know how competition works in your area of business. For example, if you run an independent bookseller then you need to be aware of how you're affected by others who sell books:

  ✔ Supermarkets and department stores, and stores at places such as railway stations and airports

  ✔ Specialist bookshop chains such as Waterstones

  ✔ Online retailers such as Amazon

As a result, you need to be able to assess and evaluate the forces of competition that are present. If your assessment is that you can't compete on price, you have to be able to offer something else – for example instant service, loyalty schemes, books of local interest.

Michael Porter, the strategy and business guru, identified five critical forces of competition:

  ✔ **Competitive rivalry:** This exists between all those who compete closely, in the wider environment or in particular clusters and localities.

  ✔ **The power of suppliers:** You have to recognise the extent and availability of supplies, and whether you have to work with single suppliers (who therefore have a great deal of power and influence over you) or you have many suppliers to choose from.

  ✔ **The power of buyers:** You have to recognise the extent to which you're dependent on your customers and consumers for your continued existence. Of course, everyone is dependent upon their customers and consumers to a greater or lesser extent. However, if you need to target a particular customer group, you can take whatever steps are necessary to ensure that they keep coming to you to do business.

  ✔ **The threat of substitution:** You need to know and evaluate how much at risk you are from people bringing alternative products and services to the markets that you serve. In increasingly internationalised and globalised trading conditions, you need especially to be aware of the likelihood of people coming in from elsewhere in the world to try to take your market away from you.

  ✔ **The threat of entry:** You have to be able to recognise when existing players operating elsewhere (not direct competitors) in the market are likely to come in and try to work in your sector.

You should also be aware of:

  ✔ **The threat of regulation:** You have to know and understand the likelihood of increased regulations and legislation in your sector.

  ✔ **The threat of changes in customer behaviour:** *Customer behaviour* refers to the bargaining power of buyers. You have to be constantly aware of the need to develop and enlarge your actual and potential customer base, rather than expecting to be able to depend on those you have for extended periods of time.

Competitor analysis

Competitor analysis considers the initiatives that your competitors may take to promote their own strategic advantage and also measures your competitors' likely responses to such initiatives.

When conducting a competitor analysis, you look at the following concerning the competitor:

✔ Its strategy and driving and restraining forces

✔ Its current business operations, capacities, strengths and capabilities

✔ The assumptions that you hold about your competitors

✔ The assumptions that you hold about the state of your industry

✔ A detailed profile of the competitor

✔ Assumptions about its current satisfaction with its current position

✔ Its likely moves and responses to moves

✔ Its position in the market

Look at the competitor's capacity to meet all its customer demands:

✔ **Over-capacity:** In a competitor, over-capacity is especially concerning because it most likely means that the competitor will look to your part of the market to try to maximise its own opportunities.

✔ **Under-capacity:** Look for opportunities to move in to their part of the market (see Figure 3-1).

Figure 3-1 shows all of the above in graphic form, and enables the information to be simply and clearly presented .You can then use this to have a detailed discussion and evaluate every part of your competitor's activities. The discussion needs to include your organisation's top and senior management and market experts, and other key people who are able to contribute. You can then draw informed and expert conclusions about the opportunities and threats that may arise from the particular competitors.

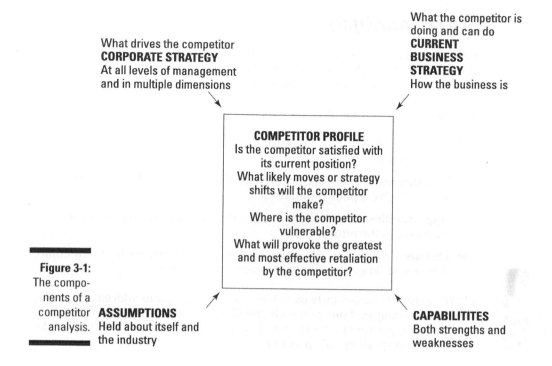

What drives the competitor
CORPORATE STRATEGY
At all levels of management
and in multiple dimensions

What the competitor is
doing and can do
**CURRENT
BUSINESS
STRATEGY**
How the business is

COMPETITOR PROFILE
Is the competitor satisfied with
its current position?
What likely moves or strategy
shifts will the competitor
make?
Where is the competitor
vulnerable?
What will provoke the greatest
and most effective retaliation
by the competitor?

Figure 3-1:
The compo-
nents of a
competitor
analysis.

ASSUMPTIONS
Held about itself and
the industry

CAPABILITITES
Both strengths and
weaknesses

Analysing the Organisation

When you analyse an organisation, you need to relate the organisation to its environment (see the preceding section). You want to obtain the most complete knowledge and understanding possible of the relationship between the organisation, its environment and its competitors.

Just as you can't have a perfect environment in which to work, you can't have a perfect organisation. You're certain to find flaws and weaknesses. What matters is what you do about them.

In this section, I look at four areas in which you can study an organisation:

✔ Strengths, weaknesses, opportunities and threats (SWOT analysis)

✔ Locations

✔ Costs and returns

✔ Value

SWOT analysis

A SWOT analysis looks at things a business does well and can capitalise on, areas it struggles with and needs to improve, and outside factors that affect the success or failure of its products or services.

SWOT is broken down as follows:

- **Strengths:** Things that the organisation and its staff are good at and for which they've a good reputation.
- **Weaknesses:** Things that the organisation and its staff are bad at or for which they've a poor reputation.
- **Opportunities:** Potentially profitable directions that may be worth exploring in the future.
- **Threats:** Potential problems facing the organisation, such as new competitors, strikes or resource or revenue constraints.

 SWOT analysis is particularly useful for understanding and addressing weaknesses. For example, if one of the identified weaknesses is slow invoicing, which in turn negatively affects cash flow, you can turn immediately to working out how to speed up this process.

Conducting a SWOT analysis

To do a SWOT analysis, follow these steps:

1. **Get your team together and generate a list of everything that comes to mind regarding the company and its products or services.**

2. **Place each item under one of the four SWOT categories (strengths, weaknesses, opportunities and threats).**

3. **Discuss and plan how to improve on these areas.**

   Talk about how you and your team can do the following:

   - Build on strengths.
   - Eliminate weaknesses.
   - Recognise and take advantage of opportunities.
   - Minimise or eliminate threats.

 Also consider carrying out a SWOT analysis on one of your competitors – ideally the industry leader or one of the fastest-growing firms in your sector. Concentrate on the competitor's strengths as well as its weaknesses so that you see for yourself what you have to compete with, as well as the opportunities presented by what it doesn't do so well.

Knowing what to do with the results

After you come up with your results, test them on trusted colleagues, key customers and clients, and other stakeholders. Doing so enables you to gain valuable insights into what everyone else thinks about the state of your business. And most importantly, you can discover why they think that particular things are strengths, weaknesses, opportunities or threats.

In practical application, a persistent limitation of SWOT is lack of insight, foresight and objective breadth. For example, many middle managers, fearful of offending top management, daren't suggest that their product is viewed as second-rate by customers, even when that's exactly the case!

Make sure that you understand the likely reception of your SWOT analysis. If sensitive issues are revealed, such as the CEO's pet project going wrong or an IT system that's plainly not working, have clear evidence ready to back up your findings.

Finally, make sure that you relate the SWOT findings to the company's goals and objectives. Especially look at the weaknesses and threats and their likely and potential effects on your ability to reach those goals and objectives.

Justifying your categorisations

So a SWOT analysis is easy, right? All you have to do is identify factors within the organisation and list them under relevant headings – and you suddenly achieve full understanding! Actually, no. Although you do (hopefully) identify lots of strengths and opportunities, you're also revealing to everyone where the organisation's difficulties truly lie. After you identify your problems and everyone knows that you do indeed have them, you need to move on to the truly challenging job of tackling and resolving them.

SWOT analysis is also not simple because you must be able to say *why* the things that you list as strengths, weaknesses, opportunities and threats are indeed so. You can justify your categorisations by:

- ✔ Explaining how political, economic, social, technological, legal and ethical forces will affect your business. For example, if you work in the travel business, you'll always keep a watchful eye on the political, economic and legal situation in the destinations that you serve, to ensure that they remain safe and secure for your customers.

- ✔ Describing the threat created by potential new competitors and market entrants. For example, if you're any form of retailer, you have to be aware of the ever-expanding retail ranges and alternatives offered by providers on Amazon and eBay.

- ✔ Estimating the strength of forces that drive your business and the extent to which you can control them. For example, if you work in financial services, and you've 20 excellent customers for mortgages, but only funds for 10 of those customers, then you have to find ways of prioritising what you offer and to whom, and why.

Putting on your analysis SPECTACLES

In his book *Mastering the Organisation in its Environment* (Macmillan Masters), Roger Cartwright takes a detailed approach to environmental analysis. His analysis requires managers to take a detailed look at each key aspect of their operation within its particular environment. He identifies the following ten-point approach, summarised with the acronym SPECTACLES:

✔ **Social:** Changes in society and societal trends; demographic trends and influences.

✔ **Political:** Political processes and structures; lobbying the political institutions (within the country and larger governing bodies); and political pressures brought about by market regulations.

✔ **Economic:** Sources of finance; stock markets; inflation; interest rates; and local, regional, national and global economies.

✔ **Cultural:** International and national cultures; regional cultures; organisational cultures; cultural clashes; culture changes; and cultural pressures on business and organisational activities.

✔ **Technological:** Understanding the technological needs of a business; technological pressures; relationship between technology and work patterns; communications; e-commerce; technology and manufacturing; and technology and bio-engineering.

✔ **Aesthetic:** Communications; marketing and promotion; image; fashion; organisational body language; and public relations.

✔ **Customer:** Consumerism; importance of analysing customer bases; customer needs and wants; customer care; anticipating future customer requirements; and customer behaviour.

✔ **Legal:** Sources of law; codes of practice; legal pressures; product liability; health and safety; employment law; competition legislation; European law; and whistle-blowing.

✔ **Environmental:** Responsibilities to the planet; pollution; waste management; farming activities; genetic engineering; cost–benefit analyses; and legal pressures.

✔ **Sectoral:** Competition; cartels and monopolies; competitive forces; cooperation within sectors; differentiation; and segmentation.

Any analysis technique can yield difficult truths and questions, but SPECTACLES analysis is likely to raise precise and sometimes uncomfortable questions that many managers (especially senior managers) may prefer not to address. For example, after considering cultural factors in great detail, an organisation may have to face the fact that it doesn't actually understand the effects of particular customs on buying patterns or on its ability to recruit staff.

✔ Estimating the effects of forces that may limit and restrain any changes you may want to implement. For example, you may want to introduce new technology that will be greatly beneficial to your business, but you know that you don't have the expertise to exploit it to the full.

✔ Prioritising and justifying your findings and conclusions so that you can argue your points credibly with top and senior managers. For example, if you've a point to make to top and senior managers, you must always include the costs and benefits – because they value these factors the most!

✔ Constructing ways forward to address and resolve the issues that you've identified. For example, if your company produces retail products and you lack a channel to convenience stores, make sure that you've credible and practical suggestions for opening channels of distribution to these outlets; don't just leave it as a statement of weakness.

Locations

Analysing and evaluating locations of activities used to be easy, especially for those involved in manufacturing. If your product gained weight during manufacturing (that is, you assembled it from components that you brought in), you'd locate close to your markets. If your product lost weight during manufacturing (that is, it was made from a raw material such as iron or steel), you'd locate close to the suppliers of raw materials.

Now the process is more complex. With the ability to engage in mass, standardised and containerised transportation has come the ability to locate more or less where you choose. In general, this freedom has led to:

✔ Local and regional distribution networks and depots for products

✔ Extensive web-based provisions for services

✔ Localised service deliveries based on regional office support

✔ Restructuring of public services to try to ensure that the overall coverage remains as full and adequate as possible, while closing down some service provisions

Organisations therefore make active choices about how they structure and where they locate. In some cases, the question of location is also driven by the need to 'have a presence' for some reason. For example:

✔ Financial services companies find themselves having to have premises and a presence in the major financial centres of the world.

✔ Companies needing rural locations need to be aware of possible problems relating to the supply of raw materials, access to transport networks, and access to customer and client bases.

✔ Companies needing urban and metropolitan locations need to be aware of transport facilities that will enable staff to get to work; they also need to be aware of constraints placed by traffic volumes and delivery restraints.

✔ Companies entering developing markets and locations normally find that having a physical presence in the new location is essential because it means that people can physically recognise them, rather than just being generally aware of their presence.

So you locate where you choose and where you need to be rather than being constrained by specific manufacturing processes or access to technology. Whatever the reason, if you do have to have a physical presence somewhere, it becomes a cost that you have to accept and then cover with the volume of activities generated.

Analysing locations is therefore driven by your needs and wants as well as those of your products and services. In the analysis, you need to evaluate:

- ✔ Access and egress for supplies and your own finished products and services
- ✔ Access to key resources (such as technology, raw materials and transport fleets)
- ✔ Availability of staff and expertise, and your ability to attract and retain them
- ✔ Convenience and desirability in terms of the markets you serve
- ✔ Recognition that the conditions in the chosen location can and do change
- ✔ Willingness and ability of backers to support you in particular places

You then put a value on each of the areas detailed in the preceding list. If, for example, your priority is expertise then you have to go where this expertise is, and everything else then has to fall into place behind this.

Analysing your location or locations provides the basis for establishing your fixed cost base. Wherever you locate, you have to be able to pay for everything that goes with it! And if, for example, you do need a presence in a capital city or financial centre, then this presence is certain to drive up your fixed costs. So you must make sure that you know and understand everything that you're letting yourself in for, in advance of opening activities.

Costs and returns

Analysing costs and returns means establishing an understanding of how you're going to meet and pay for all your commitments. This understanding in turn means knowing and understanding where the cost pressures lie, and how you're going to meet your commitments, as follows:

- ✔ What the fixed and variable costs are and where, why and how they're incurred
- ✔ Where the returns are coming from
- ✔ Where, why and how value is added and lost

So your evaluation is based on itemising every cost and every source of income. You balance these factors in combination with what you know and understand that you should be seeing. You then need to look at:

✔ Where obvious imbalances exist

✔ Where costs are rising for no apparent reason

✔ Where revenues and income are falling for no apparent reason

In every case, you need to understand 'no apparent reason' as quickly as possible. You need to find out what the actual reasons are. You then decide whether or not these reasons are necessary factors in present trading conditions or whether you're going to do something about them – and if so, what, why, how and when?

When you're looking at costs and revenues, you do so from the point of view of evaluating how and why each is moving as it is. You do, however, need to be careful about cancelling products and services that seem to be underperforming without assessing also what value they bring into the organisation overall. You also need to be careful about boosting products and services that seem to be overperforming without also understanding where the value is coming from.

Value

Value is one of those overtly nebulous concepts that nevertheless has to be defined precisely in every set of circumstances. In general, *value* means what something is worth to someone at a particular time. Value is a combination of:

✔ The cost of producing the product or service

✔ The prices that can be charged and the prices that ought to be charged

✔ Convenience and access to customers, clients and end-users

✔ Branding activities

✔ Packaging and presentation of the product or service

✔ The perceptions that customers and clients have of the product or service

✔ The perceptions that the public at large have of the product or service

Value and perception are totally interlinked at a variety of levels:

- ✔ If you think that you're getting good products and services, you look at the 'good bits' to reinforce your perception.

- ✔ If you think that you're going to get bad products or services, you look out for the 'bad bits' so as to reinforce your perception and preconception.

Distinguishing between value and price

The critical aspect of value is that a clear distinction exists between value (what something is worth) and price (what people will pay for it). Value and price are normally the same for consumer goods and services; you put a price tag on the item, and people buy it because it reflects the value that they place on the item and the price that they're prepared to pay. Value is more of a problem with property, expertise and capital goods, as follows:

- ✔ **Property:** Property is valued according to the perceptions and expertise of property managers and estate agents; it's also valued according to what the householder or owning company thinks it's worth, or wants it to be worth.

- ✔ **Expertise:** You may have to overpay for specific expertise because of the value that it delivers to your overall range of activities or to your organisation overall. This value is described as 'economic rent' and reflects the prices and costs that can be charged by those who have specific, scarce or highly sought-after expertise, skills or knowledge.

The UK National Health Service (NHS)

Managing bad service perceptions is a major concern for hospitals and other medical services within the UK NHS. The vast majority of people using the NHS actually get good service, especially at the point of delivery. However, because of a combination of adverse media coverage and the consequent uncertainties and anxieties generated, people go along for medical treatment expecting the worst in many cases. If hold-ups or delays then occur, or the patient has to wait to be examined by medical staff, this causes stress. Instead of looking at things like this as 'one of those things', the patient rather assumes that he's getting bad service.

And so it goes on from there. When his friends and family visit the patient in hospital, they ask how things are going. Instead of saying 'not too badly', the patient now launches into a tirade against the whole service, citing everything (great and small) that has gone wrong.

This is all because of the ways in which perceptions and preconceptions have been influenced by media and other external coverage prior to the patient being admitted.

None of this is to underestimate bad service or bad treatment wherever and whenever it occurs. It's to illustrate the need to recognise and be able to work within people's perceptions and preconceptions when trying to deliver value.

✔ **Capital goods:** Hi-tech industrial and commercial goods and IT projects are valued according to how quickly they can be delivered and installed and so begin to produce the value that's required by those who have ordered them; and so (for example) you tend to pay more for capital goods and IT projects if you want them working quickly.

The value chain

One way of looking at value is to look at where value is gained and lost during the manufacture and delivery of products and services within the value chain. The *value chain*, as illustrated in Figure 3-2, examines every aspect of a business and its structures and operations, showing where value is gained and lost. As a result of this examination, you know and understand the over-all contribution – positive or negative – of everything that you do.

Business strategist Michael Porter devised the value chain as a key part of identifying areas for improvements in business structures and performance. According to him, the value chain shows the detailed examination necessary to carry out a full assessment of where value is gained and lost, building full knowledge and understanding onto the outline given in Figure 3-2.

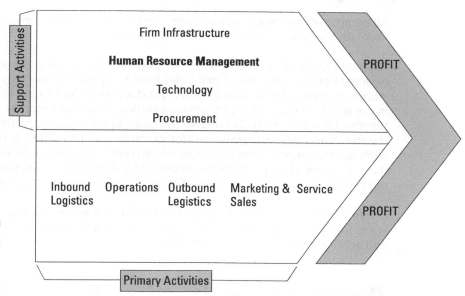

Figure 3-2:
The value chain.

From the value chain examination, you can see where value is being gained and lost throughout the production and service delivery process. You can then begin to evaluate the most critical activities that take place and the contribution made by each to the value of the product or service that's ultimately produced. You can begin, in turn, to classify all activities as:

- ✔ High value – high cost
- ✔ Low value – high cost
- ✔ High value – low cost
- ✔ Low value – low cost

The position of each may, of course, be essential to the overall product or service delivery; but you'd normally at least examine in detail the low value – high cost activities just to check whether you can do things differently without losing overall value.

Analysing Products and Services

All companies and organisations have product and service portfolios that make up the basis on which business is generated.

The complexity of product and service portfolios is almost endless. Some organisations (for example, Coca-Cola) have few products but they're constantly renewing and rebranding their products in order to keep them fresh in the minds of consumers. Other organisations – for example, car manufacturers – have few products but give the impression of having many through the use of add-ons and ancillaries (for example, limited editions). Others, such as retail stores, have hundreds of different products on the shelves at the same time; their performance is driven by their effectiveness in convincing people to buy as much as possible from them each time they visit.

Product and service portfolio analysis therefore requires that you've measures for classifying what you have: product and service lifecycles, product and service clusters and the Ford Matrix.

Product and service lifecycles

You can analyse the lifecycles of products and services to see how far into maturity (and old age) each is. As products and services work their way through the lifecycles, you assess them for continuing effectiveness. At the point where the lifecycle appears to be declining, companies and organisations then take the decision to rejuvenate, regenerate, repackage or somehow otherwise re-energise the particular products or services – or they take the decision to kill them off.

Product and service clusters

Product and service clusters exist in all industries and sectors. Product and service clusters consist of specific items that relate to each other. For example:

- ✔ Supermarkets that sell bread also sell butter, jam, cheese, meat products, herbs and spices because these items are understood to go together.
- ✔ Online travel companies sell excursions, car hire, upgrades and insurance, as well as hotel rooms and transport, because these things are deemed to go together also.

Clusters exist to serve the needs and convenience of the customers and clients, and especially to add value to everything that you do. You therefore continuously analyse the clusters that you have, to see where value is being added and lost. You also look to see whether you can add to or enhance your clusters so as to add value wherever and whenever you can.

The Ford Matrix

Ford, the car manufacturing company, analyses its products as follows:

- ✔ Products that attract
- ✔ Products that sell
- ✔ Products that make money
- ✔ Products that lose money

Ford continues to produce top-of-the-range and high-performance cars because it attracts people to the company overall. Top-of-the-range and high-performance cars lose money for Ford; however, they remain an essential marketing tool in attracting mainstream customers and clients. The mainstream customers and clients buy the mainstream mid-range: the Fiesta, Ka, Mondeo and Zetec.

Above all, Ford makes money from selling finance and service plans, add-ons and ancillaries, and persuading people to upgrade their car after two or three years of ownership.

Analysing Customers and Clients

Tom Peters, the management guru, stated, 'If you make good products and services, and service them well, you will make a fortune.' In a nutshell, this statement is the key to understanding your customers and clients. You need to be clear about what they want and expect from you, and what they don't. At the very least, ensure that you deliver to the standards that they require. Doing so means that your products, services and service arrangements must be available in the quantities and locations requested, to the quality required, and at prices that your customers and clients are willing to pay.

To analyse customers and clients, you start by looking at the volumes of business that they do with you. You gain data on their spending patterns. You examine how often they come to you and how much they spend on average, and on what, each time. Additionally, you establish surveys, cluster and focus groups in order to find out

✔ Why they come to you, and why others don't come to you

✔ What keeps them coming to you and what would drive them away

✔ What would cause them to come to you more, or less, often

✔ What would get them to change their buying and spending habits with you

---

Customer and client types

You need ways of describing your customers and clients so that you can know and understand their attitudes towards you, and their behaviour when they do business with you. Think of customers and clients in the following terms:

✔ **Apostles:** Those who think that you're the most wonderful organisation (and manager) in the world and who'll hear no evil and speak no evil of you under any circumstances.

✔ **Loyalists:** People who have a strong affinity and feel a sense of identity with you and your products and services, and who'll continue to do business with you as long as you maintain and support that loyalty.

✔ **Mercenaries:** Those who do business with you purely on an economic basis – your quality is excellent, or your prices are low.

✔ **Browsers and passing trade:** People who call in on you out of interest or because they happen to be looking at things that you sell; you need to turn them into loyalists.

✔ **Terrorists:** Customers who understand and perceive themselves to have been badly served by you; they seek compensation or do their best to tarnish you with a bad reputation by covering your misdeeds in the media.

Make sure that you know and understand what category your customers fall into, and therefore how to manage them! If terrorists are evident, address their concerns before they sully your reputation. Also bear in mind that you need a great number of loyalists to make your company economically viable and sustainable.

It's also best to have a clear view of where customer service lies in your own order of priorities.

A bit of empathy goes a long way! For example, how do you feel when you try to speak to someone about a customer service issue, only to be put on hold or told that the person you need is on holiday or unavailable? Discontented, I imagine.

If you outsource customer service to another organisation, make sure that this service adheres to your own high standards. Make sure that you write service levels and quality assurance measures into the contract that you agree with the provider, so that they do things in the ways that you want, and to the standards that you set.

Analysing Risks

Business risk is a major area of concern; therefore, understanding how to analyse risk is essential so that you keep the chances of anything going wrong to an absolute minimum. You have to be able to analyse all the results of the other analyses from the point of view of risk. The outcome is that you know and understand:

- ✔ The risks associated with the environment, and possible or conceivable developments, and their effects on you
- ✔ The risks associated with competitive activities to the viability of what you're doing
- ✔ The risks that the organisation itself may be carrying internally

You then look to locate each risk you've identified on a matrix, plotting the likelihood of something occurring against the consequences of what would or could happen. You're establishing:

- ✔ The possibility or likelihood of something happening
- ✔ The consequences if it does happen

You then choose which of the risks you're going to:

- ✔ Accept
- ✔ Avoid altogether
- ✔ Accept, but take steps to minimise their impact

Figure 3-3 shows you how to do this. For each event or possibility, you ascribe either a numerical value or a perceived/agreed strength of risk on one axis, and the likely or possible severity of the consequences should the event or possibility occur on the other. You then decide, as above, whether you are going to accept the risk, avoid it, or accept it and take steps to mitigate its outcomes if it does occur.

Risk analysis is the most critical of all analyses. You have to know and understand what you're assessing and analysing. This in turn means that you have to have enough knowledge and understanding to be able to form a judgement. It also means that you have to decide where the gaps in your knowledge and understanding are and take steps to fill them.

Remember also that a human aversion to risk exists. If something is flagged up as a risk, it means that you have to do something about it. All the time that it remains 'just one of those things', people will leave it as it is.

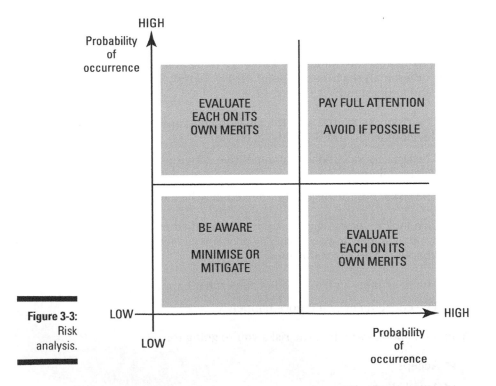

Figure 3-3:
Risk
analysis.

Effective risk analysis means that you're constantly testing your perceptions and preconceptions, and that you're constantly adding to the fund of overall knowledge and understanding that exists within the organisation. Effective risk analysis also means that an ever-decreasing chance exists of organisations and their managers taking leaps into the unknown or going off on exciting corporate adventures that ultimately prove unprofitable (or even fatal) to the future well-being of the organisation.

And never ever forget the three greatest risks to all organisations and business well-being:

- ✔ Complacency. 'It cannot possibly happen to us.'
- ✔ 'We couldn't be bothered.'
- ✔ 'We didn't get around to it.'

Chapter 4

Making Decisions

All business is driven by decisions. Some decisions are strategic and far-reaching, attending to both the immediate issues as well as the long term; these decisions set the course of the organisation for the foreseeable future. Other decisions are operational – they're about implementing and developing strategy. Then you have monthly and weekly decisions that set the course for the immediate future. And finally, you have daily decisions, which set the course for the day and sort out the problems that arise on, well, a daily basis. Thus decision making is a series and pattern of activities, and a process based on the best possible information available at the time.

Decision making also takes place proactively (the organisation and the people in charge try to impose their way of doing things on their environment and the market) as well as responsively (the organisation responds to what's going on in the outside world). And decision making happens in response to crises and emergencies.

In practice, a business has to be able to make effective decisions that cover every eventuality. You can't simply impose yourself on your environment and markets all the time, no matter how powerful or expert you may be. In uncertain markets and trading conditions, the more flexible, dynamic and responsive you can be, the better. And every business needs crisis management systems because they all face crises from time to time. (The goal, of course, is to organise yourself so that crises happen rarely and due to totally unforeseen circumstances, not circumstances that are under your control.)

In this chapter, I walk you through the decision-making process – how decisions are made in the real world. Then I explain the role of top management in decision making, and outline the various pressures they face when making decisions.

Following the Decision-Making Process

Decision making is a process (see Figure 4-1) that looks something like this:

1. **Identify the question you're trying to answer.**

   The starting point of the decision-making process is defining the problem or issue under consideration. You have to define the problem or issue before you can begin to understand the likely effects, opportunities and consequences of various courses of action.

2. **Determine who needs to make the decision.**

   Should one person make the decision and simply communicate it to the team? Or should a group of people, working together and in consultation with others as appropriate, make the decision?

   Be sure to consider the expectations of those directly affected by the decision. If they expect to be consulted, you need to do so or else explain why consulting them isn't possible. On the other hand, if they expect the people in charge to make decisions, and you want to consult them as part of your decision-making process, you need to explain why this consultation will take place – otherwise, they may see it as dithering and a cause of uncertainty, which may lead to a loss of confidence in your leadership.

3. **Be clear on how much time you have.**

   You need to know the deadlines involved. If you've a lot of time to work with, you can gather as much information as possible. If you have to make a decision quickly, all you can do is evaluate the information you have on hand.

4. **Identify your options.**

   You always have at least two options – doing something, or doing nothing. Usually, however, various courses of action present themselves, and you have to choose the one that seems best.

   The final choice always affects the future of the business, so make sure that you consider the possible ramifications of each option before you decide.

5. **Implement your plan.**

   You can only implement the plan after you've worked through each of the previous steps.

At each stage of the decision-making process, take a few minutes to think (and possibly consult and involve others) about where you're heading and why. Even if you set out on one course, you want your decision-making process to be rigorous, so that you don't overlook other possibilities.

Decision trees: If you were a tree, what kind of tree would you be?

You can help inform your decision making through forecasting and extrapolation techniques, which can lead to the building of decision trees like the one in this sidebar.

To create a decision tree, you identify each possible course of action, and then work through all the possible opportunities and consequences that you can identify. Doing so helps you gather as much information about the likely and possible outcomes, projecting what may happen as far into the future as possible.

In this way, you build up a strong understanding of the widest range of options possible. With this information, you can make fully informed decisions. If something is a bit risky, you know in advance what may happen, so you can equip yourself to deal with any issues when they do arise. If something goes well, you can work back through the decision tree and understand why. And if something goes badly, you can work back through the tree and see what went wrong, where and why.

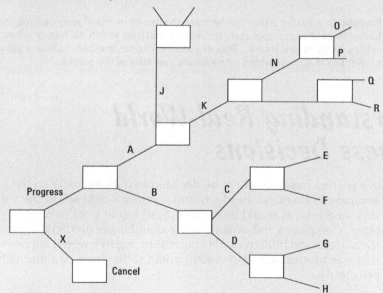

Purpose: to illustrate proposed courses of action, and likely and possible outcomes of them, from a given starting point.

In this particular example, option X - CANCEL - is evidently not on the agenda, as the consequences of this are not extrapolated.

What is illustrated are the ramifications that accrue once the decision is taken to progress; and assuming two positive choices (i.e. other than cancellation) at each stage.

The tree is a useful illumination of the complexity and implications of the process, and of the reality of taking one decision.

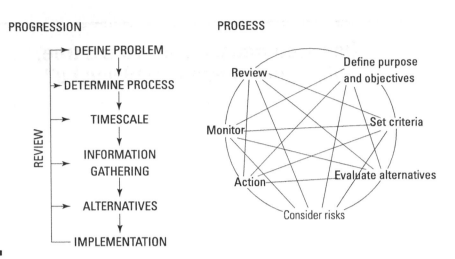

PROGRESSION

PROGESS

DEFINE PROBLEM

DETERMINE PROCESS

TIMESCALE

INFORMATION GATHERING

ALTERNATIVES

IMPLEMENTATION

REVIEW

Define purpose and objectives

Review

Set criteria

Monitor

Evaluate alternatives

Action

Consider risks

Figure 4-1:
A decision-making model.

Purpose: to draw the distinction between the two elements of progress and process. The former is a schematic approach; the latter is that from which the former arises, and which refines it into its final format. Effective and successful decision-making requires the confidence that is generated by continued operation of the process.

Understanding Real-World Business Decisions

In a perfect business world, all decisions would be made on the basis of a full assurance of success. Products and services would sell in the volumes necessary, and returns would be assured. Staff would work in harmony with each other. Companies and organisations would make predictable responses to the actions and initiatives of competitors. Figures would support everything that was proposed, and everyone would settle down to a mutually assured prosperity.

This 'perfect world' is quite clearly a fantasy. And yet people – even top managers – seek it. They fall back on the mantra 'The figures speak for themselves', trying to convince themselves that a perfect world can, indeed, be attained. But the thing is, figures *never* speak for themselves. Figures are just symbols on a page. It's how you use figures, and why, that matters.

In practice, business decisions are rather different. Of course, decisions are made in the best interests of the immediate and long-term viability of the business. But they're also made on the following bases:

✔ **In short-term interests only, often as the result of crises or enduring market and economic uncertainty:** In these circumstances, you're working to ensure the immediate survival of the business. You have an eye on the future, and ideas and plans in place for when things do pick up. But your immediate goal is survival.

✔ **Less than adequate information and background:** This situation can occur for good or bad reasons. For example, perhaps something that looks like an opportunity has presented itself, and the business has to move quickly in order to take advantage of that opportunity. In this situation, you evaluate the limited information you have, and if it seems like a good idea, you go ahead.

On the other hand, sometimes decisions are made with not enough information because information is being withheld. Maybe a manager has her heart set on something being a great opportunity for the business, so she shuts out any information that may indicate otherwise.

If you decide to go into new ventures (even for the best of reasons), you need to follow a decision-making process at each of the following stages:

- When you decide to go ahead in the first place

- When it's clear that the new venture has life or that it doesn't

- At future phases of activities and expansion – which again means that you have to evaluate whether the idea has life and, if it does, determine what you're going to do next

✔ **For purposes of triumph or prestige:** Most organisations engage in _vanity projects_ from time to time – projects that garner attention or praise but don't really add to the coffers. **_Remember:_** Any vanity project has to be paid for out of the sales of products or services.

✔ **To enter into new markets, products, services and activities:** Here, the key question is why you're engaging in the new venture. If you can genuinely support and justify the new venture in business terms, go ahead. But if you can't, make sure that you've the best possible information on which to base your decision.

✔ **Excitement and adventure:** If you're all set to do something that looks pioneering, make sure that it is, in fact, pioneering – and not just exciting because it's new!

A senior manager at one of the world's top airlines cites excitement as one of the main reasons for bungled business initiatives. He says:

Once you strip the airline industry of its perceived glamour, some managers – some very senior managers – regard everything as being mundane. All that they see is the sales of tickets, the management of passengers and their luggage, and nothing else. So they set out to create excitement for themselves using the company's money. And the results are nearly always disastrous.

The concrete airplane

What if all the pioneering airliner manufacturers came up with something that looked like an airliner and had all the features of an airliner, except it was made of concrete? If this happened and if you were an airliner manufacturer, you would have several choices to make:

- Whether to try to build engines big enough to get the concrete airplane off the ground and keep it in the air

- Whether to junk the whole project on the grounds that, whatever it looked like and felt like, it was never going to work

- Whether to experiment with different materials in case the idea could be made to work, as long as it was not made of concrete

The point is that each and every project, product or venture needs to be evaluated on its own merits. If your project is 'nearly right', then how much is actually wrong? Is what's wrong a critical factor, or just a minor detail? If you had indeed made an airliner out of concrete, you would have to decide whether the fact that it couldn't fly was because the engines weren't powerful enough or because it was made of the wrong material.

Remember: When products and ventures are 'nearly right', they're often given the green light in the hopes that the last few details are going to somehow 'sort themselves out'. If you're truly considering details, fair enough. But if the so-called 'detail' is something substantial (as with the concrete airplane) then make sure that you consider it fully *before* you go ahead! Otherwise, your venture may – like the concrete airliner – never get off the ground.

Reviewing the Role of Top Management in Decisions

Top management is responsible for making strategic and operational decisions on the part of the organisation and its stakeholders. So, people in top management or senior positions within the organisation need to know how the organisation works and where their help is needed most. When it comes to making decisions on behalf of the organisation, top management needs to be clear on stakeholder pressures and managerial pressures in order to make the best possible decisions.

Stakeholder pressures

In Chapter 1, I identify the stakeholders that are part of all businesses, and in Chapter 6, I look at stakeholders in detail. In this section, I take a detailed look at stakeholder influences on decisions and the decision-making processes.

All stakeholders have a legitimate interest in the future of the organisation, so you can bet they're going to want a say in the decision-making process. In general, three basic situations develop when it comes to stakeholders:

- The organisation serves one stakeholder group to the exclusion of all others (or at least makes one stakeholder group a priority ahead of all the others).

- Different groups of stakeholders hold sway at different times.

- The organisation does its best to treat all stakeholders as equally and fairly as possible.

As you can see, managing stakeholders in decision-making processes is complex. This complexity becomes even greater when you consider that the organisation may have to make decisions that don't always line up with stakeholder interests. For example:

- Water, gas and electricity companies may jack up their prices – which is very much against the customers' interest – in order to raise funds to invest in infrastructure for the future.

- Retailers may cut prices – which is very much against their financial interest (in the short term, at least) – in order to induce customers to shop with them.

The key to effectively managing *all* stakeholders is communication. Stakeholders need to understand what's happening and why. They start to get anxious if they're left in the dark, especially when major decisions are being made. So top management has to focus on being as open and transparent as possible. In particular, top management needs to pay attention to:

- **Staff:** Their interests are served by the assurance of the fundamental long-term, as well as immediate, viability of the business.

- **Shareholders:** Their interest lies in getting the returns and dividends that they anticipate from the business.

- **Suppliers:** They want to know why you've decided to place a particular volume of business with them and how long this demand may last.

- **Customers:** They need assured after-sales, maintenance and customer support, as well as the ability to buy the products and services they've come to expect.

Ideally, top management finds ways to keep all the stakeholders happy. But when pleasing everyone isn't possible, everyone still needs to be kept fully informed.

Tesco

When he was CEO of Tesco, Terry Leahy grew the company from a minor supermarket chain to the largest retailer in the UK and the third largest in the world. He achieved this feat by recognising the legitimate demands of everyone involved – staff, customers, suppliers and shareholders. Ultimately, however, Leahy took the view that if there was a priority stakeholder group, it was the customers – and in order for excellent customer service to take place, the whole operation had to be staff-intensive. Tesco couldn't provide excellent customer service without staff.

Leahy was Tesco's CEO for 22 years. As the company grew, initially everyone respected and admired his attention to each stakeholder group. Then the company started to show particularly high levels of profit. Business analysts in particular started to question Leahy's

approach to staff. For the last five years of Leahy's time as CEO, Tesco's results continued to beat records. Each time the company reported its results, analysts would say, 'The company is overstaffed and needs to cut costs.'

Leahy's response was always: 'If we cut staff costs, our service will decline and people will stop coming to us. And even with all these staff, we are still breaking turnover and profit records each year.'

So, clearly, sometimes you have to go against what your stakeholders say. In this case, even though the general wisdom was that Tesco was overstaffed and that costs should have been cut, Leahy was able to provide a fully informed counterargument as to why – in this case – the stakeholders were wrong and shouldn't hold sway.

Circumstances and environmental pressures, as well as stakeholder demands, change over time. What may be appropriate or in one group's interests today may not be in their interests down the road. So in addition to looking out for stakeholders' interests at present, you need to be fully mindful of how and why these interests may change in the future, and how you may have to respond.

Managerial pressures

Consider the kinds of pressures faced by managers in the NHS: hospital managers are responsible for managing budgets, organising and rostering work, and ensuring that patients get the best possible treatment while they're in the hospital. The hospital medical staff is responsible for delivering medical treatment when it's required and for ensuring that patients get the best possible treatment while they're in the hospital.

So, immediately, you can see that managerial pressures exist that have a potentially great impact on those responsible for making decisions. From this example, you can identify pressures not only from the operational side (to deliver the treatment when it's needed), but also from the managerial side (to stay within budget).

Most managers don't find themselves in such life-or-death situations, of course. But even so, they face conflicting and divergent pressures that they have to reconcile. A decision-making process that factors in conflicting and divergent pressures and issues looks something like Figure 4-2 in practice.

Your organisation has to be both capable and also willing to implement your decision. Figure 4-2 shows that you need to take into account everything that causes pressures and limitations on what you would like to do in terms of internal and external capabilities, as follows:

✔ The capacity of your organisation and its resources to implement the decision

✔ The ability of your markets and shareholders (the external limitations) to accept what you are going to do

✔ The ability of the operating and commercial and trading environment to sustain what you have chosen

✔ The willingness of your staff to implement the decision

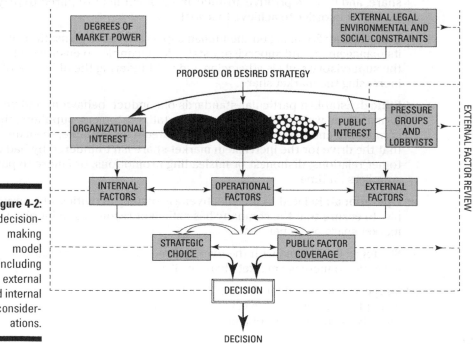

Figure 4-2:
A decision-making model including external and internal considerations.

This approach to decision making also represents the context in which you go about:

- Setting objectives
- Assessing and determining priorities
- Identifying responsibilities and accountability

Setting objectives

Top management needs to set objectives for every aspect of organisational performance so that everyone understands the roles they play and what they're contributing to the organisation.

Companies and organisations have objectives that fall into the following categories:

- **Attitudes and values:** Concerned with the psychological focus of the organisation and how it's developed – for example, to ensure that everyone knows and understands the reason for the drive to increase market share, and has the positive attitude and commitment required to play their part in order to achieve this goal.

- **Behavioural:** Focusing on the human aspects of the organisation, and its management and supervisory staff – for example, to ensure that the supervisory style is advancing and not hindering the objective of increasing the market share.

- **Ethical:** Establish particular standards of conduct, behaviour and performance, as well as the ways in which staff, customers, suppliers, the community and the environment are treated – for example, to ensure that the drive for the increase in market share isn't hindered by bad customer relations, dishonest or misleading promotions, or failure to pay suppliers on time.

- **Operational:** Related to the effectiveness of daily activities – for example, to ensure that the company has sufficient resources to increase market share by 35 per cent.

- **Strategic:** Concerned with the overall direction of the organisation – for example, to increase market share by 35 per cent by the end of the year.

- **Support:** Translated for the individual members of staff to follow – for example, to ensure that everyone has individual objectives tied in directly to all the other objectives.

The point of setting objectives is to ensure that everybody is clear about the goal of the organisation, how it sets out to achieve that goal, and their role in the organisation achieving the goal.

When you're setting objectives, think of the acronym SMART. Objectives should be:

- ✔ **Specific:** People should be able to tell what they need to do to help the organisation reach the objective.

- ✔ **Measurable:** You need to be able to tell whether the objective has been achieved, and you can't do that unless you can measure it.

- ✔ **Achievable:** The resources and time available must be enough that the objective can be reasonably achieved. If the objective is impossible to achieve, that's a problem.

- ✔ **Recognisable:** People should understand exactly what the objective is and why it has been set.

- ✔ **Time-constrained:** This component of objectives is key. People need to know exactly when they're expected to deliver on their part of the operation. Don't just say 'as soon as possible' – outline a specific day and/or time when you need something done. If you're working on a long-term project, set up interim milestones along the way.

Men are from Mars . . .

For many years, the chocolate company Mars tried to make international one of its main brands. In some parts of the world, this particular product was called 'Snickers'; in other parts, it was called 'Marathon'. The Mars company charged its marketing department to produce a strategy to harmonise the whole product under the 'Snickers' name.

A project group was formed, and it quickly met, producing a set of papers and agreeing to meet again in three months. Three months later, more papers were produced and again the group agreed to meet in three months. This process went on for over a year. The company took on a new marketing director, who asked to be brought up to speed on the progress of the 'Snickers' strategy. He was horrified to find out that, for all the papers that had been produced and the meetings that had taken place, the company was no farther along than when it had started the project well over a year ago.

The marketing director called the whole team to a meeting. He said that by the end of the meeting, a strategic approach would be produced, enabling the company to generate and structure marketing activities so that the brand would be both unified and well received in every part of the world.

And guess what? By the end of the meeting, a strategy was in place! What they had failed to implement for months was now implemented right away, simply because the project team had been given a time frame to work with.

Assessing and determining priorities

People need to know what they should do first, and what they can put off for another day. The same rule applies to organisations. Organisations and their staff have to prioritise their activities in order to ensure that everyone's interests are served.

Top and senior managers are there to ensure that the whole organisation functions as effectively as possible. To do this, they have to assess the following:

- What needs to be done
- What investments are required in terms of staff and technology
- How to ensure the continuity of supplies, products and services

In other words, they have to prioritise – setting all demands in an order of priority and ensuring that everyone understands why and how the order of priority has been established.

Ideally, top management establishes priorities to ensure that organisational resources are used to the best possible advantage in the pursuit of long-term goals. In practice, though, it's rarely possible for an organisation to achieve everything it wants or needs to achieve. It has two fundamental positions:

- That you can either tackle your top priorities in full, and other things are not addressed at all
- That you can tackle everything, but inadequately (see Figure 4-3)

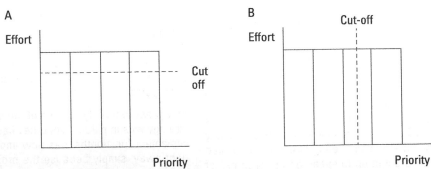

Figure 4-3: Establishing priorities.
A Everything is attempted but unsatisfactorily
B Those things which cannot be completed satisfactorily are not attempted

From time to time, top management has to decide where the organisation's priorities lie. You probably don't have the resources, the staff or the technology to do _everything_ you want to do. So, you can choose to do as much as possible (and drop the rest), or set out to achieve everything (knowing full well that you don't have the resources to do it). If you go with the latter approach, you're basically hoping that 'something will turn up' that will somehow enable you to do everything down the road.

Priorities can and do change from time to time. They can be thrown into turmoil by any or all the following:

- **Changes in customer demand:** For example, when Apple started to produce the iPhone, this change put pressure on all phone manufacturers to develop their own products.

- **Obsolescence of one of your major products or services:** For example, the bottom dropped out of the UK holiday industry when cheap flights and packages became available in cheaper and sunnier places.

- **Changes in costs on the supply side:** For example, increases in component prices in the West have caused all electronics manufacturers to try to source these products in China.

- **Entry into your market of competitors and alternatives:** For example, the entry of Ryanair into the short-haul European airline sector has caused other operators to reduce their prices and improve their short-haul services.

- **Exit from your market of a major player:** For example, the closure of Woolworths in the UK has left a major gap in the cheap/good-value confectionery and gift sector, causing losses for those companies manufacturing for these sectors as they struggle to find alternative outlets for their products.

If a major company leaves your market, it may seem like manna from heaven! Suddenly, the field is wide open, and all you have to do is fill it. But in reality, doing so isn't always that easy. If a major company leaves the market, the company's customers may go with it – especially if that company held a strong cost or brand advantage, or enjoyed high levels of customer and consumer confidence. If you've always been a niche player, then even if the market has suddenly become wide open you still have to convince many more people that you're able to supply them all, and not just your niche.

Identifying responsibilities and accountability

Now we come to the overarching pressures on top management: responsibilities and accountability. In business, everything is done in the name of the organisation, and top management is accountable for the decisions. The top managers are the ones who answer to shareholders, backers, staff and all stakeholders for the results, performance, profits and losses that have occurred.

Top managers have to account and answer for the decisions they've made, and for the outcomes of those decisions – good and bad. Because of recent political and economic crises, the question of accountability has come into sharp focus. Especially in the inquests into company failures, it has been hugely difficult for the authorities to pin down exactly who was accountable for what as the performance of organisations declined.

Ultimate accountability has to remain with top management. Even so, those in top management should be able to rely on the people working for them to:

✔ Tell them the truth

✔ Point out where crises and difficulties are likely to emerge

✔ Keep them posted on the performance of products and services

✔ Highlight any areas of concern that the organisation as a whole should be aware of

Everybody is perfectly happy to be accountable for things when they go well. The key is to establish the points of responsibility and accountability for specific decisions and initiatives so that everyone has a point of reference to which any concerns can be addressed.

Part II
How Business Works

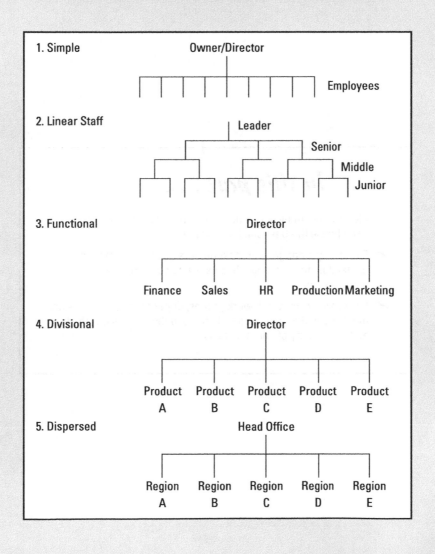

1. Simple   Owner/Director   Employees

2. Linear Staff   Leader   Senior   Middle   Junior

3. Functional   Director   Finance   Sales   HR   Production   Marketing

4. Divisional   Director   Product A   Product B   Product C   Product D   Product E

5. Dispersed   Head Office   Region A   Region B   Region C   Region D   Region E

Go to www.dummies.com/extras/businessstudies for free online bonus content.

In this part . . .

✔ Identify and analyse company and organisational structures and choose the best one for your business.

✔ Effectively manage your stakeholders and their demands to maintain their interest, business and support of your organisation.

✔ Explore ways in which work groups, departments, divisions and functions make critical contributions to the success, viability and profitability of your business.

Chapter 5

Structuring and Evolving Organisations

- -

In This Chapter

▶ Looking at the various types of companies and organisations

▶ Considering the impact of outsourcing

▶ Preparing for takeovers, mergers and privatisation

- -

*O*rganisations large and small are organised in one form or another. Whether you're one person working on your own on your laptop in your living room or a multinational commercial enterprise, you have a business structure. In this chapter, I walk you through the various types of organisations – including commercial businesses, not-for-profit organisations and more.

As your organisation grows, you may start to consider outsourcing as a way to cut costs or focus on the things you do best. In this chapter, I explain the pros and cons of outsourcing.

Finally, over time, your business will evolve. Being able to respond to your business's needs is key to staying afloat. So in this chapter, I also take a look at takeovers, mergers and privatisation – key changes that many businesses have to face.

Identifying the Various Structures and Types of Organisations

Organisations can be, well, organised in a variety of ways. In this section, I take you through the various types of organisations and explain when and why they're most useful.

Commercial organisations

Commercial organisations have a legitimacy, life and legal entity of their own. In other words, they go on in spite of personnel changes, developments in technology, equipment and working practices, and changes in the world around them. Because of this 'permanence', the following situations apply to companies:

- ✔ If customers get bad service from the company, they sue the company rather than the staff.

- ✔ Employees depend on 'the organisation' for their pay, work and opportunities.

- ✔ Backers support 'the organisation' and may ask for changes in top and senior staff if they don't get the returns they expect.

- ✔ Communities complain to 'the organisation' about issues such as noise and pollution.

As entities in their own right, commercial organisations must have their own statutory and legal structures. In addition, they have to be insured, which means that those who are responsible for running them have to be recognised as 'fit and proper persons' for this purpose.

In terms of size, commercial organisations fall into two camps:

- ✔ **Large enterprises** which have large and/or dominant market shares and values, and large and complex workforces following a range and variety of occupations and expertise. Large enterprises have great influence on working practices and trading activities in every sector in which they operate.

- ✔ **Small and medium-size enterprises (SMEs)** which are normally defined as employing 250 people or fewer and/or having revenues of less than $5 million. In the UK today, over 90 per cent of companies and organisations employ 50 or fewer people. SMEs are found in all forms and sectors – their activities, conduct and expertise know no boundaries.

Commercial organisations – large and small – fall into one of the following categories:

- ✔ **Sole traders:** Sole traders (also called sole proprietorships) operate as one-person entities and carry out the chosen activity of that person. For example, a writer may be a sole trader – he may write for a variety of publications and not be on staff, nor does he receive a regular salary and benefits from anyone.

✔ **Partnerships:** Partnerships operate with more than one person. They often occur between family members or professional colleagues. For example, two or three attorneys may open a law practice together. Although each attorney has his own clients, the clients pay the firm as a whole, and the attorneys are given salaries by the firm.

✔ **Private limited companies:** In private limited companies, the people who own the company structure the organisation around shared ownership. Private companies exist in all sectors and come in all sizes. For example, Virgin is a private company, as is Boots, the retail pharmacy chain.

✔ **Public limited companies (PLCs):** These companies are just like private limited companies, except shares of the company are offered for sale on a stock market. The great advantage of offering shares on a stock market is the amount of money that can be raised.

On the downside, you can end up losing control of the company when you offer shares. Dominant shareholders – those who buy the biggest share values – appoint their own top and senior management, and from this position they clearly (and quite rightly) exercise control and direction over what the company does, when, where, how and why. Having put their money in, they want (and need) to see returns on their investment in terms of the share price rising and dividends paid. So they seek to influence the direction of the company in ways they think provide the best possible chance of these returns.

You may need to go public if you're selling something that is highly technologically advanced, or expensive to produce, market or sell. If you want to become a large and physically dominant organisation with a presence across the globe, you may have little choice but to go public. However, the question of control is a serious one. Unless you secure your own position by remaining the majority shareholder, you may lose everything that you've built up.

What's the difference between a partnership and a private limited company?

The main difference between a partnership and a private limited company is the 'limited' part. In a partnership, partners are liable in full for losses incurred, which means that if things go wrong, partners may have to sell other assets and possessions to make good on the losses. This situation applies to all partners – even if particular individuals weren't the ones responsible for the losses. With a private limited company, on the other hand, liability for losses only extends to the value of the shares held by the owners.

Another form of partnership, called *limited liability partnership* (LLP), allows partners to limit their liability for losses by agreement with the other partners. Normally, however, at least one partner accepts unlimited liability.

The question of control is the key issue in determining whether to be a private or public limited company. In a private company, the existing shareholders retain control and influence according to the percentage of shares owned. In a public limited company, shares are traded on stock exchanges so, theoretically, the dominant share ownership can change at any time – which means that control of the company can change also.

Whatever the form chosen, legal issues exist. The structure has to be determined and delivered so that all those involved in the organisation know and understand their position, obligations and responsibilities. All companies and organisations face the crucial question of accountability and governance. This means having a structure, articles and legal documents that state clearly how the business is to be conducted, as well as a clear definition of the nature of the business.

Whatever its status, every organisation has to produce accounts at the end of the year, and state clearly their income, expenditure, turnover and profit (or loss), and PLCs are required to publish their accounts.

Rewards to the owners, backers and directors of the business have to be stated as well, and these rewards must be in line with legal obligations and responsibilities for the future of the business, and (for partnerships and private companies) in accordance with the status of the partner or shareholder.

Going global

If you want your company or organisation to go global, you must have at least one of the following:

✓ **A global presence:** You have physical locations – and therefore, ready access – all across the world.

✓ **Global technology:** You have the technological capacity to produce and deliver your products and services anywhere in the world.

✓ **Global influence:** You produce one of the (few) products and services demanded by everyone everywhere in the world.

✓ **Financial size:** You can back and support the sheer volume of resources necessary to maintain and develop a global presence.

✓ **Technological command:** You can underpin and support everything that you do through a top-quality and secure technological infrastructure.

✓ **Market influence:** You can persuade people anywhere in the world to adopt and use your products and services.

✓ **Command of expertise:** You attract and retain the nature and levels of skills necessary to deliver your products or services anywhere in the world.

✓ **Command of supply and distribution chains:** You can get not only the raw materials that you need, but also your products and services to market in every location in which you operate.

Remember: The fact that you have a website and can be accessed from anywhere in the world does *not* mean that you will be able to do business anywhere in the world. Many companies have made this mistake. For example, Lastminute.com called itself 'the global provider of last minute travel solutions'. So anyone going to the website would expect to be able to travel anywhere in the world 'at the last minute'. But, in practice, the company really only operated in the UK, and it never had contacts in more than ten countries around the world. Similarly, Boo.com called itself 'a global shoe retailer'. It mistook completely the fact that most people buy shoes because they need and want them, and it was never going to be able to sell shoes to people in Tahiti from its bases in Sweden and the UK.

Besides, what works in one country won't necessarily work elsewhere. For example, Tesco has had great trouble establishing a viable operation in the USA and has now pulled out. Aldi and Lidl, major German supermarket chains, have managed only a niche presence in other countries, despite their serious price advantage relative to domestic UK and French providers.

So, if you're looking to expand overseas, you have to be absolutely *certain* that the proposed new locations and markets want what you have to offer. After all, they've managed without you so far!

Public service bodies

Public service bodies are constituted for specific purposes by governments so that people get the health, education, police, energy, infrastructure, transport, emergency, military, security and social services that they need.

Fundamentally, two basic approaches to public service bodies exist:

- The government determines the **size and scale** of the public service at the outset. Then the government finds the funding from tax revenues and delivers it in order to support the size and scale of the service.

- The government determines a **budget** for the service at the outset. Then the government matches the size and scale of the service to what the budget can support.

Choices have to be made in terms of:

- **Location of services:** Whether services are provided on the spot for everyone, or whether those who need the services have to travel to get them.

- **Timing of services:** Whether services are provided on demand, or whether waiting lists and/or priority given exist.

- **Quality of services:** Whether services are equipped with the latest technology and expertise, or whether an 'acceptable' (whatever that means) level and quality are determined for a period, and then not upgraded until the end of that period.

Under construction

A few years ago, one of the UK's largest construction companies sent a delegation to Malaysia to tender for work. A building boom was just beginning, and this company wanted to be a part of it.

The delegation arrived and started to look around for work to bid on. Their first round of bids wasn't even acknowledged, let alone accepted. Finally, someone suggested that they go to see the different departments in the Malay government that were offering work. Eventually, they met the minister, who inquired politely who they were.

Affronted, the delegation leader, the company's project director, replied, 'We are the largest UK building contractor, and we are a global organisation.'

Politely again, the minister asked, 'How many countries do you work in?'

'Seven,' came the reply. 'We are staggered that you haven't heard of us.'

The minister said, 'You are right. I do apologise but I have not heard of you. Indeed, I cannot name any UK construction company except Balfour Beatty. How many Malay construction companies can you name?'

Defeated, the delegation left. The company never did any work for the Malay government, although it did subsequently pick up contracts in North and South America.

It missed out on the Malay opportunities because it did everything wrong. It went in with preconceived ideas rather than proper knowledge and understanding. It didn't know or understand the local business culture. It assumed that because most people in the UK had heard of the company, everyone in the world had heard of it. It assumed that because it had done work in seven countries, it was therefore a global operator. This kind of presupposition – and the perceptions of vanity that are clearly attached – is no basis for any form of international or global expansion.

Service demands are also skewed by local and regional factors; the size, density and age of the population; and the ability to deliver the level and quality of services demanded in specific areas.

Within this context, a public service organisation has to be created, staffed and equipped to deliver its particular service. The quality and volume of the service as a whole also has to be assured. And everything then has to stay within budget and deliver for the taxpayer and the country.

Responsibility and accountability for governance and transparency in public services are determined by statute and constituted through a combination of political interests from central and local government. The purpose is to ensure that the combination of local and national interests, service quality and value, and financial accountability are maintained.

The general public ultimately pays for all public services. One point of view is that taxes should be kept as low as possible and public services should be kept as a core rather than total provision. The other view supports establishing a taxation regime in order to pay for the service levels determined and demanded. This latter point of view demands that people's perceptions are managed in terms of getting value for money from the tax burden rather than constantly seeking to reduce it.

NGOs and quangos

Non-governmental organisations (NGOs) and quasi-autonomous non-governmental organisations (quangos) are organisations constituted by government and/or special interest groups for a stated purpose. Having been constituted, NGOs then operate fully independently of government, while quangos remain integrated with the arm of government which created them.

Typically, both NGOs and quangos are given a budget and a specific remit to work to; then, within these constraints, they carry out their duties in the best interests of those who have constituted them.

NGOs and quangos have proliferated in the UK recently. The main reason for this growth is the amount of work existing that mainstream public service bodies can't easily deliver (see the preceding section 'Public service bodies').

Many NGOs and quangos tend to be specialised. The great advantages of constituting organisations in this way are:

- Flexibility in terms of the roundup of the expertise required
- A measure of freedom in how the expertise is deployed

These advantages – flexibility and freedom – have to be tempered with full accountability and transparency. In many cases, this balance isn't easy to achieve. The problem lies in ensuring that the expertise and remit are delivered as fully as possible, while at the same time maintaining budgetary control and transparency.

NGOs and quangos are normally overseen by government representatives and a board of governors. Depending on the remit, representatives from industry, commerce and other public service bodies are involved, to ensure that what the NGOs and quangos are doing remains in the interests of everyone directly concerned and in the wider public interest as well.

The not-for-profit sector

Of all parts of business organisation, the not-for-profit sector is the hardest to pin down. The term *not-for-profit* is a contradiction in itself: all organisations have to run at a surplus, especially not-for-profit organisations. Indeed, they need to raise enough to make a full and effective contribution, and they normally have to do so without the benefit of full government support, or the capability to trade on a fully commercial basis. They have also to maintain the absolute confidence of their supporters and those who make donations in order to deliver the services as they meet their particular remit.

Not-for-profit organisations have to be legally constituted for a clearly stated purpose and then registered with the appropriate authorities. They have to declare the activities that they're going to pursue, and they have to make clear the ways in which they're going to allocate and spend funds. They have to account for the money they raise and where they spend it, in exactly the same way as commercial organisations and public service bodies.

The largest and most powerful not-for-profit organisations are major players and influencers in their field. They have to be professionally and expertly run. Those who lead and direct not-for-profit organisations require the same levels of expertise and responsibility that are demanded in top positions in commercial organisations.

National Society for the Prevention of Cruelty to Children

The National Society for the Prevention of Cruelty to Children (NSPCC) is a major flag carrier for the rights of abused, neglected, deprived and displaced children. The NSPCC is also one of the major influences on childcare and settlement policies in the UK. It acts as a lobby and influences the development of national and international children's policies.

Some years ago, recognising the influence that it could potentially have, the NSPCC shifted its whole focus from the direct provision of children's services to be able to maximise its potential power and influence. It would continue to provide direct care and other children's services. But a big part of the funds raised would now be used explicitly for campaigning, political lobbying and awareness-raising of the horror of child abuse and neglect.

This shift in emphasis can be clearly understood. However, it alienated many of those who conducted fundraising activities on the NSPCC's behalf and were prepared to leave endowments to it. In particular, fundraisers felt that if they were no longer directly supporting abused, neglected and deprived children, they would no longer contribute. The consequence was a falloff in individual donations. However, this falloff was more than tempered by increases in corporate donations.

Other organisational forms

You need to know about a couple of other organisational forms that have arisen for a variety of reasons, including the following:

- ✔ **So much work being commissioned and carried out today is too big for a single company or organisation.** This fact doesn't just apply to commercial organisations. In many parts of the world, for example, you see famine relief and infrastructure development being carried out by a combination of not-for-profit organisations and NGOs, as well as commercially driven companies.

- ✔ **A lot of work requires a range of technology and expertise that single companies simply don't have.** This means that companies and organisations from all sectors have to be prepared to work together. This cooperation can happen even when they're competing with each other for work elsewhere.

- ✔ **A lot of work requires companies and organisations to go into locations and activities that they've never been involved in before.** This requirement means that they have to be able to find local partners with the specific knowledge and market understanding required.

- ✔ **Many bodies, especially government and international institutions such as the United Nations (UN) and International Monetary Fund (IMF), have preferred lists of companies and organisations from their own countries and elsewhere in the world that they normally turn to for work.** Companies and organisations on these preferred lists can then invite others to partner with them on particular ventures and activities; other companies and organisations lobby those on the preferred lists to get into new activities and locations.

So all kinds of drives for new and changing organisation forms exist, further driven by technology, the proliferation of information and the ease of travel. In this context, the two key organisational forms you need to know about are the following:

- ✔ **Federations:** Organisation federations come together for particular reasons (including those in the preceding list). Federations normally form as the result of a bid for a large and enduring contract of work, which then leads to other prospects and opportunities. The federation consists of suppliers; distributors and transport organisations; consultants and specialists; technology firms; those with local knowledge, understanding and presence; as well as the originating company. As soon as they're involved with each other, the companies in the federation have the opportunity to explore further areas for collaboration.

Federations also come about as the result of national, local and regional development. Such programmes can be generated by NGOs and the not-for-profit sector; then it becomes necessary to engage those with the specific expertise required. This need leads to the opportunity for further collaborative and cooperative work.

✔ **Joint ventures:** Joint ventures exist where two or more organisations come together to create an organisation for the purpose of delivering a specific product, service, project or venture. This coming together happens where the work is too large, complex or diverse for one organisation to carry out on its own.

The difference between a joint venture and a federation is that the joint venture is disbanded after the work is completed (though the partners are likely to seek further opportunities while the joint venture is in place).

A joint venture is always the subject of a legal constitution with clearly stated responsibilities and obligations that apply to each member. A federation may include legal definitions, but is much more likely to be governed by a memorandum of agreement or understanding that exists simply as a definition of the nature of collaboration, but without otherwise being legally binding.

Outsourcing Work to Other Companies and Countries

Outsourcing (the practice of contracting out work that either you do not have the capacity to carry out yourself, or that isn't the specialty of your particular organisation) is one of the major influences on business today. On the one hand, it has led to a lot of generic work in transport, catering, security, technology services and component manufacture being contracted out; on the other hand, it has led to a proliferation of companies and organisations that specialise in these areas and deliver their specialty to other organisations on a contracted basis.

On the surface, outsourcing appears to be a huge advantage for the following reasons:

✔ Every organisation sticks to its own specialty.

✔ Organisations pay a fixed and assured fee for the outsourced products and services.

✔ The length and cost of the outsourced contract and relationship are known and understood.

✔ Everything that is outsourced is one thing less to worry about, leaving organisations free to concentrate on their core priorities.

However, outsourcing has a downside too. If you're considering outsourcing, ask yourself the following questions:

- Are you outsourcing to get better value for your money, or are you doing it because you can't be bothered to do the work in house?

- Are you outsourcing because doing so is the best use of your fixed costs, or are you doing it just to get otherwise peripheral staff off your payroll?

- Are you doing it to reduce your headcount as a percentage of capital employed, and therefore using it to try to manipulate your share price?

Then you have the question of who you outsource to. Outsourcing needs to work as a partnership that brings mutual benefits. Anything that you outsource carries the following potential pitfalls:

- You lose control over the quality and value of the outsourced products and services.

- If the outsource provider goes broke, you have to find a replacement quickly.

- If you outsource purely for a cost advantage, you need to be sure that you get the cost advantage that you seek – and you need to make sure that this advantage doesn't come at a cost to your reputation.

The right reasons?

If you don't outsource for the right reasons, you may live to regret it. Here are some examples of organisations that outsourced for the wrong reasons:

- One of the UK's top universities outsourced its catering and conference functions in return for a fixed fee of £250,000 per annum. In the first year of outsourcing, the catering company made £9.5 million.

- One of the UK's leading car companies outsourced the manufacture of its plastic components. Then it drove down the prices paid to the outsource provider – which went broke, leaving the car company with ten days' lost production while it frantically renegotiated the contract!

- One of the UK's largest telecommunications firms outsourced its HR function to one of the big four consultancies. The result: problems that had previously taken a few minutes to resolve escalated into major disputes and grievances, accompanied by huge delays, and conducted by an HR function that was now detached rather than involved. After nine months, the telecommunications company paid the three years of the outsourced contract in full and took the HR function back in house.

The lesson? Be clear and honest about what you want and why, and make sure that you know what you're getting yourself into.

How cheap is that cheap labour?

Most of the top clothing suppliers outsource production to parts of the world where the products can be manufactured (allegedly) much more cheaply than in developed countries. Most of them at some stage have had to face accusations of local exploitation, child labour, slavery and oppressive working conditions. The first of these accusations was levelled against Adidas in 1987, but a variety of companies have faced this type of allegation in the years since.

Each time the question has been raised, the companies have promised to remedy the situation and that these things will never happen again. Dealing with these scandals on a regular basis has to be paid for out of the (alleged) cost advantage that locating this work in these parts of the world supposedly delivers.

Changing Ownership and Activities

Change is the only constant in life and in organisations. A variety of factors can drive that change – from competition to technology, new markets to products and services. Two specific forms of change have to do with business types and structures: takeovers and mergers, and privatisation.

Takeovers and mergers

Companies and organisations have a life and permanence of their own, and they also have a value. This value may come in the form of any or all of the following:

✔ **Staff and technology expertise:** One company has highly sought-after staff and/or technology that another company is prepared to pay for.

✔ **Locations of work and activities:** A company wants to be involved in a particular location, so it buys a company (or multiple companies) in that location in order to gain a presence.

✔ **Customer and client bases:** One company targets another company for its (usually high-value) customer or client base.

✔ **Industry specific value:** One company targets another company for some reason specific to that industry. For example, British Airways took over BMI for its landing slots at Heathrow, and Starbucks took over the Seattle Coffee Company in London in order to gain a substantial and immediate physical presence there.

All the above are assets that other companies may want to buy up. When this situation occurs, a value is placed on the asset, and then, after an agreement has been made, the organisation is sold.

Valuing a takeover target is always complicated! The value is arrived at in one of the following ways:

✔ Negotiation and agreement between the company wanting to make the takeover and the target organisation

✔ Approaching key shareholders in the target for takeover and seeing what price they'll accept for their shares

✔ A *hostile takeover*, in which the company wanting to make the takeover buys the shares of the target company on the stock market, until it has enough to gain full control

Whatever the approach, after a sale a new organisation comes into being. Even if no immediate change occurs for the employees, they're under new direction, and before long they're sure to notice some changes.

What's the difference between a takeover and a merger? Well, a *takeover* is exactly what it says: one company buys up the other and then takes control of all its activities for the future. A *merger* is where two or more companies agree to come together on an equal footing, with no control assumed by one of the pre-existing parties.

Although coming to agreement on a takeover or merger can take a lot of time, the hard work really doesn't begin until the takeover or merger happens. The people in charge need to convince staff that the takeover or merger is in their best interests too. And if the takeover or merger is accompanied by staff restructuring, redundancies and layoffs, these changes have to be done in such a way that the overall viability of the organisation isn't changed.

Privatisation

Recently, governments have sought to offload some of the public services they've traditionally offered. In many cases, they've done so through *privatisation* – valuing the particular public service activity and then selling shares on stock exchanges, or inviting companies to tender for parts of work that were previously run by public service organisations.

The theory behind privatisation is that the private sector is driven by profit, so is much more likely to be cost-effective in the delivery of public services. The reality, certainly in the case of privatised services in the UK, is that prices and charges have gone up, while the service levels, access, convenience and quality have all gone down. Transport infrastructure, water, gas and electricity have all been privatised, which has resulted in an increase in charges for these services – not only for individuals, but for companies and organisations.

The greatest problem with privatisation remains the ability to assure the quality, volume and value of services that are no longer under the purview of the government.

Chapter 6

Meeting Stakeholder Demands

. . . .

In This Chapter

▶ Identifying your stakeholders

▶ Assessing stakeholders' priorities

▶ Taking an ethical approach with stakeholders

. . . .

*S*takeholders are the individuals, groups and organisations that have an interest in the business. *Internal* stakeholders are staff, managers, owners, shareholders and directors. *External* stakeholders are suppliers, customers, the locations in which the business operates and the communities from which the suppliers, customers and staff are drawn. External stakeholders also include the media, government, statutory bodies and regulators. You also have to be aware of lobbies, vested interests, pressure groups and their interests in business activities and how these interests are carried out.

Stakeholders influence the ways in which a business operates. For example, businesses respond to customer pressures for new products and services, and improved levels of service. Businesses respond to changes in laws and regulations by altering their reporting activities. Businesses respond to lobbies and pressure groups by addressing their concerns, and modifying business activities if the concerns are legitimate.

Stakeholders influence wider business issues. A business can lose reputation if its industry or sector is known for bad working practices or mistreatment of its suppliers. So when these concerns are raised, they have to be dealt with in full, even if the particular business has in fact done nothing wrong.

All stakeholders are entitled to be treated with honesty and fairness. You need to be clear that if you start to gain a reputation for being dishonest with your stakeholders, you're going to find your reputation really hard to repair.

In this chapter, I take you through each of the types of stakeholder in turn, and take a look at stakeholder priorities and ethical issues, so you've a good grounding in how best to manage relationships with all kinds of stakeholders.

Knowing Who the Stakeholders Are

Everyone has a number of different interests (*stakes*) in different parts of society, business, companies and organisations. And everyone has expectations and aspirations that differ depending on the range of roles that people hold, and their capabilities and interests.

So, for example, a woman who has a husband and children, who works as an accountant and who likes gardening and going on holiday to Spain has a stake in:

- ✓ Her employer and that of her husband
- ✓ Schools, colleges and leisure facilities for the children
- ✓ Gardening companies and suppliers and the availability and quality of products for the garden
- ✓ Road, rail, sea and air travel, and the reliability and value of these services

She also has her own perspective on the universal demands and expectations of society: healthcare, security and policing, and the ability to live comfortably and to go about her daily activities.

The following sections take you through all of the different stakeholders in business. I cover their expectations and interests, and also show some of the ways in which you must behave towards them and treat them.

Backers

Backers (also called financiers or shareholders) are people who put money and resources into a business in order to receive one or more of the following returns on their investment:

- ✓ **Financial returns:** Backers expect to increase their investment in commercial ventures, projects, products and services.
- ✓ **Product and service sales volumes:** These enhance reputation and standing, as well as providing financial returns for the backer (ideally, causing even greater and increasing returns for the future).
- ✓ **Reputation enhancement:** Backers expect to have their reputation enhanced as the result of backing particular business and ventures, and they expect also that they will be recognised as being trustworthy and valued as an integral part of the business.

✔ **Value:** For example, government departments who put money into public services expect a return in terms of the quality and availability of the service, and the frequency with which it's delivered; the development and enhancement of the overall quality of life; and the attention being paid to factors that are presently of value to society as a whole and/or the particular groups for whom the services are being provided.

✔ **Economic returns:** Backers looking forward to high and enduring levels of return depend on a combination of your ability to command the market (or the part of it that you serve) and the extent to which you have a captive market – the greater the degree of market captivity, the greater the potential returns. If you dominate your market, you've a responsibility: do you want to gain a reputation for exploiting (or even fleecing) your customers, as well as providing high levels of returns? In most sectors, someone eventually offers a better value proposition to the customers and clients, and so the level of returns enjoyed up to that point has to change (downwards).

If you're a backer, then know your markets! Know whether the market is growing, declining, stagnant or captive, and what this means for your investment and returns. Backers of businesses that operate in captive markets have to take a fully informed view. This is because customers and clients know when they're in a captive market. As well as price rises, the other key indicator is the quality of products and services; and if quality and value are going down at the same time as prices are rising, this strategy is ultimately one for failure (see Chapter 8 on strategy).

Additionally, if your market is rapidly changing or developing, or where there is a whole string of new products coming along, be aware that not everyone might like them. In such cases, some people resent changes, so they oppose them, complaining about every minor shortcoming and delay. In many cases, they form lobbies and pressure groups to try to get things into more of a steady state. So if you're backing something that operates in a rapidly changing market or environment, you need to be prepared for this kind of opposition.

If you are a backer or investor, you need to keep in mind that if you want particular returns, you have to invest in the things that provide those returns. And if you want to invest in particular sectors, activities, products or services, you have to be prepared to take the returns that are on offer.

Whatever results and returns you seek or demand as a backer, simply piling resources or throwing money at something doesn't of itself bring success. However much money and resources you invest, resources still have to be spent as effectively as possible and targeted precisely at the results that you want to achieve. Of course, in many cases backers do get the returns that they seek. In other cases, however, backers have to conclude that they are not going to get high levels of returns from some investments.

Being a backer: The story of David Parkin

For the past nine years, David Parkin has been a director of one of the UK's major domestic fuel suppliers. In this position, he has presided over the trebling of consumer prices. David is also a non-executive director of one of the UK's top retail chains. As such, he's had to explain to the retail chain shareholders the effects of the activities of one of his employers on the other.

The lesson? If you back something or are involved in something, business is never straightforward! You have to be able to see what's often a particularly complex picture. You have to be able to recognise that an action you take for the interests of one group of stakeholders may have detrimental effects on others.

Staff

Staff are a key stakeholder group and they play a critical role. They combine together into teams and groups, departments and divisions to produce and deliver the organisation's products and services. They make the difference between success and failure, progress and stagnation, change and inertia. And crucially, the average staff cost across all organisations is between 60 and 70 per cent of capital employed.

Of all the parts of business that managers hate, attending to the staff is top of the list. People are unique and individual, and they have their own hopes, fears and aspirations that those in charge have to recognise and deal with – which is stressful, but necessary.

Here are the first steps toward understanding the staff as stakeholders:

- ✔ Respecting and valuing their contribution

- ✔ Taking all steps necessary to ensure that their contribution is as effective as possible

- ✔ Valuing them as a resource

- ✔ Respecting them as individuals as well as the investment that the organisation has made in them as a workforce

- ✔ Rewarding them – financially, of course, and also in terms of satisfaction, fulfilment and development

The forms of organisation and management, and the mix of collective and individual aspirations and ambitions, form the basis for recognising the staff as stakeholders in particular ways. Consider these key questions:

✔ Why do companies and organisations staff and structure themselves in the ways that they do?

✔ What are the organisation's ambitions, and how are these integrated with those of the staff?

✔ What aspirations does the organisation have and how do the staff deliver them (and how should the staff be delivering them)?

It sounds like a lot of hard work. However, if managers take the time and trouble to find out what staff truly expect and to recognise what they can and can't offer, they save a whole lot of trouble later on in terms of staffing problems and collective and individual motivation – and therefore in managing performance.

Customers and clients

No business has any reason to exist except because of its customers and clients. So you have to understand exactly what the customers and clients of any organisation require and expect.

Recognising customers and clients as legitimate stakeholders means that you're completely clear about the price, quality, value, volume and time mix:

✔ **Price:** What customers are willing to pay for particular products, services and service levels.

✔ **Quality:** Durability, usefulness and benefits that the purchase of the product or service brings.

✔ **Time:** A reflection of how quickly customers can gain access to the products and services available, and how long it takes to get to the location where products and services are delivered.

✔ **Value:** The position of the product or service in the eyes of the customers and clients.

✔ **Volume:** The ability to access the numbers of products or services demanded.

Look at the full range of reasons that customers and clients use particular organisations, and why they don't use others. Above all, don't make assumptions about price and charges. If it were the case that the only thing you had to do to bring in customers was to bring your prices down, then everyone would use cheap supermarkets and stores, and not the more expensive ones like John Lewis or Marks & Spencer.

Batchelors Foods Ltd

Batchelors Foods Ltd specialises in producing soups, noodles in pots and other ready meals for the retail grocery sector. The company has taken a precise view of what it can offer people in terms of career progression and development: none of these things! Instead, Batchelors offers

✔ High salaries relative to other parts of the food industry, and also in relation to what's on offer elsewhere in the locations where it operates

✔ Identification of a steady stream of people who come to work for the company as and when required

Batchelors has taken the view that it can't offer anything except the work and money. Identifying that on average people stay with the company for just over seven months, Batchelors has therefore taken steps to ensure that it has a steady and reliable stream of labour rather than trying to offer other motivations for people to stay.

Customers and clients expect to:

✔ Be treated with politeness, courtesy and respect

✔ Have their concerns and questions addressed with respect when these are raised

✔ Have problems put right as soon as possible when these arise

Stew Leonard, Inc

Stew Leonard, Inc is a small supermarket company based in Norwalk, Connecticut, USA. The company was founded by Stew Leonard and each of the three stores is run by one of his children. His son, Stew Leonard Jr, is the CEO. The company is the highest performing supermarket in the world in terms of income per square metre, income per product line and income per product cluster.

The company carries out regular consultations with customers and all staff have to participate. One customer said: 'The fish you sell isn't fresh.

It is always hygienic because you shrink-wrap it and keep it on ice. But from time to time, I would like to be able to buy the fish fresh off the ice.'

The company's first response was to assert that the reason it shrink-wraps the fish is to make sure that it stays fresh. However, it then decided to try selling fresh fish too.

The company lost no sales of shrink-wrapped fish. It gained sales of fish straight off the ice worth between $15,000 and $50,000 per week, depending on the season.

Suppliers

Of all the key stakeholder groups, *suppliers* – those who provide you with the raw materials, expertise and other resources that you need to be fully effective – are those that people tend to neglect. Yet if you want to conduct effective business, you have to know and understand the supply side in full; and understanding it means recognising suppliers as a priority stakeholder for every organisation, whatever their activities.

Suppliers include those of:

- Components and raw materials

- Information, information technology and other technology-based services

- Business support functions (for example, catering, security, transport and accounts)

- Customer service functions (for example, web support and telephone helplines)

- Specialist services (for example, expertise, consulting and technology support)

All organisations recognise that managing the supply side is a key expense, and so they try to ensure that they get the best possible service from their suppliers as cost-effectively as possible. They create relationships based on:

- Costs and charges that are sufficiently low for the purchaser to remain viable, and sufficiently high to be commercially worthwhile for the supplier

- Enduring confidence in the viability of the other to continue in the relationship for as long as it suits everyone concerned

- Effective management of problems related to variability in the supplies required (on the one hand) and available (on the other)

- Adaptability if prices, charges and volumes have to be varied

In practice, many organisations go to a lot of trouble to 'manage' the supply side as follows:

- Playing off one supplier against others to try to get the lowest prices

- Cancelling contracts at short notice in favour of a fresh, new and supposedly cheaper (better value) supplier

- Driving down prices because they can, because they're in a dominant position

- Delaying payments to suppliers as a matter of company policy

REAL WORLD EXAMPLE

Helmont

Helmont is an English fish-processing and cannery company. Until recently, it took its supplies of fish from Ocean-Going Trawlers Ltd, a fishing fleet based in Liverpool. Helmont Ltd was a highly successful and profitable company and supplied to all the main retail brands.

Following new quota arrangements, the prices of landed fish catches in the UK rose by 10 per cent. Accordingly, Helmont decided to look around for alternative suppliers. After extensive research, the company found that the port and fishing fleet of Cadiz, Spain were prepared to supply them with the volumes of fish and the regularity of deliveries required at a cheaper price. So Helmont cancelled the contract with Ocean-Going Trawlers and took up with Cadiz.

But the fish from Cadiz tasted different, and many of Helmont's customers changed supplier. And transportation slowed due to refrigeration units on the lorries breaking down, plus hold-ups with the border authorities between France and Spain, in the Channel ports in northern France and on the motorway network in England.

In order to remain viable, Helmont had to return to Ocean-Going Trawlers in Liverpool and do its best to renegotiate the contract. This they did, but the conditions in the new contract were much less beneficial to Helmont.

Superficially attractive as each of these strategies is, they're no basis for building an enduring and mutually profitable relationship. If a business wants a genuinely secure supply side, it needs to treat suppliers as a priority stakeholder and build effective and enduring relations with them.

The public and the media

The public and the media are stakeholders because of the influence that they have on everyone. Businesses have to understand and manage public perceptions so that everyone understands what the business does and has confidence in it.

The public and the media have clear expectations of organisations, and comment whenever they've cause to do so. All businesses seek public support and always want positive media coverage. Businesses try to manage public and media perceptions by ensuring that:

✔ They gain the best possible media coverage and that every story is positive

✔ They're honest and transparent at all times

✔ They're prepared to contribute to the public and to the communities in which they work

✔ During a crisis, they face the public and the media, stating as clearly as possible what's gone wrong and why, what they're going to do to put it right and how long it will take

A more or less universal truth is that everyone likes to be liked and respected, and companies and organisations are no different! Managing relations with the public and the media helps to build respect, trust and confidence – and means that if (when) a business runs into trouble, the publicity is likely to be less negative.

Pressure groups

Pressure groups, lobbies and vested interests spring up to advance their point of view on any matter at all, and they exist in all parts of business. Essentially, pressure groups take one of the following positions:

✔ **Internal lobbies and vested interests:** They exist within companies and organisations. Such groups include professional and managerial clusters, trade unions, staff interest groups and people working at a given location in large and complex organisations.

In addition, in the UK and USA specific shareholder pressure groups are created within the banks and financial houses to ensure that rules and regulations about risk, compliance and due diligence are indeed followed. Some of these groups call company directors and top managers to account for their actions taken in the name of the particular company.

✔ **External groups:** These groups have a direct interest in what goes on in particular organisations. Groups include:

- Patients' groups in health services.

- Groups of parents of children at schools and colleges.

- Consumer groups related to particular products and services.

- Local environmental action groups that have concerns about the ways in which companies and organisations are conducting their business. These groups are especially concerned with waste disposal and effluent management.

- Groups opposed to specific business consequences, such as transport and traffic congestion, that are caused by particular activities.

- Wider environmental action groups, raising more enduring concerns about pollution and waste management.

- Organisations that themselves act as lobbies and vested interests, such as employers' associations, trade unions, Greenpeace and Friends of the Earth. They've a legitimate (indeed statutory) obligation and interest in how other organisations conduct themselves in relation to their own stakeholder groups, and to the business operations and wider environment.

HBOS

One of the matters that brought the financial crisis of 2007–08 to a head was the corporate attitude of Halifax Bank of Scotland (HBOS), the UK retail banking group, to a journalist's story that stated that HBOS's assets were over-valued. Rather than responding to the concern, HBOS tried to vilify the journalist, stating that he was a reprobate and a drug user who frequented sleazy bars.

Everyone now knew that the story had substance – if there were no truth in the tale, HBOS would have dealt with it at face value. So journalists began to dig for new information. And quickly it became apparent that the assets of the company were indeed greatly over-valued.

Lobbies and vested interests also spring up in response to particular concerns at different times. For example, at present in many parts of the world farmers' lobbies are doing their best to ensure that supermarket chains don't drive their prices down to the point at which farming activities no longer remain viable.

Whatever the vested interest or pressure group, dealing with any concern need not take long provided that those in charge of the particular matter or issue are determined to work hard to address it.

Some pressure groups can simply be ignored or slapped down. In these cases, however, you do have to be sure that they will not simply come back at you another way. Otherwise, in many cases failure to deal with matters fully or effectively means that the particular lobby or vested interest simply assumes that their concern has substance, and so they dig for more information anyway.

Understanding Stakeholders' Priorities

All stakeholders have legitimate concerns and issues, and any stakeholder that raises any issue at all does so because it's of importance to them. So businesses must recognise and deal with the issues that stakeholders raise.

WARNING!

A business doesn't have to cave in to every last demand that a stakeholder makes. But it does have to prepare for anything that comes its way, from any source at all. Knowing all your stakeholders and their concerns reinforces overall standing and respect with everyone, which in turn helps to build confidence and reputation. And if businesses don't deal with issues openly and honestly, people simply assume that the particular business has something to hide, or is incompetent (or both).

Businesses need to consider the priority order for stakeholders – whether the organisation places the interests of one or more groups above the others.

Nothing's wrong with having one group of stakeholders as the priority. For example, if from time to time a company manages its share value so that people continue to back it, then the shareholders are the legitimate priority and the company can be totally open about this.

In some places, the staff are accorded the same standing as the backers and financial interests. In some sectors, a statutory obligation gives the staff the same standing on the direction and development of the organisation of business as the financial interests.

In public services, successive governments have sought to put:

✔ Patients at the heart of the NHS (patients are the priority stakeholder)

✔ Parents at the heart of the school system (because they have the major interest in the education of their children)

Each of these positions is clearly stated and justified so everyone knows and understands the priority order, even if they don't necessarily agree with it.

Writing in 1987, Wheeler and Silanpaa proposed The Stakeholder Corporation, in which the only true path to enduring success is recognising the full diversity of legitimate demands made by backers, customers, clients, staff and suppliers – and then making sure that you serve the interests of everyone. Wheeler and Silanpaa argued that if you try to prioritise one group in favour of others you create an imbalance; and that this imbalance in turn leads to the destabilisation of organisations.

So, if a business prioritises stakeholders in terms of how it treats them, the business needs a rationale. For example, in the Virgin organisation, staff come first, because, as Richard Branson stated on the BBC's *Money Programme* in 2002, 'Only by having highly capable and motivated staff can you deliver the quality of service that our customers expect. If you do this, then the customers will keep coming back.' For South-Western Airlines, conversely, customers are the priority, and the company lobbies on behalf of customers in areas such as fuel charge rises.

Considering Ethical Issues

Most of the dealings that a business has with its stakeholders have ethics at their heart. Dealing with matters openly and honestly when they arise reinforces perceptions of overall integrity. Failure to deal with issues quickly and comprehensively gives rise to the belief that the business is prevaricating or that it has something to hide.

So, for example:

- If you're a manager and a member of staff asks for a pay increase, you need to able to say whether or not this is going to be possible. If you're going to agree, you need to be able to state clearly how much the increase is going to be – and why it is to be this much and no more or no less.

- If your business is having to put up the prices of products and services, you need to be able to explain why.

In general, therefore, businesses need to be as open and honest as possible in dealings with stakeholders. Especially, they must make sure that everything they do meets with legal as well as moral standards. All organisations are accountable for their actions, and anyone who breaks the law must ultimately answer to the legal systems of whatever country, state or region they're operating in. Anyone who becomes involved in litigation knows that legal action is expensive, time-consuming and stressful. The best approach, therefore, is to maintain standards that result in a much-reduced chance of being sued.

For more on ethics, flip to Chapter 2.

It's much easier and quicker to lose a reputation for fairness, trustworthiness and honesty, than it is to build one. Therefore, managers have to:

- Uphold standards of conduct and behaviour, performance, and product and service delivery

- Manage shareholders and other financial interests

- Work within the law, regulations and statutes

- Work within the culture of social norms of the locations in which they operate

- Set and maintain the highest possible standards of integrity and transparency

- Manage dishonesty

If managers commit to each of these aspects, they effectively manage stakeholders and deal with problems as they arise.

Chapter 7

Organising for Success

In This Chapter
▶ Understanding the concept of organising for success
▶ Seeing how to organise work and work groups
▶ Handling major staffing issues
▶ Knowing the use and value of technology and assets

*O*rganising for success means getting together all the resources required and then deciding how to combine them to best advantage so that you can achieve your goals and objectives. It gives the basis on which you serve your customers. It provides the platform from which you meet your obligations to all your stakeholders, giving them what they need, want and expect from you. In particular:

✔ Customers get the best possible products and services whenever they need and want.

✔ Staff get long-term job and work security and the resources to work as effectively as possible on their given tasks.

✔ Backers and financiers get the returns that they need, want and demand from their investment in the company.

✔ The company or organisation itself makes a good contribution to the locations in which it bases its activities.

So if you put the nature of companies and organisations and the purposes for which they exist together with the interests and demands of all stakeholders, you have the best possible basis for success, as follows:

✔ Delivering profitable products and services in the commercial sectors

✔ Ensuring the highest possible levels and coverage of service in public sectors

✔ Ensuring that the groups and interests using the not-for-profit sector get the very best services possible

In this chapter, I look at everything necessary to organise for success. You have to build your own foundations for this. You go on to determine the particular form of organisation that you need and want. You determine the places where you are going to operate, the nature of the work groups that you need, and the technology and expertise that you are going to employ.

Building the Foundations for Organising for Success

In any sector, in order to organise for success, a business has to focus on the following:

- **Knowing what success means to the organisation and the stakeholders.** Success is a value judgement. You can't call on any sales figure, profit margin or percentage increase in income or turnover in isolation from everything that's going on around you.

- **Setting out a vision.** *Vision* is intangible, but it means having clearly in your mind's eye a picture or impression of what you want to do, how, when, where and why. The business needs to know what it wants to achieve overall, and then define the steps to get there. Then everyone knows what the business stands for and how it operates. Vision creates certainty and clarity, which people like.

- **Defining objectives.** You can't measure anything as a success unless you were clear about what you set out to achieve in the first place. You can ask:

  - What did we set out to achieve? Did we achieve it? If so, why? If not, why not?

  - What else did we achieve along the way? Why are these achievements and not consequences?

  - What did we not foresee, and why? Could we have foreseen it?

  - What are we going to do now and next? Why? How does the next part of progress shape up?

- **Knowing that organising for success is a process.** You never actually stop; you can never ever say: 'We have arrived; we can rest on our laurels.'

- **Being clear about the standards you're setting.** Be especially clear about conduct and behaviour – these things determine what people actually think of a particular company. Especially if you're known or perceived to be achieving things at the expense of morals or ethics, your conduct and behaviour may be questioned. Being in this situation can, and does, lead to adverse media coverage, and you may then have to manage declining sales and commercial performance, as well as the coverage itself.

Having a clear vision

You can state a vision in simple, clear terms. Here are a few examples:

✔ **The Body Shop:** When Anita Roddick was founding The Body Shop, she said that all she ever wanted to do was to make enough money to feed her family.

✔ **Rolling Stones:** Asked about the enduring success of the Rolling Stones in 2009, Mick Jagger said, simply, 'All we ever set out to do was to give people a good night out.'

✔ **Swatch:** When Nicholas Hayek, the founder of Swatch, was asked in 2002 what made the company so successful, he said, 'We were always very clear what the Swatch watch stood for. It is good value; distinctive appearance; fashionability; something that people wanted to be seen wearing.'

Understanding the Nature of Organisation

How companies and organisations structure themselves in order to give themselves the best possible chance of success is very much a matter of individual choice, but in every case the following have to be in place:

✔ **Coordinating activities** so that people work toward delivering the vision and meeting the objectives (refer to the preceding section 'Building the Foundations for Organising for Success').

✔ **Planning for the present and future** by determining the mix and volume of activities, as well as planning the kind of organisation and the skills, knowledge, attitudes, behaviour and expertise required.

✔ **Controlling the ways in which staff carry out activities** to ensure the required standard of production, service delivery and service levels.

✔ **Controlling the finances** to ensure that costs are kept to a minimum and revenues to a maximum.

✔ **Directing and developing the performance levels** required and demanded.

✔ **Managing location issues** so that all the pressures of being in a particular location are addressed and accommodated. For example, if public transport is restricted, you have to ensure that your work patterns fit in with people's ability to get to work. Organisations that work in many locations have to create work patterns that fit with each place of work, which may mean that you have to have hours of work that vary between locations – it may not be possible to put everyone on the same schedule. For more on location, head to the next section.

REAL WORLD EXAMPLE

Olympic athletic wear

In the run-up to the London Olympics, the conduct and behaviour of Adidas, the supplier of athletics equipment for Team GB, was questioned. Adidas was faced with questions about how the equipment was being produced. A team of reporters uncovered an alleged scandal about the manufacture of the rowing, boxing, football and hockey kits that were being produced for Team GB, and for the merchandising of replica kits.

The reporters had been told to go to a factory in Indonesia where they found people working 65 hours a week for $2 per day. They also found evidence of child labour and the physical abuse of staff by supervisors.

The reporters took the issue to Adidas, who first declined to comment. When presented with the evidence, the company agreed to review its commissioning processes and factory supervision. However, it refused to close down the Indonesian operation and move production elsewhere.

There have been regular scandals among clothing manufacturers. Over the years, all the major companies have been found to have used child, slave and low-paid labour to produce high-value branded goods.

In the case of Adidas and Team GB, however, the attachment to the alleged Olympic ideal of fairness and conduct caused the team bosses to consider whether to change suppliers even at that late stage.

In this case, neither Adidas nor Team GB had fully organised for success. They had all the external paraphernalia and trappings of success – but they had failed to consider that how things were being produced was as critical as what was being produced and delivered.

Considering Locations of Work

When considering locations of work, you've a range of factors to take into account. You need to ensure that wherever you set up, you can do the work (or have it done) effectively and profitably, whatever the constraints.

All parts of the structure need equal treatment and consideration; you don't want people working in remote locations forming the impression that what they do is of no consequence because nobody appears to take any notice of them.

REMEMBER

Wherever you locate, you must have a cost-effective approach, even if you've non-standard or unsynchronised operations. If you need to have some harmonisation across different locations, then make sure that people are able to be there when you need them.

Weighing up a location

The following are considerations businesses make when it comes to the location(s) of their activities:

✔ Do we have to compete for staff with those already operating in an area?

✔ What are the property prices, rentals and values? You need to be able to answer this question both from the point of view of affordability to your own business, and also affordability to staff whom you might want to recruit in the future.

✔ Is the location easy to access for deliveries, dispatch of products/ services and customer visits?

✔ Are the premises equipped to the standards of furnishings and technology that enable people to do their jobs fully and effectively?

✔ Will people want to come and work for us here, and be proud to be associated with the organisation?

✔ Will backers, suppliers and customers be impressed by the premises?

✔ Are the premises secure and safe, and able to store products, services, data and equipment without fear that anything will be stolen or compromised, or that accidents or disasters will happen?

If you're looking to expand, consider the costs incurred. You're paying out of your existing volumes of business and organisation resources. The income generated from the new activities and locations hasn't yet arrived!

Of course, creating the ideal work location is only possible in an ideal world. So, you have to temper the crucial issues with a dose of reality. If you need staff in difficult locations, then you have to be prepared to help them get in and away from these areas. If your staff depends on public transport to get to work, you have to be prepared to operate within any constraints that the transport networks impose. If you've traffic problems related to your access and egress route networks, you have to be prepared to schedule your supplies and deliveries at times when traffic is less of a problem.

Working via the Internet

An ever increasing number of organisations have their own virtual location, enabling people to work for their company wherever they happen to be. However, people working offsite means that the website has to deliver the equivalent of everything that's available from physical premises. From the point of view of staff usage and access, the virtual location must:

- Be comprehensive

- Be user-friendly for everyone who comes to the site

- Give clear and simple directions for usage

- Provide all the links that anyone is going to need

- Provide meeting forums where required

- Protect confidential commercial and personal information

- Give points of contact that people need when working from remote locations

- Give points of contact that people need when working with you, including customer, supplier, backer and media interests

Businesses must keep websites up to date. Preaching perfection, a business updates the website on a daily basis. Preaching reality, the business puts in place inspection schedules so that staff examine the site often and update it when necessary. The website must be supported and serviced by technology and expertise so as to make an enduringly viable contribution to overall performance and represent the company's 'virtual headquarters'.

Boo.com

You can't organise anything in isolation, but you can't have an effective and enduring web presence unless you recognise the nature of the environment and markets in which you have to be able to conduct profitable activities.

Boo.com was a Swedish online shoe retailer. Working from premises just outside Stockholm, the company purported to be able to sell shoes to anyone, anywhere in the world. The company raised over £300 million in start-up capital. However, it quickly ran into difficulties on all fronts:

- Boo.com realised that people bought shoes on impulse, or because they needed them. Therefore, the Internet business model that assured people that they would get their shoes in seven to ten days was not a sound basis for conducting activities.

- Staff conditions and the working environment were of the highest order, but the volumes of business conducted could not pay for the costs involved.

- Boo.com had no customer support telephone lines or physical access, which meant that the company quickly gained a reputation for providing a slow and poor service.

The company was forced to acknowledge that it can effectively only supply shoes on a commercially viable basis to the immediate locality – which removed much of the rationale for having a fully web-based activity.

The best and most commercially viable web-based activities are fully integrated with the needs of customers, as well as with any physical presence held by the company or organisation. So, for example:

✔ Web-based grocery sales are integrated with what's provided in supermarkets. Customers move around a virtual store, make their choices and pay for them. The only difference is that the groceries are then delivered rather than taken home by the customer.

✔ Travel and holiday purchases made online result in the delivery of the tickets and confirmation of accommodation at the moment the payment is made. So everything is delivered at exactly the same speed as if the customers had gone into a shop and made the purchases.

On the other hand, the contribution of some overtly web-based activities isn't always clear. For example:

✔ NHS online invariably gives advice to seek the advice of your doctor or consult your pharmacist.

✔ Airport support websites invariably ask you to check with your airline to see whether air travel problems exist.

✔ Police websites give phone numbers to report crimes and concerns – sometimes after the telephone line has requested that you go online in the first place.

The key issue, therefore, is that the website as location has to have its own value for those using it. Part of that value is the fact of its existence, but this in itself isn't enough. As a result of visiting the website, users must be able to do something or gain something that they didn't have before.

Organising Work and Work Groups

Many different forms of organisation exist, driven by size, location, products and services produced and delivered, ranges of activities and the need to accommodate staff and equipment. (For more on organisation types, take a look at Chapter 5.)

Every organisation is different, and each has its own ways of structuring and organising work and *work groups* (the teams of people who work together to deliver the activities required). But all organisations require order so that the collective effort is effective, valuable and profitable. So individual tasks bundle up into jobs; jobs bundle up into departments, divisions, functions and work groups; and all this, in turn, gives you the size and structure of the organisation that's going to deliver everything that it promises – in the volumes, quality and locations chosen, to the satisfaction of staff, customers and backers.

Within this complexity, a business carries out the following tasks and activities:

- ✔ Producing and delivering products and services, and providing customer and client service in support of them
- ✔ Managing the supply side, ensuring that everything needed gets into the organisation
- ✔ Managing the distribution side, so that products and services reach those who need them
- ✔ Keeping records and files on every aspect of the organisation
- ✔ Providing everything that staff members need to be able to do their jobs
- ✔ Providing means of supervision and control
- ✔ Meeting legal and statutory obligations in terms of making reports to governmental and other public authorities

In order to achieve all of this and still deliver the best products and services, companies and organisations are usually broken up into departments, divisions and functions. These departments, divisions and functions are then staffed by people capable and willing to work in them. And to work effectively, they are then given the technology and equipment required to do their jobs to the best of their capabilities.

Departments, divisions and functions

The purpose of an organisation structure is to break down all of the work that is required, into something manageable and effective. Normally, doing so means that you organise everything according to one of the following:

- ✔ **Function:** What a department is there to do, for example, marketing, sales, accounts, production and HR.
- ✔ **Location:** For example, the London office and the Paris factory.
- ✔ **Activity:** What a company actually does, involving the work of both individual departments and also across the whole organisation, for example, the IT project and the new market in Shanghai.

Large and complex organisations need additional structuring, as follows:

- ✔ **Regional offices,** responsible for a part of the market or country in which activities are carried out.

✔ **Divisions and divisionalisation,** in which activities are grouped together to form a recognisable whole. For example, Ford has manufacturing divisions; easyJet has sales divisions; Dell has research divisions – and these divisions are structured as such because of the sheer size of the operations.

✔ **Subsidiaries,** which carry out specific activities in given locations.

Thus you produce a management and directional structure to ensure the optimum control and coordination of activities, control of resources and ability to operate wherever required. In other words, you produce an organisation chart – a representation of the organisation that you can see and that you can make available to everyone (see Figure 7-1). You need this representation so that you and everyone else in the organisation have a clear view of what is being managed and organised.

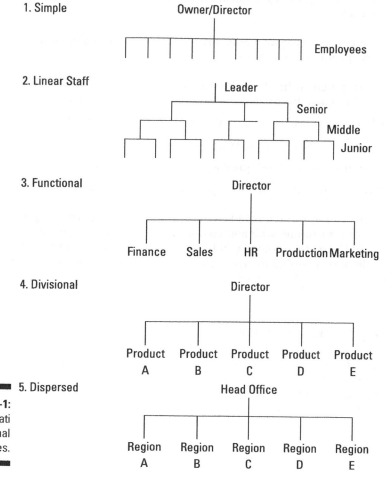

Figure 7-1:
Organisational structures.

You have an organisation structure that everyone understands. You use this to allocate the different activities that have to be carried out on the most efficient and effective basis possible, in accordance with your stated targets, objectives and priorities. This form of organisation also means that you are clearly stating:

- Areas of responsibility, authority and accountability
- The creation of working relationships and operating mechanisms
- Division and allocation of work, responsibility and authority
- Patterns of management, supervision and work control

The nature of the work, the size of the organisation and the technology and equipment available affect the structure. For example, an organisation may break down large staff groups into subgroups so that someone can keep control of them.

When it comes to departments, divisions and functions, businesses have a few key questions to address:

- How much authority and autonomy are we going to give to individuals, and to each group, department, division and function?
- How are we going to arrange the basis of overall control?
- What kind of reporting relationships do we put in place?
- What standards and quality of performance do we require?
- What is our approach to supervision and management?

Any organisation also has to be capable of addressing what happens on a daily basis, including staff and customer relations issues, production hold-ups, and IT and technology glitches. It also has to be structured so as to be capable of responding to crises and emergencies and any sudden opportunities that present themselves.

Spans of control

A *span of control* is the relationship between each work group and its supervisor or manager. Large spans of control mean that businesses have few managerial layers and fewer levels of hierarchy; smaller spans of control mean the contrary. Figure 7-2 shows different spans of control.

REAL WORLD EXAMPLE

The case of the invisible job

After graduating from business school, John went to work for a large manufacturing corporation. This organisation was tightly structured and controlled, with manuals, procedures and policies for every eventuality. This first job provided an excellent grounding for John; however, after two years, he decided it was time to move on, so he went to work for a smaller but fast-growing finance house.

John was welcomed into his new job with open arms. He met his new colleagues and settled down to work. But he couldn't quite work out what he was meant to be doing. He asked a colleague. He didn't know. So he asked to see his line manager. The colleague wasn't sure who the line manager was either. Eventually, John went to see one of the partners to ask where the rules and procedures for governing his behaviour and performance were.

The partner replied: 'We don't have any procedures and regulations like that. We want you out in the field, looking for ideas, finding clients, generating business. You're expected to use your own knowledge and expertise in deciding what are good ventures for us to be involved in.'

The story illustrates the effect and influence that organisation structure can have on individuals, and their behaviour and performance. In this case, John now found himself having to get used to a different way of doing things quickly. The structures were indeed there, but they were different to what John had been used to. The lesson is that whatever the structure, everyone needs to know and understand how it works, and how it supports and enables the work that has to be done.

With spans of control, businesses need to consider some key issues:

- ✔ How closely do we want staff to be supervised?

- ✔ How many layers of supervision and management can we afford, both from the point of view of paying for them and also in terms of their contribution to operational efficiency and effectiveness?

- ✔ To what extent do we need supervisory and managerial layers for the purposes of career development and promotion paths?

An organisational and managerial fashion exists at present for *delayering* (removing levels of supervision and management, and giving additional responsibilities and autonomy to frontline staff alongside their main duties). Superficially, delayering is attractive. Where it can be made to work, it saves costs and adds variety and enrichment to people's jobs. But reporting relationships and controls still have to be in place and capable of operation in the new delayered structures. Otherwise, businesses don't keep to budgets and resource allocations, and consequently they leave a mess that's expensive to clear up. And keep in mind that delayering means training and briefing the frontline staff for their new responsibilities, and paying them more.

A. (4-person span of control)

A. (4-person span of control)

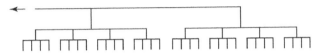

Spans of control (1)

A. 4:1 (32 persons, 8 suservisors, 2 managers)

B. 8:1 (32 persons, 8 suservisors, 0.5 managers)

Figure 7-2:
Spans of
control.

Spans of control (2)

Whatever the approach taken, everyone must be clear at all times about what they need to do, how, when, where and why. So long as the span of control, method of supervision, reporting relationships and ability to account for everything are effective, any approach is fine.

Spans of control look great and it is very reassuring to see them. However, the real world isn't always so simple. Watch especially for these two key problems in all sets of circumstances:

✔ How to manage effectively someone (individual or group) who has two or more bosses – for example, when they're working on steady-state work in one area but carrying out project work in another.

✔ How to supervise and manage effectively those who don't attend the place of work often – for example, those who work in the field or in remote locations, those who telework from home or those on permanent night or weekend shifts.

Businesses need to devise patterns of supervision and management that include all staff in communications, consultations and information exchanges. Staff away from the place of work need to get hold of managers whenever they've problems and issues. And managers need to have regular email and phone contact with everyone.

Dealing with Staffing Issues

Organising for success means recognising the vital nature of effective staffing. Businesses have to:

- ✔ Define the people they need and then go out and find them

- ✔ Develop opportunities for staff in terms of career prospects and personal, professional and occupational development

- ✔ Relate staff effort and staff development to organisational growth and progress

If you can identify and target the kinds of people who want to work for you and then go and build relations with them, you greatly enhance the cost-effectiveness of your staffing effort.

For more on human resource management, head to Chapter 16.

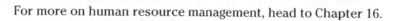

Federal Reserve

During one of the many meetings about staffing matters, and especially about the ability to attract and retain good people, a senior manager at the Federal Reserve said, 'Our trouble is that we are unable to compete for top-quality staff. We simply don't pay enough. Anyone who is any good will go and make their fortune in the commercial sector.'

Everyone in the meeting agreed that a problem existed. However, one of those present went away and set to work. She returned to the next staffing meeting with a set of proposals. She said, 'We need to look at what we do offer, not what we don't offer. After all, we are offering the chance to be involved in federal policy;

international, economic and monetary development; relations with the European Central Bank, World Bank and International Monetary Fund. And the salary of $200,000 isn't bad, even if it isn't as high as the commercial sector. So I suggest that we concentrate on using these factors to find the people that want to come and work for us, who want to be involved in this way.'

If you think about the staffing effort in terms of what you offer, rather than worrying about what others offer, then targeting the right people becomes much more effective. And it also, crucially, gives a huge boost to your chances of organising for success and making the structures that you have work well for you.

Investing in Technology and Assets

Organising for success involves making sure that people have all the technology, equipment and resources that they need to do their jobs effectively, and that staff are trained and expert in the technology and equipment.

Sounds obvious, doesn't it? And yet companies in all parts of the world buy in technology because technology is the next corporate 'must have' – and then they're faced with having to junk what they already have, install the new technology and retrain their staff, or operate it alongside what they have and hope that the two systems are compatible.

Whatever technology you need and use, when organising for success you have to obey some rules:

 ✔ Businesses have to buy technology out of existing resources – the return on investment only occurs when the technology is up and running, and producing and delivering what's required.

 ✔ To be effective, all technology and technology replacements and upgrades need to be able to do the volumes and quality of work better, more quickly and to higher standards than what is presently in use.

 ✔ The business has to invest in staff training, development and familiarisation, and staff have to accept the new technology as the preferred way of doing the work.

Investment in websites, networks and organisation intranets has to have discernible and stated returns. And although complex websites and networks are likely to be technologically superb and show off the expertise of those who design them, their chief purpose must be to do the job.

Keep in mind that technology has a limited useful life, so it will one day have to be written off and replaced. A businesses needs to know the boundaries of the useful life before buying the technology. Therefore, return on investment has to be achieved within the boundaries and timescales envisaged. If this doesn't appear to be possible, then you shelve the idea and consider other possible approaches.

Moore's Law states that the capacity of technology doubles every 18 months. This doubling is an essential lesson for all organisations and their managers. If it turns out that a business gets a greater useful life out of its existing technology and equipment, so much the better. But a technological advancement may render uncompetitive what the business is currently using.

REAL WORLD EXAMPLE

Barbie

When Mattel designed the first Barbie website, it took into account the following:

- ✔ The nature of those who would be using and accessing it: girls ages 3 to 11 and their mothers, aunts, friends and sisters

- ✔ The speed and simplicity with which all of the website links could be used

- ✔ The security of payments and personal details

- ✔ The colours and images on the site

Mattel then had to relate the key points of the website to the company's own approach to organising for success. So the systems had to be easy to use, user friendly and accessible for customers and small children. They also had to be easily used by the staff. The website had to support the standard retail effort, and provide customer and user support whenever required. This fact meant, in turn, that staff had to have access at all times. Customer response times and the quality of response remained the priority in terms of organising for success. Everything that was implemented had to enhance sales, customer relations and the brand. Whatever the technology used, this kind of focus needs to always be the driving force when organising for success.

Part III

How to Be a Business and Do Business

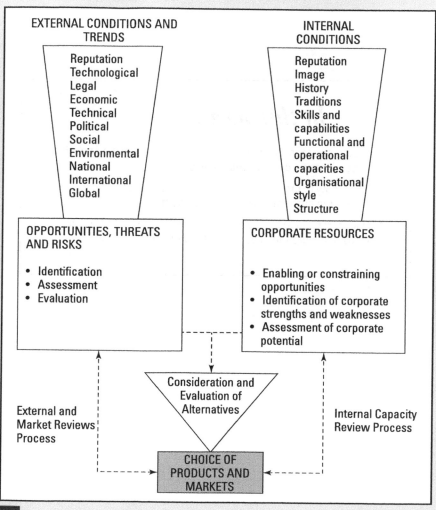

In this part . . .

- ✔ Create a core foundation or generic strategic position on which to conduct and develop your business.

- ✔ Know how to create great products and services in order to attract the customers you need and want.

- ✔ Use marketing to build an identity for your products and services to ensure the enduring viability of your business.

Chapter 8

Understanding Business Strategy

Spend any amount of time in boardrooms or flying business class, and you're sure to hear the word *strategy* bandied about. Well, there's a reason for that: an organisation's strategy has everything to do with its success. If you're not clear on your strategy, how are you going to know whether you're on the right path?

Strategy is the subject of this chapter. I start by telling you what strategy is (and what strategy isn't). Then I walk you through how to define your organisation's strategy and implement it.

Knowing What Strategy Is (and Isn't)

Business strategy is about deciding what you do, when you do it, where you do it, why you do it and for whom. Business strategy is also about deciding what you *won't* do. In other words, strategy is about setting the course for the organisation, and then guiding and directing the organisation along that course, advancing and developing to meet changing markets and operational conditions, and ensuring short-term and long-term survival.

My friend Peter Antonioni (he of '*Economics For Dummies*' fame) describes strategy as 'the long view of the big picture'. This is as good a summary as you are ever going to get. And you need to be able to see and understand all parts of the long view, and every detail of the big picture at all times, so that you know how the whole hangs together.

You may have seen 'strategies' that look glossy and productive – for example, 'We aim to be the world's fastest-growing online retailer,' or 'We will seek opportunities wherever they may arise.' But dig a little deeper and you see that these words lack substance – they don't say anything about what the organisations will do, when, where, why and for whom. Strategies aren't about corporate boasting.

Strategy is a process: a combination of the vision that you have for the present and future, and the full range of decisions that you have to take to move things forward. The strategy process is evolving continuously, and it has to address:

- Matching what you're capable of with what your customers, clients and backers want, need and demand.

- Looking for opportunities for new ventures, and for developing what you already have.

- Responding to opportunities, problems and crises that come up on hourly, daily and weekly bases.

- Being competitive: what you do has to at least be an alternative to what others are doing in your industry or sector.

In order to be effective, a strategy needs to be:

- **Clear and specific:** A clear, accurate and well-defined strategy is at the core of all successful organisations. When an organisation isn't successful, the reason is often because the organisation lacks clarity of purpose. When you know what your purpose is, you can effectively and efficiently manage your resources to develop new products and services that the market wants.

- **Flexible:** Strategy isn't a rigid plan or course of action that you follow blindly once you have it in place. Any organisation must be flexible and responsive to opportunities as they arise.

- **Evolving:** Strategy does not stand still. You have to have an eye on how markets, products and services are evolving, and to be able to respond if you need to or want to. You have to evolve your organisation alongside this, so that you remain capable of exploiting any opportunities that come your way.

- **Devised in-house:** Strategy needs to be owned by the organisation overall. Responsibility and accountability for strategy remain with the top and senior management. The execution of strategy is down to everyone in the organisation – they have to know why they are doing the work they do.

Strategy is not (or ought not to be) the product of consultants or focus groups. You can't hire a consultant or assemble a focus group in order to come up with your organisation's strategy and then just blindly follow what other people tell you. All organisations need to be in control of their own direction and destiny. If you outsource your strategy, you are outsourcing the keys to your own future. Many organisations hire consultants and use focus groups to advise on strategy development; responsibility for the strategy itself must remain house.

Virgin Cola

One of Virgin's earliest ventures was into the soft drinks market, with its very own cola. Before the product went on the market, Virgin undertook extensive product testing, conducting taste tests pitting its cola against the world's two top cola brands, Coca-Cola (Coke) and Pepsi.

In blind tasting tests, Virgin consistently came out on top – taste testers rated its taste as the best, better than Coke and Pepsi. So Virgin went straight into full production and waited confidently for the profits to start rolling in. Unfortunately for Virgin, the high-volume sales and profits never materialised. The question is, why?

Although Virgin tasted good, Coke and Pepsi remained acceptable to the markets that they served. Virgin failed because it concentrated on the taste rather than the brand and everything that was associated with Coke and Pepsi. As long as the taste of Coke and Pepsi remained acceptable to their markets, any company trying to enter the market would have to compete with the Coke and Pepsi *brands,* not with the taste of the drink, and that's what Virgin hadn't done.

This story just goes to show that defining strategy is about attention to all the details, as well as overall clarity. You can't have a great idea and just go with it – you have to make sure that everything else is right, which means investigating and evaluating the results of your own strategic analyses. In this case, Virgin got everything right except the customer demands, and the results were fatal.

Defining Your Organisation's Strategy

Now that you know what strategy is (see the preceding section), you're ready to tackle setting the strategy for your organisation. Where do you begin? Think about the definition of strategy: deciding what you do, when, where, why and for whom. When you break it down, defining a strategy is really about being able to answer five key questions, which I cover in this section.

What do you do?

In order to devise your business strategy, you start with a *core strategic position* that your entire organisation understands and supports. Strategy guru Michael Porter identifies three core positions from which all effective and profitable activities arise:

- **Brand leadership or brand advantage:** You offer products and services on the basis of creating a strong image or identity. Investment is required in marketing, advertising, developing brand strength and loyalty, and the high values that are associated with these activities.

✔ **Cost leadership and cost advantage:** You strive to be the lowest-cost operator in the field or to operate from the lowest possible cost base. To be a cost leader, you need to invest in production technology and staff. Cost leadership organisations have small hierarchies and large spans of control so that everything can be concentrated on the critical activities of delivering excellent products and services.

✔ **Focus:** You concentrate on specific niches and take steps to be indispensable in those niches. The purpose is to establish a long-term and concentrated business relationship with distinctive customers and clients based on product and service confidence, high levels of quality, utter reliability, and the ability to produce and deliver the volumes of products and services sought by customers when required.

If you can't clearly compete on the basis of cost, brand or focus, then you need 'something else'. This something else is likely to be one of the following:

✔ **Convenience:** People can easily get to you, so you set out to serve their needs and wants whenever they come by.

✔ **Customer loyalty:** People continue to come to you because they've always done so.

✔ **Other relationships:** For example, maybe an enduring family tie has helped to generate business between yourself and your customers.

✔ **Personal liking and confidence:** People come to you because they prefer to do business with you over other organisations.

You need to define what you do right from the start. Everything flows from this information. Defining what you do clarifies everyone's understanding of how you're going to do things, as well as what you're going to do. And if you aren't clear about this, you can't expect your backers, staff and suppliers – and, crucially, your customers and clients – to be clear either.

When do you do it?

When do you devise and begin to develop and implement your strategy? Right from the beginning! When you start to devise your strategy, alongside your core position, you have to be clear what your mission and vision are, and what goals you're setting. Mission and vision reflect how you see the business growing and developing. Goals give you a set of targets and milestones to reach, and you use these goals as a check on progress – and as a reality check.

This clearly applies to companies that are in the start-up phase. It also applies to mature organisations: as strategy evolves and develops, so the mission and vision advances also. It does not mean that you lose your core position and everything that is of value to the organisation. It does mean that you are moving with the times – and with the markets and customers also.

Mission and vision are not daydreams – they're the beginnings of hard and expert work. To have an idea isn't enough; you must be able to translate that idea into something that is of value to customers, and something that attracts finance and support.

Mission

When it comes to your organisation's mission, you need to be able to answer a few critical questions. These questions have to be answered at the 'when' stage as well as at the 'what' stage:

- What do you want to do?
- What can you do?
- What can't you do?
- Who are you going to do all this for?
- What do your potential customers, clients and backers want from you?
- How are you going to deliver everything that you promise?

The answers to these questions become your mission. You set out along a path to deliver the products, services, service and expertise that you have on behalf of your stakeholders and at a profit to yourself and everyone else involved.

Vision

Vision exists in your mind's eye, but you have to translate it into something that all those around you can aspire to, follow and deliver. You have to be able to put something that is possibly a bit dreamy or idealistic into words and pictures: to portray (or describe) an organisation that clearly states the contribution that you and everyone else involved are going to make to the markets, customers and clients. You have to be able to do these things in terms that attract backers and financial support, and that are going to make people want to work for you.

Funds and backing are hard to come by, and getting harder. One Wall Street trader sums up the situation particularly succinctly:

> 'Those who still have money to invest are those who have not squandered it on the madness that went on during the early years of the 21st century. If, therefore, you are going to persuade these people to back you, you have to have every detail in place up front. If you cannot put into words what you want to do, when, where, why and for whom, and if you cannot state what the returns ought to be, potential backers will simply walk away. In particular, they will walk away if you are not quite sure when you are going to need or want their backing.'

Of mice and men: The Airbus A380 'Superjumbo'

The Airbus A380 airliner, nicknamed the 'Superjumbo', was commissioned in 1996. The first planes were scheduled to roll off the production line in 2000, and Airbus developed detailed schedules and milestones to reach that goal. Everything tied back to Airbus's goal of building the biggest, best and most cost-effective airliner in the world.

The first plane was completed in 2006, more than five years late. Airbus hadn't built any slack into their schedule. They had assumed there would be no holdups, delays or other glitches in any part of the manufacturing or delivery process. In other words, the assumption

was that everything would go according to plan. You know what they say about the best-laid plans: they often go awry.

When you're setting timelines and schedules for reaching your organisation's goals, assume that things are going to go wrong – lots of things. That way, if everything goes right, you beat your deadline and become a hero. And if some things go awry, well, you still stand a good chance of meeting your goal on time. And as with this particular case, if you don't get the goals and timeframes right for one aspect of the work, it throws everything into chaos.

Goals

As a part of the strategy process, you set goals. Goals are a combination of the what with the when – goals have to have time frames and deadlines for their achievement.

All organisations need short-, medium- and long-term goals. As the organisations progress, so do the goals. You use the short- and medium-term goals as checks on progress. As you progress, the longer-term goals then become medium-term goals and so need additional detail. You're integrating your goals in a variety of ways. Goals are the basis of monitoring and reviewing what you're doing and how you're doing it. Goals are a check on actual achievements. They're also benchmarks and milestones along the path of progress. They serve as a check on your own forward-looking and forecasting expertise.

Where do you do it?

Strategy takes place in places: the organisation itself, and also its markets and locations of work. Invariably today, strategy also takes place on the Internet.

So you 'do' strategy wherever you see or perceive a demand for what you've envisioned and decided. To be effective, you have to know all of the detail about what you propose, how you're going to deliver and what your own vision is for the immediate and enduring future.

You have to know the detail of how the markets work in their particular locations. You also have to know how the Internet works in your particular sphere of activities.

You also need to know the logistics of where you are setting up activities and delivering your own work. Depending on the nature of your activities, this may include delivery issues, the ability of staff to get into work, and the ability to attract and retain staff. All of these factors are driven and influenced by the locations of work that you have chosen. And they become limiting factors on your ability to implement your strategy in full.

Why do you do it?

The question 'Why?' in terms of defining your strategy needs to be considered as follows:

- Why do you have the particular strategy that you have?
- Why do you produce the products and services that you do, in the ways that you do, for the customers that you serve?
- Why do you work in the particular locations that you do?

You do it because a clear and effective strategy is at the core of all successful and enduring business activities. If you don't have a clear and effective strategy, people come to understand that you've no clear direction or idea about what you're trying to achieve, and the basis on which you're trying to attract customers.

However, this is only part of the answer. You do it because you have the combination of size, resources, technology, premises and expertise on the one hand, and the ability to attract and serve customers on the other, that has given you your present market position.

So, in practice, why you have the particular strategy that you do have is founded on your present position. From here you develop your strategy in line with your ability to match your own resources and capabilities with the opportunities that present themselves, and the opportunities which you go out and look for.

You work in particular locations for a variety of reasons, as follows:

- You have actively decided that it is the right place, or you can develop profitable business there.
- You once saw an opportunity there, and now you are established the location provides additional opportunities for you to explore.
- You are close to your major customer bases.
- You can command the resources that you need and want.
- You have to be there because the rest of the industry is located there.

You can find yourself under a lot of pressure to locate where others in your sector are located. There are sound business reasons for this, in that expertise is likely to be available in those locations. There are also behavioural pressures that you have to recognise: if you are not in the particular location, you may get ignored by your customer bases in favour of those who do locate there. You may also get pressure from shareholders and backers to locate in those places because there is a belief or perception that 'everyone else is there'. For example, when considering finance companies:

- It is very expensive for any company to locate in the city of London, Wall Street, or Singapore, yet finance companies do so because not to do so would mean loss of prestige, reputation – and business.

- Finance companies that outsource customer service and technology development activities to India are now faced with steeply rising staff and premises costs. Yet they continue to maintain their presence there in case they get marginalised by the rest of the industry if they move out.

Matching external opportunities with internal capabilities

When you've devised your business strategy, you have to consider all the following:

- The necessary finance, investment, budgeting and resourcing activities

- Staffing approaches designed to match the workforce and its capabilities with the operational requirements of the organisation

- Marketing activities, designed to ensure that the organisation's products and services are presented in ways that give them the best possible impact and prospects of success

- Investment in technology and capital equipment to ensure the continued ability to produce the required value, volume and quality of output to the standards required

- Ethical factors, where you set the overall standards of conduct, attitude, behaviour and performance

What you're doing is matching external opportunities to your internal capabilities as an organisation.

The figure indicates the ways in which you match internal capabilities with the opportunities that exist in markets and the environment.

Externally, you are taking the results of environmental analyses (see Chapter 2), and then evaluating the findings as risks, opportunities and threats.

Internally, you are assessing your capabilities, resources and strengths alongside the external results. You then decide, by relating your capabilities and resources:

- What you are prepared to be involved in, and what you are not.

- Which opportunities you are going to follow up on, and which you are not.

- The effects of undertaking new activities on your existing work.

- The effects of taking up new activities in terms of your reputation.

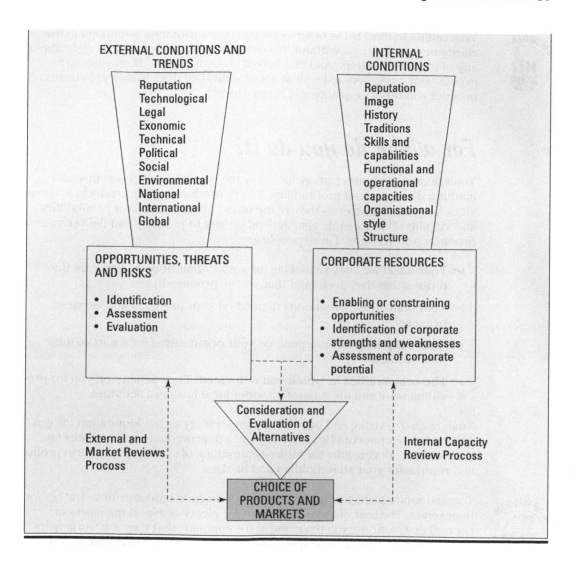

EXTERNAL CONDITIONS AND TRENDS

Reputation
Technological
Legal
Exonomic
Technical
Political
Social
Environmental
National
International
Global

INTERNAL CONDITIONS

Reputation
Image
History
Traditions
Skills and capabilities
Functional and operational capacities
Organisational style
Structure

OPPORTUNITIES, THREATS AND RISKS

- Identification
- Assessment
- Evaluation

CORPORATE RESOURCES

- Enabling or constraining opportunities
- Identification of corporate strengths and weaknesses
- Assessment of corporate potential

External and Market Reviews Procoss

Consideration and Evaluation of Alternatives

Internal Capacity Review Procoss

CHOICE OF PRODUCTS AND MARKETS

You do what you do also because you've obligations that you have to meet:

- To your customers in delivering the products and services that they seek from you
- To your backers in the promise to repay and deliver returns on their investments in you
- To your suppliers in ensuring extended and viable business activities with them
- To the places where you work in providing jobs and prosperity

Your ability to meet these obligations and responsibilities is founded in the clarity of your strategy. Without this overall clarity, you cannot be clear about any of the other matters. And crucially, if you aren't clear, then you can't expect your customers to be clear about what they'll get from you in terms of product and services quality and service levels.

For whom do you do it?

You are devising your strategy for everyone who has an interest in your continued success and profitability. You're producing your products and services for your customers – they're the ones you depend on for profitability and viability. Other people also depend on you to produce and deliver your products and services. These people are:

- ✔ **Your backers:** They're looking for your organisation to generate the returns that they seek (and that you've promised!).

- ✔ **Your staff:** Their livelihoods depend on your products and services being sold.

- ✔ **Your suppliers:** They depend on your organisation for a part of their own business.

- ✔ **The communities in which you're located:** They depend on you for providing work and for generating wider local business activities.

You are also devising and delivering your strategy as the foundation for generating future opportunities for everyone – new products and services for customers, enduring jobs for future generations of staff, and long-term profits and returns for your shareholders and backers.

Top and senior managers are of course devising and implementing strategy for themselves. The best of them (and there are plenty of expert managers of course) devise strategy in the name of the company that they are working for. They do however want to be recognised for the successes when these come along!

The worst managers devise strategy to make a name for themselves – and if the company does happen to succeed as a result, then this may be little more than a happy accident.

RBS: The importance of due diligence

One of the main factors in the corporate failure of the Royal Bank of Scotland (RBS) in 2008 could be traced back to the bank's acquisition of ING Baring, the Dutch bank, in 2006.

Under the guise of a strategy for growth and expansion, RBS bought ING Baring for $50 billion. This initiative was led entirely by a domineering top management team. This team considered the takeover 'a good idea' and so it went ahead – on no more substantial basis than this. By taking over ING Baring, the future of RBS would be assured; moreover, it would become a major player on the world banking stage.

Prior to the takeover, there was no due diligence – investigation of the true standing and quality of the business of ING Baring. RBS and its management took the valuation of $50 billion at face value and duly paid up.

Only when they had acquired ING Baring did RBS investigate in detail what they had already bought. They found that they had vastly overpaid for the acquisition, and could not indeed afford it, in terms of the returns that they were going to get from ING Baring customers.

Implementing Your Strategy

So you have arrived at the point where you are clear about:

- Your core strategic position
- What activities you are going to conduct, when where, why and for whom
- Matching your resources and capabilities to the opportunities available

You have now come to the point of implementation. Implementation of strategy has two basic parts: formulation and execution.

Formulation

Strategy formulation takes everything that you have done so far, and adds the details.

This means first deciding what you are going to do, and what you are not going to do. There are always more opportunities than resources, and in practice you cannot do everything.

Second, you decide how you are going to proceed. You have a range of choices, as follows:

- ✔ Growth: expanding your business to take in new markets, products and services, or growth from selling more to your existing customer bases.

- ✔ Consolidation and retrenchment: using resources to protect the customer bases and business volumes that you already have.

- ✔ Cashing in on a saturated or declining market before you lose your edge and position.

- ✔ Pioneering and opening up new opportunities before others have thought of them.

- ✔ Diversification into new product and service lines.

- ✔ Price leadership, in which you are going to start price wars to try and take market share away from your competitors.

- ✔ Branding, in which you develop the real and perceived quality of your products and services – and company – so as to be able to (invariably) increase prices.

- ✔ Market or location domination, measured by sales volumes, customer numbers and/or sales revenues received.

Third, you have to decide whether you are going to do things gradually and incrementally, or whether you are going to blitz everything all at once.

Finally, you have to have a basis for making your decisions at the formulation stage. It doesn't matter what this basis is, so long as it works for you.

Execution

You have now arrived at the point of putting everything into action. This is as the result of having identified the opportunities and risks afforded by the environment. You have also assessed your capabilities.

Turning this into reality means that you have to do all of the following:

- ✔ Identify and prioritise the key tasks
- ✔ Implement effective decision-making processes
- ✔ Establish systems for monitoring and evaluating progress
- ✔ Assign tasks to the workforce, and integrate the work of the different departments with each other
- ✔ Make available the right expertise and technology

✔ Integrate activities so as to ensure the effective completion of the tasks in hand

✔ Install management and supervisory systems to ensure coordination of efforts and activities

✔ Implement information and other management systems

You have to integrate all of the above into a series of tasks, actions and schedules. In everything that you do, there will be goals and deadlines that you need to meet. The extent to which you meet or miss your goals and deadlines forms one of the bases on which you assess your strategy for success or failure. You are also setting out the ways in which the longer term likelihood for success can be looked at.

You have also to integrate the following into the execution phase:

✔ Maintenance, repair and upgrade schedules.

✔ Research and development, improvement and enhancement schedules.

✔ Any additional financial, technological and staff resources required.

Measuring the results

You need to be able to measure what is happening as you implement your strategy, You need to be able to measure actual performance against forecasted, projected or budgeted activities.

Above all, you have to look to the finances. You need to assess them in terms of what actually happened, compared to what your projections and forecasts were. You are comparing:

✔ Actual overall returns against projections.

✔ Actual costs of sales, and product and service delivery, against projections.

✔ Any effects of unforeseen circumstances on particular costs. For example, did the cost of raw materials rise during implementation? Did you have to replace technology earlier than you had thought?

By doing this, you are also improving your own strategy processes for the future. You use the information gained when measuring the results to inform your projections for the next phases of your activities.

Virgin's business strategy

The Virgin Group's approach to involvement in new ventures is based on the following basis for strategy and business development:

✔ The proposed new sector of activities is already well established and served by other providers.

✔ The service provided by other organisations falls short in some way – especially perceived customer satisfaction.

✔ There is a commercial and profitable potential for engagement in 'the Virgin way'.

✔ There is potential for developing the sector using the existing Virgin customer base.

✔ There is a sense of fun and adventure (enabling Sir Richard Branson to add his own personal touch wherever possible!).

Everything that Virgin does or contemplates is assessed along these lines. Virgin state that they will look at any proposition that they can match at least four of the above conditions to, when deciding on future strategy formulation.

Alongside the finances, you carry out measurement and evaluation against the pre-set aims, objectives and goals that you had. You are looking at:

✔ What went according to plan and why?

✔ What failed and fell short of success and why?

In simple terms, the key overall questions that you ask yourself are:

✔ What did we do well and why?

✔ What did we fail at and why?

✔ What else did we get out of this strategy and why?

The last question is especially important. Everyone gets results from activities that they couldn't easily have predicted when they were devising their strategy. For example:

✔ Waitrose generated increases in sales to its core and affluent customers as the result of introducing cheaper value-line products to try and expand its customer base.

✔ BSkyB developed a niche selling replica cycling shirts to people who never cycle as the result of the successes of Bradley Wiggins and Christopher Froome.

✔ The Harry Potter phenomenon made its major revenues not from book sales (which were very high, to be sure!), but from merchandising and product development once the books were made into films.

However, you can only ever assess and evaluate unlooked for successes like these. They never provide any form of certainty for the future. For example, the Teenage Mutant Hero Turtles phenomenon was so successful that the owners decided to develop the next generation, introducing child turtles. This bombed – it was not what customers wanted! What they wanted was the originals and nothing more.

So evaluate the great successes, and then form your own judgement for the future – but don't try to predict the future!

Strategy evaluation is both a continuous process, and also the subject of more formalised regular reviews at required and appropriate intervals, and at each stage where goals are reached or supposed to be reached. By doing these reviews, you build a framework for everyone involved to judge what has happened, and to inform how things are to proceed for the future.

You have some points of inquiry to make also, as follows:

- The extent to which everyone clearly understood what you set out to do, and the effects of any lack of clarity.

- Consistency with the organisation's capabilities, resources and aspirations.

- Any risks and uncertainties that you failed to identify in relation to the opportunities you explored.

- Evaluation of the actual contribution of what you did, to the long-term future of the organisation overall.

You need to look at how the market responded. You do this both in terms of any specific initiatives in isolation, and the effects of these initiatives on your overall market standing and reputation – and profitability.

You also look at the effects – positive and negative – of the drives of dominant stakeholders and personalities on what was achieved.

Looking for the warning signs

Of course nobody ever sets out to fail. However, you have to know and understand that if you do pursue certain courses of action, you are likely to end up either failing or else falling short of the success that you are seeking.

In addition to this, you also need to be aware that any or all of the following are likely to end in failure if you do not address and remedy them:

✔ Rising costs and falling sales revenues and sales volumes, which squeezes profit margins

✔ Rising prices while product and service quality either remains the same or else declines, which has adverse effects on your reputation

✔ Increasing differentials between top and bottom salaries across the organisation, which is damaging to staff morale and motivation

✔ Failure to reward productive output from staff and investor loyalty and commitment, which is failing to recognise and reward those who have committed themselves to your company

✔ Overpricing your products and services to a captive market, which is expedient and therefore unwholesome

✔ Using dishonest sales practices to entice people to buy from you, which you will have to remedy when (not if) you are caught

✔ Failure to deliver the product and service quality that you imply in your marketing and promotional efforts, which is also dishonest

If you see or notice any of these factors or points as you assess company strategy, you need to address them as soon as possible.

Strategy is a process. As an organisation, you're never done with your strategy. Instead, you have to take these same steps over and over again as the organisation moves forwards, and as the products and services brought to market grow, develop, mature and decline – you never quite arrive! You try to do everything better, more quickly, more cost-effectively than you've done it before. And you seize opportunities to progress and develop. But in order to be fully effective, the strategic approach must be one of constant development and improvement.

Chapter 9

Creating Great
Products and Services

*O*rganisations wouldn't exist if it weren't for products and services. Part of running an organisation is maintaining your current line of products and services, as well as developing new ones. In this chapter, I walk you through both scenarios, giving you the information you need to stay at the top of the heap when it comes to your offerings.

What's in Your Stable Today? Evaluating Your Existing Products and Services

Products and services are at the core of all organisations. Without a product or service, the organisation has no reason to exist. Creating great products and services is about matching what you do to what your target market wants. You also need to be aware of the lifecycle of products and services, so you can plan ahead. Finally, you need to deliver the quality that your customers have come to expect.

Beer at breakfast

One sunny morning in June, London commuters coming off the trains at Euston railway station were delighted to find that one of the major beer-producing companies was offering free samples! The trains had been hot and stuffy, and a cold glass of beer (even at that hour) was a welcome treat.

As the samples were being handed out, the beer company was asking questions: Do you like this product? Would you buy it? In the context of that hot, sunny morning, the commuters responded favourably. So the beer company decided to greatly increase its production of its existing product.

And then – you guessed it – the product development failed. Sales turned out to be disappointing. And yet those responses at Euston station had been so positive. What had gone wrong?

Simple: the beer company had tested the product in the wrong place, at the wrong time, under the wrong set of circumstances. And most importantly, it had asked the wrong questions. Sure, it had generated a strong response to the questions 'Do you like this product?' and 'Would you buy it?' But the questions should have been: 'Would you buy this product? If so, how much would you pay, how often would you drink it and under what circumstances?'

Of course, asking these direct follow-up questions is difficult, because you're more likely to get negative, as well as positive, comments. But you must be direct if you want a clear picture of market demand.

Offering a range of products and services

Most organisations offer a range of products and services – few do only one thing, or sell only one product, with no variations. These products and services fall into two main categories:

- ✔ **Core products and services:** These are the products and services for which your organisation is known and valued. They're the ones you've built your reputation on, the ones that rake in the dough.

- ✔ **Peripheral products and services:** These are the products and services that bring in marginal income. They have marginal, satellite or ancillary value, but they're not the meat and potatoes of your operation.

Just because you make the bulk of your income from your core products and services doesn't mean that you should ignore the peripheral ones. Peripheral products and services can add value for your customer, and support your broader goals. For example, most airlines don't just sell plane tickets – they also sell trip insurance, car hire, and luggage and airport transit services. These other products and services are marginal, but essential, sources of revenue. And they make travel more convenient for the people who buy plane tickets. Be sure to consider what else your organisation can provide as the result of your mainstream activities.

Analysing the contribution of products and services

If you're trying to evaluate your products and services in terms of the contribution that they truly make when it comes to growth, market share and income, a really useful tool is the Boston Matrix (see Figure 9-1). Using the Boston Matrix, you evaluate your products and services against two criteria – growth and market share – and then plot them on the chart where you think they belong.

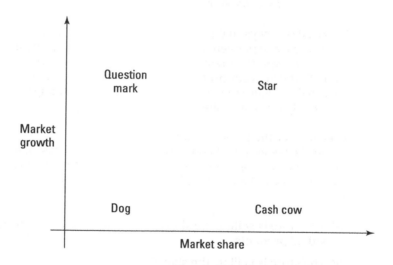

Figure 9-1:
The Boston
Matrix.

Cash cows: High share of low growth market; today's breadwinners; the main source of income.
Stars: high share of high growth market; today's and tomorrow's breadwinners from which future cash cows will come; normally need high investment and support to maintain position.
Question marks: low share of high growth marketl tomorrow's potential breadwinners; not all will succeed.
Dog: low share of low growth market; normally only kept if they have some distinctive positive feature (e.g. something on which a traditional or enduring reputation has been built, and without which, the present reputation may be diluted).

You're looking for a mix that shows clear and regular sources of income (stars and cash cows) and plenty of potential for the future (question marks). You're also identifying the products and services that you have to tackle eventually:

✔ **Question marks:** The question marks need constant evaluation to see whether they're really going to come on-stream and become your next generation of stars and cash cows.

✔ **Dogs:** The dogs need constant evaluation in terms of whether you may be able to reinvigorate them, or whether the time is coming to kill them off.

Not every product or service you offer will be a powerhouse in the income department. Some products or services make money and others lose money, but just because a product or service loses money doesn't mean that this product or service isn't valuable for your organisation. It may be part of what attracts customers to buy the products or services that are more profitable for you.

But what if you have a product or service that no one is buying? Shouldn't you stop carrying it? This point is key: if you stop offering products or services that nobody buys, you're removing choice. Even if customers never actually buy those products or services, you may still need to offer them to maintain the *perception* of choice for the customer.

The 80–20 rule says that people are attracted to an organisation's products or services by 80 per cent of what it offers. They only buy from a limited range – however, the presence of the large range is what has attracted them to you. Reducing your product and service lines may make sense, but be sure that you don't jump to conclusions without determining whether your money losers really are losers after all.

Also consider the power of *clusters*. Product and service clusters exist around the wider actual and perceived benefits to customers. What does this sentence mean? Consider this example: a department store selling shaving cream, razors and aftershave lotion can take one or the other of the following views:

- ✔ The store is selling the shaving cream, razors and aftershave as individual products.
- ✔ The store is selling 'the shave'.

By selling the shave rather than the individual products, customers are attracted to the one-stop convenience and satisfaction and will spend to this effect. And if you only sell the shaving cream and razors (but not the aftershave lotion, which perhaps makes a loss), people may not come to you for any of these products.

Looking at product and service lifecycles

All products and services have a lifecycle – a beginning, a middle and an end. Technically speaking, the lifecycle of any product or service has five stages (see Figure 9-2):

✔ **Introduction:** When you bring a new product or service onto the market for the first time.

✔ **Growth:** When the product or service takes off and its true potential begins to become apparent.

✔ **Maturity:** When the product or service is a familiar and well-loved feature on the market – people are happy with it, and continue to buy it.

✔ **Saturation:** When the product or service has reached its maximum sales level, and no further development is possible.

✔ **Decline:** When the product or service has run its course, and no more value or profit is to be gained from it.

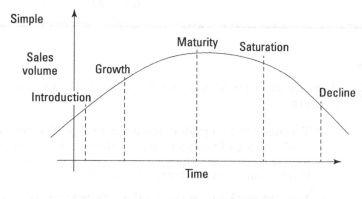

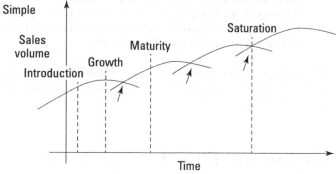

↗ Marketing efforts, strategies, campaigns

Figure 9-2:
A product or service lifecycle.

The model indicates the conception, growth, regeneration, renewal and extension of the effective and profitable life of particular products and services. The Figure also indicates relationships with successful and effective marketing activities.

A rolling stone gathers no moss

Even products and services as iconic and supposedly stable as those provided by Coca-Cola and McDonald's are always tweaking and developing their presentations to reflect seasonal changes – for example, the Coca-Cola Santa Claus packaging at Christmas time, Happy Meals that tie in with kids' movies, and so on.

In these ways, they keep their brands and the limited ranges of products and services that they deliver fresh in customers' minds. If they didn't, Coca-Cola, McDonald's and others like them would become 'ordinary'. Any time you see an iconic company change things around, you can bet that they're attempting to keep the public interested. And the fact that they do so is what sells their products.

Being aware of a product or service's lifecycle is important for a couple of reasons:

✔ **You need to accept that no product or service lasts forever.** When you're aware of this fact, you're willing to devote your time and energy to new product development (see 'Creating the New Kids on the Block: Product and Service Development', later in this chapter).

✔ **You can work to rejuvenate the product or service at each stage along the way.** For example, you can try to enhance performance, repackage and redesign the product or service, or rebrand it and engage in other marketing activities (see Chapter 10).

All products and services can be developed, improved, transformed and replaced. The key is knowing when to intervene, and what developments and improvements to make.

Paying attention to quality

No matter how much your product or service costs, quality matters. Just ask your customers! Quality is a combination of the following:

✔ **The overall and absolute reliability of the product or service to do what it says it does:** People expect products and services to be reliable and deliver what they promise or infer. People increasingly expect extended longevity and durability, especially from products such as electrical and electronic goods. They expect accuracy and speed of service from things like healthcare services and financial and insurance services too.

- **The value that customers place on the product or service's performance:** The amount of money that people pay for a product or service reflects the priority or importance that it has for them. And by paying this amount, they expect also the peace of mind that goes with being sure that the product or service will perform when required.

- **The perceptions and expectations people have of the product or service:** Products and services should meet the expectations of your customers, as well as your organisation. If you fail to meet everyone's expectations, you can't charge a price low enough or that people will be prepared to pay. If you get the right mix between product performance, price, value and quality, you give yourself the greatest possible chance of delivering products and services that are of enduring commercial viability.

Researcher Benjamin Garvin identified eight dimensions of product and service quality that you have to be able to assess and define in order to deliver products and services of genuine quality:

- **Performance:** The actual performance delivered by the products and services.

- **Features:** Appearance, desirability and more.

- **Reliability:** How long customers can reasonably gain value from a product or service.

- **Conformance:** A reflection of what customers expect to see and receive when they buy a particular item.

- **Durability:** A reflection of longevity.

- **Serviceability:** The extent to which something can be repaired and upgraded.

- **Aesthetics:** The general appearance of the product.

- **Perceived quality:** How well the expectations of customers are met.

Another researcher, Alexey Parasuraman, identified gaps in customer perceptions that have to be managed if they're to be persuaded that products and services have a particular quality. Parasuraman used the acronym RATER – reliability, assurance, tangibles, empathy and responsiveness. In this, he identified five gaps that have to be managed:

- **Gap 1:** The gap between a customers' expectations and what the organisation thinks that customers expect.

- **Gap 2:** The gap between an organisation's definition of service and the level of service demanded by customers.

- **Gap 3:** The gap between expected service and actual service.

- **Gap 4:** The gap between the service delivery and what customers are told is service delivery.

- **Gap 5:** The gap between customers' perceptions of service and expectations of service.

REAL WORLD EXAMPLE

NHS treatment

The question of quality arises in the delivery of public services. In recent years, the NHS has had such poor press that people now *expect* bad service and poor treatment. In particular, they expect:

✓ To have to wait, often for hours, beyond their appointment times

✓ To receive rushed and inadequate treatment

✓ To receive treatment that suits the authorities rather than the patient

These perceptions of the quality of service have been developed and reinforced by the combination of media coverage and scandals. So the question then becomes how to manage that perception and, indeed, any perception of bad-quality service.

If people have come to expect poor service, you have to recognise the position you're in, acknowledge what has gone wrong and then take steps to put it right. In this case, the NHS needs to:

✓ Reschedule appointments and make sure that everyone sticks to them

✓ Make it clear what treatments do and don't do

✓ Make it clear the extent to which treatments are driven by what the authorities will permit

At the core is active communication, related directly to people's concerns about the products and services the public services provide.

Both of these approaches – Garvin's and Parasuraman's – are extremely useful in terms of trying to pin down the nebulous concept of quality. Paying attention to both of these approaches gives you real insight into what customers expect, as well as what you actually deliver.

Creating the New Kids on the Block: Product and Service Development

Effectively developing new products and services depends on the creativity, inventiveness and imagination of the organisation. But what exactly is entailed in new product or service development? What does that term even mean? When I talk about developing new products and services, I'm talking about all the following:

✓ Developing new products and services for existing markets

✓ Taking existing products and services to new markets, and repackaging and rebranding them if necessary

✓ Developing peripheral products and services so that they become core

> ✔ Making improvements in product or service design and presentation
>
> ✔ Developing, enhancing and improving the performance of existing products and services

Product and service development generally involves several steps. I cover each of them in the following sections. First, I take a look at what motivates development.

Finding reasons for development

Two factors tend to drive the development of products and services: the products and services themselves, or the market.

Product- and service-led developments

These developments occur when you see the potential to move the business forward by improving what you already do. Because your products and services are already successful, as you enhance them they should become even more sought after. So, you may consider:

✔ Improving the design and appearance of what you already do

✔ Improving the overall performance of what you already do

✔ Producing ranges of add-ons and ancillaries that you've decided are beneficial to customers and clients

✔ Introducing new product and service ranges alongside what you already do so that customers and clients buy these innovations on the basis of the confidence that they already have in your products and services

An example of a product- or service-led development is the one-stop-shop concept that was pioneered in the UK by Tesco at the beginning of the 21st century. Having established its position as the leading grocery retailer, the company moved into clothing and outdoor goods. It expanded its range of electrical goods. It moved into financial services, bookselling and telecommunications. The line of reasoning was that customers would find an ever-increasing range of products and services available under one roof and would have ever more reason to come to Tesco. And if they came to the store, for example, to pay the insurance premium, they may just go and pick up groceries or a new shirt at the same time!

Market-led developments

These developments occur when you introduce new products and services as the result of your market research and analysis. This analysis brings you to the conclusion that there are gaps that you can profitably fill.

There are always gaps in any market. For example, recognising that there was a huge unmet demand for low-cost air travel, Ryanair, Southwest Airlines and others stripped down what you get for your ticket to the seat only. Gone are all the ancillaries, including food and drink – if you want those, you have to pay extra.

In order to engage successfully in market-led product and service development, you have to know and understand your market. Successful market-led developments can only be sustained if you can find the gaps, assess their viability and then fill them with what the customers want. Plus, when you've given the impression that you're going to fill the demands identified, you need to do it! You don't want to give the impression of promising everything but delivering nothing.

Producing a prototype or mock-up of your idea

Coming up with the idea for a new product or service is such hard work that you may feel like that's the end – but the idea is really just the beginning. After you have your idea, you need to produce a prototype or mock-up of what you have in mind. The prototype enables other people to see your idea in action, and to begin to form their own judgements about whether the idea is viable.

Examples of prototypes include 3D photographs of any new product: for example, cars, food packaging, toys and games. Architects produce models, both on screen and also physically, of the buildings that they envisage. When produced, these prototypes enable everyone to see how they might look when finished, and what the possibilities might be for developing them.

At this stage, you may produce something that looks beautiful to you, but flawed to everyone else. Don't worry – this is normal! All it means is that you don't yet have a full understanding of the strengths and weaknesses of your idea.

You're producing a prototype or mock-up because you *want* feedback. Negative feedback only helps to make your product or service stronger.

Getting to market

Getting new products and services from the prototype stage to market is expensive and time-consuming. Once you have agreed on the prototype, you then have to test it out on customers to see if they might like it. You also have to cost everything out in full; and then you have to test it out to see if backers might be prepared to support it.

This part is therefore critical. You have data now about your prototype; if the data supports further development, then you are starting to commit organisational resources to something that is going to enhance your product and service ranges.

You therefore have to take a view on how you are going to get it to market. Are you:

- ✔ Going to try it out in a few locations only, or are you going to hit every location at the same time?

- ✔ Going to commit production and service delivery resources on something which may or may not succeed?

- ✔ Support everything with marketing activities?

This phase needs full organisational backing, together with a sustainable commitment of resources. If you go in half-heartedly you are likely to fail. If you underestimate the scale of demand, you are likely to lose out to imitators and substitutes.

The getting to market phase is also the one where many initiatives fail. Why? Usually, ideas fail for one of the following reasons:

- ✔ It takes too long in practice.

- ✔ It becomes clear that getting the new product or service to market will be too expensive.

- ✔ By the time the new product or service gets to market, people's tastes and demands will have changed.

Ask yourself the following questions:

- ✔ How quickly do we need to get the new idea to market? Why?

- ✔ What are the consequences of delays on the one hand and glitches on the other?

- ✔ How quickly can we get the new idea to market? What are the resource implications? Will we have to take resources from what we're already doing? If so, what are the consequences?

Shoot 'em down, turn around – come on, Sony

For the first 16 years of its life, what is now Sony operated out of the garage of Akio Morita's father. Morita had spent time in the Japanese navy during the Second World War. He had come to the conclusion that there was a commercial market in the communication and recording technology that had been used in the navy. However, it had to be of a commercial standard.

So, for 16 years Morita spent every waking hour getting the recording technology up to a commercial standard. Only then did he launch the first range of products to the market. From there, he grew what is now Sony. And crucially, the company has never stopped this pioneering approach. From the earliest days, it has recognised that everything that has been produced has been capable of development and improvement.

This approach and attitude is the same one you have to take when your organisation is trying to get something new to market. And if – as happened for a period after Morita died – you do lose either your impetus or fundamental approach, then you need to rediscover it real quick!

Building on your successes

As you come to have successful products and services, you always need to continue to look around to see what else you can do on the back of your successes. What you do isn't nearly as important as why you do it.

Here are a few examples of companies that have built upon their successes well:

- ✔ Virgin has gone from being a magazine publisher and recording studio to doing everything the company is known for today. It successfully transferred its brand values – high quality, good value, and product and service confidence – to everything that it does.

- ✔ Mars, the chocolate company, also produces Pedigree pet foods. It can use the same distribution and retail outlets for both sets of products.

- ✔ Sky and Canal Plus, the satellite broadcasters, have gone into Internet services and telephone packages because they can provide all these services via the core broadcasting technology.

On the other hand, here are a couple of examples of companies that have tried to build upon past successes and haven't seen the results they hoped for:

- ✔ easyJet is a particularly successful low-cost airline. But its attempts to use the 'easy' brand elsewhere have met with limited success. Car hire, cinemas, cruises and casinos have all failed to grow as the airline has done.

✔ Ford and General Motors have failed to develop profitable niches for electric and hybrid cars in spite of the high and increasing costs of fuel.

So how can your organisation be more like Virgin, Mars, Sky and Canal Plus, and build on your successes with, well, success? Here are some suggestions:

✔ Make sure that whatever you do is going to build and enhance the reputation that you already have.

✔ For any new idea, test, test and test again with customers, users, focus groups, anyone who can give you an informed opinion about the new idea.

✔ Get the price right in terms of what your customers are willing and able to pay. If you need them, include add-ons such as service, maintenance and upgrades to make your new idea even more attractive.

✔ Make sure that you relate what you're doing now to what you've done in the past – however revolutionary your new idea, people want to be assured that you're still 'the same you' that has given such great service in the past.

✔ Have some idea where the new product or service is going to lead for the future. It shouldn't just be a one-off.

✔ Examine everything that you do to see where improvements and developments can be made. And if people suggest improvements and developments – whoever they are – then always evaluate the ideas fully before accepting them or turning them down.

Flight of the Concorde

Concorde was developed as the world's first supersonic airliner. It first flew in 1969, and for the next 40 years remained an iconic product, the flagship of both BA and Air France.

Concorde was originally a joint venture between British Aerospace and what is now EADS. Each of the partner companies took a different attitude and approach to building on their success.

British Aerospace and BA maintained it as a luxury and exclusive product, delivered with top-class services to passengers who paid top-notch prices. From this point of view, Concorde was a successful and highly profitable luxury product and brand.

Air France and EADS also used Concorde as a luxury product. However, they used technology and knowledge gained from the Concorde to develop a mainstream airliner industry. This, in turn, became Airbus, which now manufactures and sells more than half the world's airliners.

Neither of these approaches is right or wrong. They're just clear illustrations of how you can build on what you already have, in whatever way works best for you.

Abandoning your failures

Alongside your successes, you also have to deal with your failures. But what exactly is a failure?

Success and failure ultimately are value judgements. And if you think that boundaries exist at all, remember that Mariah Carey's 2004 album *My All* was deemed a failure by her record company because it sold 'only' 18 million copies worldwide!

In the end, you have to trust your judgement and intuition when assessing if and why a product or service has failed. Sometimes you have to put your faith in a product or service that isn't yet fully tested. Conversely, you have to be prepared to abandon a product or service that looks like it may fail. Because of this, you may end up going with products or services that don't work. Or you may end up abandoning a product or service that other organisations end up having great success with.

Don't waste time thinking about what may have been. Trust your judgement. The key is to ask yourself:

✔ What caused us to fail?

✔ What could we have done differently?

✔ What should we do differently next time?

Chapter 10

Marketing Your Products or Services

*M*arketing is essential to getting your products and services in the hands, hearts and minds of your consumers. But marketing isn't as simple as some people think. Still, in this chapter I give you a good grounding of what you need to know to effectively devise and implement a marketing strategy.

I start by defining what marketing is and what it does – there's no point in trying to use a tool if you don't know what you're using it for. Then I look at whom exactly you market to. Many people make the mistake of thinking that their target market is the *entire* market ('We want to sell to everyone!'), but the reality is, whether you know it or not, you're selling to only a segment of the market.

Organisations use a variety of strategies for marketing, and I take you through these, and the variety of marketing media you can use to get your message out. Then, finally, I fill you in on a key part of your marketing strategy – branding – and tell you how to research the market to make sure that your message is heard.

Knowing What Marketing Is and What Marketing Does

Marketing is the competitive process by which goods and services are offered for consumption at a profit. Marketing combines the actual product or service with how it is presented (for example, in its packaging, colours, appearance and price), in order to engage the interest and commitment of customers and the public at large.

For the purposes of this introduction as it relates to traditional approaches to marketing, I will outline five different types of marketing here:

- ✔ **Consumer marketing:** Presentations to retail consumers in two basic forms:

  - Unconsidered purchases, which lead to instant satisfaction or dissatisfaction (these purchases may lead to enduring satisfaction also; their key selling point is instant satisfaction)

  - Considered purchases, which lead to both instant and also enduring satisfaction or dissatisfaction

- ✔ **Industrial and business-to-business marketing:** Presentations from one business to others in two basic forms that are based on the development of relationships between purchaser and provider:

  - Unconsidered purchases (for example, the office coffee)

  - Considered purchases (for example, technology, manufacturing and service delivery equipment, high-value purchases such as airliners and property, and information systems)

- ✔ **Public services marketing:** Highlights the advantage and convenience of public services, as well as clarifying what is, and isn't, on offer.

- ✔ **Not-for-profit marketing:** Focuses on drawing much-needed resources to the not-for-profit sector.

- ✔ **Internal marketing:** Encompasses activities designed to build interest, confidence and enduring workplace relations within organisations.

A major outcome of effective marketing is the building of relationships between organisations and their customers. Every interaction between an organisation and its customers contributes to the development of relationships. Therefore, every interaction is critical in generating customer loyalty and building a psychological, as well as a commercial, relationship between customers and organisations.

Customer relationships and loyalties are built, developed and maintained through the combination of product and service quality, immediate and after-sales activities, and the continued willingness of customers to buy and use the products and services in ways that are of value to them. The management and development of customer relationships and loyalties is a key aspect of marketing strategies.

Marketing is about profit, so everything that you do in terms of marketing has to be in the interests of your customers. Marketing is competitive, so if you aren't effective, people are going to gravitate toward organisations that are.

Targeting Your Piece of the Pie: Market Segmentation

No organisation serves the entire market, no matter what the market is. You may get customers from across the market at various times, but the key is knowing where the core of your business is coming from. Typically, in order to determine this information, you need to think of the market in terms of segments. Markets are segmented in two main ways:

- ✔ **Social segmentation:** Breaks down the population according to the occupation of the head of the household. Here are the social segments:

    - **A:** Aristocrats and upper-middle-class people, including directors and senior managers.

    - **B:** Middle-class and professional people, including lawyers, doctors and senior managers.

    - **C1:** Lower-middle-class people, including teachers, nurses, engineers and those who work on computers and information technology (IT).

    - **C2:** Skilled working-class people, those who have taken apprenticeships and who have a 'trade', including those doing some engineering and technology activities.

    - **D:** Working-class people, those who are semi-skilled or unskilled, who work in labouring or industry-specific jobs, call centres, retail and hospitality.

    - **E:** People on subsistence levels of income, including those who have to exist on state support, and those who are unemployed.

- ✔ **Market and social segmentation:** This kind of segmentation has existed in the UK since 1998, when the UK National Statistics Office produced the following framework:

    - **1A:** Large employers, higher managers, company directors and senior public servants.

    - **1B:** Professional people, including doctors, solicitors, engineers and teachers.

- **2:** Associate professionals, journalists, nurses, midwives, actors, musicians, junior military and public servants.

- **3:** Intermediate occupations (for example, secretaries, flight attendants, driving instructors and telephone operators), as well as professional athletes on teams (for example, footballers and cricketers).

- **4:** Small employers, managers of small departments, non-professional self-employed, plumbers, farm owners and managers, and self-employed professional athletes (for example, golfers and tennis players).

- **5:** Supervisors, craftspeople and related workers, electricians, mechanics, train drivers and bus inspectors.

- **6:** Semi-routine occupations, including traffic wardens, caretakers, gardeners, shelf-stackers and assembly-line workers.

- **7:** Routine occupations, including cleaners, waiting staff, messengers and couriers, labourers and dock workers.

- **8:** Everybody else, including the long-term unemployed, those who have never worked, the long-term sick and prison populations.

Regardless of which segmentation approach you subscribe to, the goal is to understand who your main customers are. From there, you develop your marketing activities by getting to know each of the segments your customers fall into and the associated occupations. Then you relate your efforts to what people in those segments of the market value most.

As you define your customers and their needs and desires, you begin to build a picture that includes the following information:

- ✔ The size of customer bases in specific niches and locations

- ✔ The balance of quality, volume and price of products and services that customers expect

- ✔ The value of the product or service relative to other items available for consumption

- ✔ The value of the product or service relative to other items that the customer base needs or wants to purchase

- ✔ Patterns of spending among members of the niche or customer base, and the extent to which they use cash, credit cards or purchase orders

- ✔ The demand for access to product and service after-sales facilities

- ✔ The ease of access to those places that deliver and sell your products and services (including Internet outlets)

- ✔ The frequency with which given products or services are used and consumed by the customers

Market segmentation isn't exact. What you're trying to do is define and classify people in order to target your products and services as effectively as possible. Market segmentation provides a jumping-off point, a way for you to better target the needs and wants of a particular group of people (that is, your customers).

Devising Your Marketing Strategy

Your marketing strategy is directly tied to your business strategy (refer to Chapter 8). In order to be effective, any marketing strategy needs to fit well with your overall business strategy. Here are the two main marketing strategies that organisations pursue:

- **Pioneering or 'first in the field':** Organisations who follow this strategy are all about opening up new markets and developing new products and services.

    The clear advantage of being first in the field is that you get first or early-mover advantage. You can begin to build a presence, identity, image and market share before anyone else. You set yourself up as everyone else's main competitor.

    Of course, you also have obligations and commitments. You have to set the standard of product and service quality and delivery high enough to make your organisation difficult to compete with. And you have to keep those standards high. Otherwise, those who follow will find any weakness and concentrate on that to compete with you and build their own market share.

- **Follow the leader:** Organisations that play follow the leader tend to assess the efforts of those who are first in the field, and then try to deliver something better, having learned from the mistakes of the pioneer.

    The critical advantage of being a follower is that you note the mistakes of the first and early movers, and concentrate on them to develop your own position. As you're doing so, you also note product and service improvements that can be made. Then you implement these improvements as part of the process of carving out your own position.

Whether you're a leader or a follower, you have to compete. Unless you can completely dominate a market or segment, competitors are always present. And they'll start to make inroads into your market if you don't keep your standards high.

Marketing is led by different forces. You need to know and understand which of these forces is leading the products and services produced by different organisations, so as to understand why they are being marketed and presented in their own particular ways.

As you understand the forces and how they operate in marketing activities, you come to understand how the products and services have been developed up to the present. This then gives you the best possible basis for understanding how they might be developed most effectively for the future.

It is essential that you know and understand the following marketing forces:

- ✔ **Ethics-led:** Organisations create and develop a reputation as the result of a distinctive moral or ethical stance – for example, using fair-trade ingredients (Starbucks), or presenting high quality ingredients as a promotional feature (Nestlé).

- ✔ **Market-led:** Organisations look first at a range of markets, assessing their requirements and deciding which of these markets they can most valuably and profitably fill.

- ✔ **Staff-led:** Organisations are driven by the skills, qualities and preferences of the staff in developing their products and services.

- ✔ **Supply-led:** Organisations produce products because they've complete faith in those products and know that they can sell them at a profit.

- ✔ **Technology-led:** Organisations produce the products they do because of the technology they've access to.

Marketing strategies may be offensive or defensive. *Offensive* marketing activities seek to make inroads into the competitive position and customer and client bases of others. *Defensive* marketing activities are undertaken with the objective of preserving your current position in response to the moves made by others.

Choosing a Marketing Mix

After you have a marketing strategy nailed down (refer to the preceding section 'Devising Your Marketing Strategy'), you need to choose a marketing mix.

The marketing mix is the combination of all of the features and activities that you use to present your products and services to best advantage, and to ensure that customers recognise them.

Marketing mixes are based on each of the following elements, all of which are present in marketing activities, though the balance varies between different products and services:

- ✔ **The four Ps:**
  - **Product:** Variety, design, branding quality, packaging and appearance.

- **Promotion:** Advertising, sponsorship, selling, publicity, mailshots (or bulk/direct mail) and Internet presence.

- **Price:** Basic, discounts, credit, payment methods and appearance (especially using 99p instead of £1).

- **Place:** Coverage, outlets (including online), transport, distribution and accessibility.

✔ **The four Cs:**

- **Customers:** Mailshots, Internet, television advertising, and presentation activities related to the needs and wants of customers.

- **Convenience:** Establishing the required and desired outlets, and educating customers on accessing the available outlets (including online).

- **Cost:** The equivalent of price in the four Ps, including the requirement to balance cost and price with value and benefits.

- **Communication:** Developing advertising, sponsorship, selling, publicity, mailshot (or bulk/direct mail) and online materials that are valuable to customers.

Marketing mixes arise from the combination and interaction of each of these elements. But for most products and services, one of the elements is more important than the others. For example:

✔ If a product has no intrinsic quality or durability, you can't name a price low enough to charge for it.

✔ If the product isn't price sensitive (in other words, if people buy it because they need it, when they need it), discounting it to attract more customers is pointless. (When was the last time an electric company had a sale?)

✔ Convenience has to be seen through the eyes of the customers. For example, people are only prepared to walk 200 to 300 metres in order to buy fast food. So, if your location is farther away from your customer base than this, you won't attract the trade that you seek.

You design and build marketing mixes in accordance with the benefits that the products and services deliver to customers. The marketing mixes themselves are delivered in accordance with company strategy, and structured so as to appeal to the markets and market segments served.

The marketing mix presents what you're trying to deliver in ways that will be received positively by the intended audience.

Ryanair

Ryanair's marketing continually treads a fine line between absolute expertise and tackiness. Its marketing mix combines the four Cs as follows:

✔ **Convenience:** Customers can book flights online very quickly.

✔ **Customers:** Customers know and understand the quality of service that they are getting in return for travelling with Ryanair.

✔ **Cost:** Customers know that the fares are low. Customers also know that they have to pay very high prices for hold baggage, any assistance that isn't pre-booked and the carriage of specialist equipment such as sports gear and musical instruments.

✔ **Communication:** Gaudy, cheap and tacky advertisements attract attention, raise a smile and above all make sure that the company remains firmly in the minds of consumers.

Ryanair keeps up this process through constant promotions. Customers are enticed to buy 'add-ons', including luggage, car hire, airport transit and hotel rooms – all presented on the basis of real and perceived discounts offered by Ryanair to their customers as the result of their bookings with the airline.

Selecting Your Marketing Media

A variety of media tools are available to organisations. Here's a rundown of some options you may consider:

✔ **Advertising:** You may buy ads in newspapers, magazines, online, and more.

✔ **Circulars, mailshots (or bulk/direct mail) and email contacts:** You send out promotional materials (or the electronic equivalent) in order to keep your products and services in the minds of your customers.

✔ **Direct sales:** You employ salespeople to engage in face-to-face sales activities with customers, building physical as well as psychological relationships with your customers and clients.

✔ **Packaging:** You package your product in such a way that it attracts your target customers.

✔ **Price presentations:** You set your prices so they appear attractive and valuable to your customers.

✔ **Promotions:** You attach a price, volume or value advantage to your products or services, and you do it in such a way as to make your products and services stand out from the crowd.

✔ **Public relations (PR):** You can use radio, television, the Internet and newspaper coverage to your best advantage, essentially getting third party endorsement in the process.

PR is sometimes seen as 'free advertising'. It is not. It has to be very carefully managed in order to ensure that you get the wider media coverage that you seek.

PR is the professional practice of presenting products/services/organisations and information about these products/ services/organisations through a third party with the goal of influencing the intended audience to support them in a positive light.

✔ **Service presentations:** You use attractive images to draw customers to your service.

✔ **Sponsorships:** You target events with which you want to be associated and that can develop your identity in the markets you're targeting. You give them money in exchange for prominently displaying your organisation's name at the event.

Branding: Showing Who You Are and What You're About

As you develop your marketing efforts, you begin to build a brand image and identity. Your company and your products and services gain lives of their own. Beyond the quality of your products and services, customers develop certain expectations of you. As you develop your brand and image, you build customers' confidence in everything you do, including:

✔ The actual and perceived quality of your products and services

✔ The actual and perceived quality of the customer service you provide

✔ New products and services that your customers can expect from you

Whether you realise it or not, you're building a psychological contract between your organisation and your customers. This psychological contract forms the basis of developing and building customer loyalty. Customers who are actively loyal are essential as you build your ability to operate profitably and effectively.

Never underestimate the psychological aspect of brand and image building. As you develop customer confidence and build expectations, make sure that you always deliver. People hate to be let down. If you let down your customers, you shake their confidence in you.

Thinking about the brand you want

You want to be in control of your organisation's brand – as opposed to letting your customers or the general public label you. So start by thinking of the brands of organisations you're familiar with. For example, consider the railway, telephone and electricity companies that you use. What are their brands? Are they:

- ✔ Excellent, or a necessary evil?

- ✔ Good providers, or expensive and unreliable?

- ✔ Easy or difficult to speak to if you've a complaint?

- ✔ Easy or difficult to change or replace?

Consider what influences your knowledge, understanding and perception of these organisations. Is it:

- ✔ The bills that they send you?

- ✔ The media coverage they receive?

- ✔ Other people's stories about them?

- ✔ Your own personal experiences of them?

- ✔ Your most recent experiences of them?

Meeting customers where they are – not where you wish they were

Railways, telecommunications companies and electricity companies are often frustrated with the negative media coverage they get. When questioned, their employees do their best to convey the reality. For example, they explain that 80 per cent of the trains run on time, how essential telecommunications are and how electricity is only priced so high because of fuel charges.

No matter how true these statements may be, customers think otherwise. As an organisation, you have to work on customers' perceptions, no matter how inaccurate or frustrating they may be. After all, it doesn't matter what you do or how good you actually are – it's how good or bad the customers *think* you are that's the key to your brand.

So, if you're branding one of these companies, you first need to attack each of these key points: the reliability and punctuality of the railways, the value and essential nature of telecommunications, or the essential qualities that electricity brings to people's homes.

Look at all these experiences as a starting point for understanding how your customers think when they think of your products or services, as well as your organisation. Then address each of the points that have been raised. Use all the relevant media at your disposal to present a strong and positive message and image of your company, and its products and services.

Your organisation has to be clear about the brand values that it wants to promote. And those values have to line up with the values that your customers want.

All brands must have some measure of quality and value. The key is being as precise as possible about what *quality* and *value* mean to your customers. Then, when you know that, you have to deliver additional and precise values according to customer demands. For example, here are some popular brands and the values they deliver:

- ✔ **Amazon.com:** The ability to deliver books and other products anywhere that the customer wants within a day or two, supported by discounted prices.

- ✔ **Burberry:** Distinctive design, available at prices affordable to the target markets.

- ✔ **Facebook:** A secure and reliable medium for sharing personal information and building a circle of friends online.

- ✔ **Marks & Spencer:** Good-quality food and clothing at reasonable prices.

- ✔ **Swatch:** Quality, reliability, a sense of fun and adventure, and good value.

Each of these examples has a clear identity, relating to questions of confidence and expectations. Your organisation needs to replicate the consistency, clarity, identity and simplicity of all those who build effective brands.

You use each part of the marketing media available that's relevant to your brand so as to present a unified, coherent and consistent message. This reinforces and develops the identity, image and presentation that you want to achieve to build and develop the brand you want.

Building a brand

To build a brand, you use all the relevant media available. Make sure that you include the following:

- ✔ **Your logo,** which is distinctive and usually has coloured lettering and/or an image, which you promote to ensure that people recognise the brand immediately

✔ **Promotions and presentations** of your products and services in ways that ensure that people recognise you for the specific quality, value and confidence that you purport to deliver

✔ **Associations with others** that you've chosen because they reinforce the quality, value or completeness of service with which you want to be associated

You have to ask a few key questions:

✔ What sort of a logo and image are we going to present? Why and how?

✔ Where are we going to present this logo and to whom?

✔ How are we going to ensure the consistency that we seek?

✔ How are we going to get the associations of quality and value that we seek?

This set of questions then becomes the starting point for:

✔ A strategic approach in which you determine what activities and media you're going to use, when and where

✔ An operational approach, in which you carry out all the activities that you've chosen and then evaluate them for effectiveness

✔ The foundations of a strategic and operational approach to developing the brand in the future, through both brand strategy development and the determination of specific activities

Where, when and how you use media is critical in building your brand. Ryanair doesn't advertise in expensive glossy magazines. And Burberry doesn't advertise its clothes as being for sale in supermarkets. In both cases, doing so would be wasting time and money, not to mention damaging the brand. Why? Well, if Ryanair is advertised in glossy magazines, customers are likely to think that it clearly isn't the good-value airline that it has always promoted itself to be. And Burberry customers don't buy clothes in supermarkets – they go to upmarket department stores and more exclusive outlets – so if Burberry clothes were advertised as being available at supermarkets, it would cease to be the brand of choice for its current customers.

Through this process, you're making direct connections all the time between your products and services, and the brand. You also underpin the brand itself with a structure and consistency of approach so that you're constantly reinforcing the image and identity that you want to get across.

The 'Flower Duet' at British Airways

For 15 years, British Airways (BA) structured much of its advertising around sunny and tropical images. Each of these presentations was accompanied by the music of the 'Flower Duet' from the opera *Lakme* by Christophe Delibes. In 2009, BA decided that this focus had run its course.

The problem was (and remains): what to replace it with? BA's initial focus shifted to its very proud history and heritage as a pioneering airline (it was the first to offer a truly global network) and its high standards of in-flight service. The problem: although the new approach

did, indeed, support BA's global brand, it wasn't considered special or unique. It also said very little to the 30 per cent of BA's customers who use the airline for short-haul flights only.

So, the enduring problem remains: how to replace the 'Flower Duet'? Only BA can answer this question. But the lesson to keep in mind for your organisation is that when you do decide to cancel something, you need something that is at least as distinctive to replace it. Otherwise, even if your brand doesn't suffer, it won't develop either.

Doing Market Research

The purpose of market research is to identify and maximise sales opportunities for your products and services. The goal is to get to know as much as you possibly can about your customers and their needs and wants.

Market research incorporates a variety of tools that I cover in this section.

Customer surveys

Customer surveys are about finding out what people truly think of your products and services. You conduct customer surveys to find out the value, quality, usefulness and durability of your products and services – from the customer's point of view.

You clearly establish the objectives of the survey by completing the following sentence:

The purpose of this survey is to _____.

Then you structure your questions to fulfil the stated purpose.

Surveys are most useful when you successfully target sufficient numbers of customers to give you a large volume of data from which to work.

Surveys always suffer from two key shortcomings:

- ✔ People can't be bothered to do them, so you tend to get few responses, limiting your data.

- ✔ The responses are coloured by how the respondent is feeling at the time. If the respondent is feeling positive and cheerful, you get more positive responses than if the respondent is having a bad day.

Factor the effects of the shortcomings in to each survey that you commission. And be sure to give people enough time to respond, but not so much time that they forget about it or never quite get around to doing it!

With all surveys and customer research, never ask questions that gain a generally favourable response. Generally favourable responses look great and positive at first sight but are actually noncommittal. People give generally favourable responses to general and imprecise questions such as:

- ✔ **Do you like this product or service?** The easy answer is, 'Yes, I do.'

- ✔ **Would you buy this?** The easy answer is, 'Yes, I would.'

Always ask specific and precise questions, such as the following:

- ✔ What value does this product or service deliver to you?

- ✔ How often do you or will you use it?

- ✔ Will you buy this product or service? If so, how often?

- ✔ How much are you prepared to pay for this product or service?

When you ask specific questions, the responses generate useful data. You also avoid the misperceptions that arise from a lot of general but overtly favourable data.

You can conduct surveys via the Internet or email, as well as in writing. The advantage of electronic surveys is that they're very cheap and easy to set up, and you can target a lot of people very quickly. However, the returns generated are normally tiny. People will behave as you do when asked to respond to online surveys (you likely delete them and move on!). So you have to try and make it as worthwhile as possible for people to respond to an online survey; for example, by giving out prizes, vouchers and other incentives to those who do complete the survey.

Coping with complaints, er, customer feedback

Customer feedback is great – especially when you're receiving compliments on your excellent products and services and the helpfulness of your staff. All too often, however, customer feedback means complaints! No company likes to hear complaints about the company or its products, services and customer service. Nevertheless, you have to note every complaint that comes in, respond to it and make sure that the problem never occurs again.

You have to balance the complaints that you do get against your own statistics and data. For example:

✔ If the complaint is about a product malfunction, how often has this malfunction happened? Over what period of time has it happened? Find out whether the malfunction is an isolated incident or a more serious matter.

✔ If the complaint is about poor service, was it an isolated occurrence? Or does it indicate the need for a full-blown customer service training programme?

If you're a large and complex organisation, you need to evaluate whether all the complaints are coming from one location, or whether a general problem exists across the organisation. If the former is the case, you can address that particular location; if the latter, you have to get top management support and understanding of the problems that you're facing.

Failure to do anything about complaints may lead to a more serious loss of reputation or confidence. So make sure that everyone takes complaints seriously, reports them when they occur and follows up.

Focus groups

A *focus group* is a group of people brought together for a reason – in this case, to assist you with your market research! You choose focus groups from whichever parts of the population you decide best suit your purposes. Depending on the actual purpose of the focus group, you may choose from:

✔ Particular age ranges

✔ Particular locations

✔ Specific occupations or income brackets

✔ Gender or specified ethnic groups

✔ Any other mix that suits your purposes

As with all market research, you only get the responses that you ask for! So when constituting a focus group, here's the starting point:

> The purpose of this focus group is _____.

When you can complete this statement, decide who you want to participate and invite them to attend. You may have to provide incentives (for example, a small fee, as well as refreshments).

When participants arrive, make sure that you've a proper agenda and structure, and follow it. Make it clear to participants what you're asking them to do and why. Explain what the commitment is when you invite them – nobody likes to be told later on that you're expecting them to do even more than they expected. Finally, make sure that you give them as much time as they need to respond.

The advantage of a properly constituted focus group is that you get a wealth of detailed information about the precise subject. However, if you don't set clear objectives, you get only general information and a lack of substance.

To conduct a focus group you need to lay down the following:

- ✔ Clearly stated purpose
- ✔ Rewards (if any)
- ✔ Structure for the meeting
- ✔ Statement of the feedback and contribution that you need from the group members
- ✔ Timescale – should there be one meeting or several meetings, and how long should each meeting last?

Meetings with customer groups

Meetings with customer groups are a variation on focus groups – the difference is that you target people who use your products and services. You can arrange meetings with customer groups for a variety of reasons:

- ✔ To check on the quality of your products, services and customer service
- ✔ To ask them what else they would like you to produce or deliver
- ✔ To ask them specific questions about their buying habits with you
- ✔ To ask them who they see as being your competition and why
- ✔ To ask them about the costs of your products and services and the prices that you charge

Have a proper structure and agenda for the meetings. Set up the meetings in ways that are bound to enhance customers' views of you. Get them to meet in a good quality place, somewhere that they will be pleased to visit. Make sure that you provide delicious refreshments and make sure too that they get ample opportunities to let you know what they really think of you. Be sure to follow up with polite and respectful feedback and thank them for their efforts. If you have freebies to give out, make sure that you've enough to go around!

Specialist groups involved in new product and service testing

Specialist groups constituted for the purpose of testing new products and services have to be structured as focus and customer groups are, so make clear the purpose, commitment and duration required.

You have to accept everything that the group comes up with. If they find faults, glitches or imperfections, use this data as the basis for improvements. Ideally, you should have the time and space to argue and debate the findings with the group.

The advantages of specialist groups are that you get people to hammer away at your product or service, and ideally test it to destruction before you take things to market. Plus, they're likely to tell you things that you hadn't thought of, which may prove valuable.

Tracking purchases

Everyone should practise purchase tracking! You have to know the regularity and frequency of all product and service sales. You can do purchase tracking in a variety of ways:

- By measuring the time that retail products remain on the shelf
- By measuring the time between repeat purchases
- By measuring the time taken for customers to purchase replacements and upgrades
- By identifying who is suddenly starting to use your products and services, and who is suddenly no longer using them
- By identifying what other things people buy when they buy your products and services

Most retail outlets now have their own loyalty and rewards cards, which are an accurate and invaluable record of people's spending habits and activities. You can use the information gained to target individuals and groups with offers and additional chances to purchase.

The use and value of loyalty cards in market research and data gathering is critical, so you have to make it worthwhile for people to use the cards after you issue them. Most such cards offer rewards and discounts based on the frequency of usage and/or amount of spending. Make sure that if you offer rewards for loyalty, you deliver them – think of these rewards as an investment in market research, not as a cost.

Tracking Internet buying habits

You can track Internet buying habits by retaining customer and site visitor details and their purchase histories. This information helps you:

- Target return visitors with offers and inducements
- Promote along the lines of 'people who bought this product also bought . . .'
- Identify the regularity and frequency of individual visits relative to purchases made
- Identify specific values per customer visit

Use the wealth of data that online activities generate as part of the marketing effort. Make sure that all data is assessed and evaluated for every titbit of information possible. Your ability to store, retrieve and analyse data has never been greater, so make the most of this opportunity! For more on data gathering and analysis, flip to Chapter 14.

You can get data from industry and sector sites, as well as from local chambers of commerce. You can also use sources such as the *Financial Times* and *The Economist* for more general data about the state of markets and industrial and commercial sectors and activities. And you can get data from social media sources such as Facebook, Twitter and LinkedIn. Trawl these sites to see what people are saying about you – it gives you valuable general information about your markets and customers and what they think of your company and its products and services.

Putting It All Together

As you draw up plans for your marketing campaigns and activities, you need to include feedback from your product and sales teams, web designers, those responsible for advertising and promotion, as well as your customers. You then integrate this feedback with the product and service strategies that you have decided to follow.

Here are a few tips for putting together your marketing plans, activities and campaigns:

- **Develop a list of marketing strategies and tactics.** This list helps you see the possibilities before you narrow down your choices. Know which strategies and tactics may be successful, and which may not. Look at examples from other companies in your industry and see what has worked for them. Your goal is to collect as many strategies and tactics as you can.

- **Think like your customers.** Look at your company and its products and services from the customer's perspective. In other words, look objectively at your business.

- **Know your competition.** Look at what your competitors are doing, and what they aren't doing that maybe you should be doing. Can you think of ways to improve on what your competitors are doing?

- **Analyse your options.** When you have your full list of marketing strategies, decide which you're going to use and which you're going to eliminate or defer for the moment.

- **Be clear on the purpose of your marketing activities, plans and campaigns.** Exactly what is the marketing plan supposed to accomplish? Whatever you finally choose to do, you need to advertise, present and emphasise the benefits and attractions of your company and its products and services.

Going viral

Viral marketing is essentially word-of-mouth marketing, but in today's climate, this kind of marketing is driven by the Internet and social media. Lots of companies want their marketing campaigns to go viral. But the thing is, you can't count on that happening. You need the foundations of traditional media, market research and all the topics I cover in this chapter, and you develop your viral effort from there. Take the most creative and innovative approaches that you possibly can, underpinned by a disciplined understanding of how publicity and promotional initiatives are supposed to work.

According to Jay Conrad Levinson, author of *Guerrilla Marketing: Cutting-Edge Strategies for the 21st Century* (Piatkus), the approach that you need is as follows.

✔ **The 10/30/60 rule:** According to Levinson, you should invest 10 per cent of your marketing budget in talking to everyone in your marketing sector, regardless of whether they match your ideal customer profile. Use another 30 per cent of your marketing budget to convince people who match your customer profile that they should become your customers. Devote the last 60 per cent of your marketing budget to marketing to your current customers, producing the most profits at a lower cost per sale.

✔ **The 1/10/100 rule:** This rule says that £1 spent communicating with your own staff is equivalent to £10 spent communicating in general, which is equivalent to £100 spent communicating with your customers. In other words, your employees can become the most cost-effective way to transmit your marketing messages to your customers.

✔ **The rule of thirds:** According to Levinson, you need to spend one-third of your online marketing budget on designing and posting your website; one-third on marketing the site in traditional methods; and one-third on improving and maintaining your website, keeping it entertaining, fresh and easy to use.

✔ **The rule of twice:** This rule says that remaining truly competitive online will cost you twice as much as you think. In other words, viral marketing isn't cheap.

✔ **The rule of the ruler:** Everything has to be actively developed and managed, including viral marketing. You can't simply set up a Facebook initiative and then leave it to run. If you want to ensure that viral marketing is cost-effective and does a good job for you, make sure that you keep your hand firmly on the tiller!

Part IV
Money, Money, Money

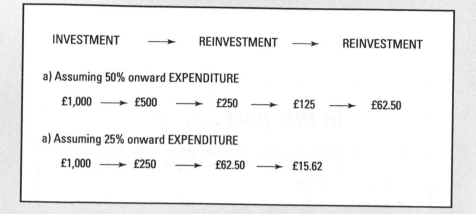

INVESTMENT   ⟶   REINVESTMENT   ⟶   REINVESTMENT

a) Assuming 50% onward EXPENDITURE

£1,000 ⟶ £500 ⟶ £250 ⟶ £125 ⟶ £62.50

a) Assuming 25% onward EXPENDITURE

£1,000 ⟶ £250 ⟶ £62.50 ⟶ £15.62

In this part . . .

✔ Understand what financial structures are and what they mean in terms of developing profitable and successful activities within your business.

✔ Brush up on your investment know-how by investing in the present and the future, ensuring your immediate business needs are met at the same time as planning for future business developments.

✔ Get acquainted with accounts and accounting and be confident in presenting and interpreting finances.

✔ Know your numbers and swat up on your statistics to understand what your finances, resources and investments are producing in quantifiable terms.

✔ Use your knowledge of numbers to make effective decisions within your business.

Chapter 11

Understanding Finance

. . . .

In This Chapter

▶ Understanding what finance is and how finance is used

▶ Weighing your assets and liabilities

▶ Allocating your resources

▶ Creating and using budgets

▶ Understanding and managing costs

. . . .

*A*nyone who studies business has to know and understand finance – finance is the lifeblood of all organisations. Without it, you can't survive – and if you don't have enough, your organisation will die. In this chapter, I fill you in on the different types of finance, how finance is used, how finances are structured, how resources are allocated, how budgets are made and how costs are apportioned. This chapter brings finance into focus.

In business, you often hear the phrase, 'The figures speak for themselves.' Nothing is farther from the truth. Even when the figures show that there are serious financial problems, it is the people involved – not the numbers – who have to work out what to do in response. So, understand what the numbers mean, and then use those numbers to inform your judgement.

Knowing What Finance Is and Where It Comes From

Finance is a combination of share capital, business loans, investments made and income from sales. All organisations need finance to support their existence, to pay for their daily activities, to meet specific obligations (for example, wages and salaries) and to meet commitments to other stakeholders. And you need enough finance to produce, deliver and support your products and services.

Public service bodies have their finances allocated to them by the offices of central and local government, and by other public sector authorities (for example, the National Health Service). Some public sector bodies are also able to raise additional funds by charging for certain services. Not-for-profit organisations have to raise the funds that they need from donors, sponsors and memberships.

The following sections outline the sources of finance for companies.

Capital and shares

Capital is required by companies for long-term finance and for making sure that resources exist to support their activities over long periods of time. Companies and commercial organisations draw their financial resources mainly from share capital and the sale of loans as follows:

- ✔ **Sales of shares:** Small companies may sell shares to family, friends and colleagues. Larger organisations may sell shares to the general public and other institutions on stock markets. A share is a portion of the company offered for sale to others so as to raise capital. Anyone buying a share becomes a part owner of the company, proportional to the share that they bought.

- ✔ **Debt capital:** Debt capital is most often used where an existing and stable enterprise effectively raises money against its existing operations and assets to fund developments, new activities, or to acquire other companies and assets.

- ✔ **Sales of loan notes, debentures and preference (or preferred) shares:** All these are short-term or fixed-term capital. This capital is finance that you may have to raise for stated business purposes, for example because you've had a sudden influx of work that has to be serviced. Usually, you raise short-term finance through a bank overdraft or loan. You agree with the lender that the finance is for a specific purpose and that you'll repay the loan by a specified date.

Here are the definitions for each of these terms:

- • **Loan notes:** A company may issue loan notes, normally to raise revenue quickly. Loan notes are papers that define the basis on which the company owes money, and the conditions under which loan note holders may call the loan in. Loan notes don't carry the rights to dividends (returns paid per share to shareholders) that shares have; they do state how much the company's going to repay at the end of the loan.

- **Debentures:** Debentures are a form of loan note, but they're issued for the specific purpose of raising money to add to the capital fund of the company.

- **Preference shares:** Preference (or preferred) shares are issued on the basis that if anything goes wrong, the company pays preference shareholders before anyone else. Preference shares may also carry a higher dividend than other shares; if so, the company must pay the preference shareholders first when they pay out dividends.

If you sell shares as above, the advantage is that your liability is limited to the face value of the shares. In other words, if the company goes bankrupt all you have to find in terms of your liabilities is the face value of the shares. If you don't limit your liability in this way, everything that you own can be added to the pot to pay for your debts if you do get into trouble.

Loans

You can raise long- and short-term finance through loans. If you take out loan capital, you have to be prepared to make the regular repayments agreed and to repay that loan upon demand, or at the end of the loan period. The advantage of loan capital is that it's normally easy enough to raise. The disadvantage is that the loan maker can call in the loan at any time if it so chooses.

Retained profits

Retained profits are those parts of your profits that you keep back to invest in the future of the business, instead of paying them out as dividends to shareholders or bonuses to staff. Using retained profits brings specific demands in terms of using them demonstrably for the development of the business. If you've excellent and consistent levels of profits coming in, these profits reduce your need to call upon additional share capital, or to raise loans from finance houses. On the other hand, every business always has demands for development and improvement that it has to fund, support and invest in.

After a highly profitable period, you may be looking at carefully and prudently investing in the future of the business. However, you need to include any residual or enduring obligations for development or investment that you have. Shareholders may demand a dividend as the result of investing in your success. Loan makers may demand repayment of a portion of what they've lent you. Staff are likely to want increased wages, salaries and bonuses. Those who have other charges on the business may also require additional repayments.

Using Finance

You can't run an organisation without finance. But what exactly do you use finance for?

Well, you've obligations and responsibilities that you have to fulfil, and finance is what lets you fulfil them. As tempted as you may be to take the money and run, your goal is the long-term survival and development of your organisation – you wouldn't have opened up shop if it weren't.

In this section, I walk you through the key ways that organisations use finance.

Investing in the business

One essential purpose of finance is investing in the business. You've heard the old adage 'You have to spend money to make money', right? Well, this is where that adage earns its keep. Part of running a successful organisation – and keeping that organisation successful – is ensuring that all the tools and resources you use to produce your products and services are working well.

For example, maybe your transport fleet needs to be replaced, maybe the cost of your supplies are expected to rise, maybe the electricity and fuel charges are going up, or maybe your place of business or factory needs to be refurbished. Sure, you may be able to overlook those things in the short term, but eventually, they're going to catch up with you, and they can hurt your organisation's chances of doing what you do so well: getting those products and services into the hands of your customers. So make sure that you do keep enough aside – and more – to support every development that comes along.

Bonuses and rewards

Finance is used to reward employees for their hard work. After all, without your employees, where would you be?

If you don't reward people for their success and efforts, you face a direct consequence: sooner or later, they stop caring, stop working hard and stop trusting you.

Boneheaded bonuses: The Brothers Lehmann

Lehmann Brothers, the US merchant and investment bank, went bankrupt in 2008. After hundreds of years of effective and highly profitable trading and investments, the company found itself unable to pay its bills.

For the previous five years, the company had been making large amounts of money. These amounts had been handed back to investors in the form of highly enhanced bonuses. Staff had also benefited from bonuses. In 2007, these bonuses reached $3 billion. In 2008, on the expectations that this level of profitability was

going to continue into the future, the company paid out $4 billion in bonuses.

However, at the end of the trading period, the company had made only $2 billion in profits. So it found itself with a $2 billion shortfall. Even a company like Lehmann Brothers couldn't carry this form of loss, especially without any assets to back it up. So it foreclosed and was taken over by Barclays Capital in 2009.

The lesson? Be absolutely clear that you can pay out what you promise. And don't pay more in bonuses than you can afford.

Make sure that any bonuses you pay out are fair. You want to reward people for their collective, as well as individual, efforts. Here are a few approaches that you can take to bonuses:

- ✔ Pay everyone the same percentage of their salary.

- ✔ Pay everyone an additional month or two months' salary.

- ✔ Pay everyone based on profit margins.

- ✔ Pay everyone for 'performance' according to pre-set criteria that apply to everyone.

- ✔ Pay sales staff on commission based on the number, volume and value of the sales they complete.

- ✔ Pay trading staff the incentives they have written into their reward packages.

- ✔ Pay production staff bonuses based on output volumes.

Be sure that all your employees understand how the bonuses are being determined, so that no one feels like he's being left out in the cold.

Dividends and returns

A major use of finance is all about keeping your backers, shareholders and investors happy. Quite legitimately, your financial backers are entitled to expect returns on their investment – and you owe them for their support.

Typically, you pay out a set dividend per share. Where you've large numbers of low-face-value shares, a dividend of a few pence per share is typical. Where you've lower numbers of high-face-value shares, the dividend per share is much higher.

Payments of dividends and returns is further complicated by the fact that, usually, investors can sell their shares at any time. You may have to be prepared to buy back shares in private companies where the investors want, or need, their money. Some companies have had to pay dividends in bad years from the retained profits of past good years in order to maintain the share value and stock market confidence.

Structuring Finance

Companies and organisations structure their finances so that they can carry out their activities as effectively and efficiently as possible.

Businesses typically use a variety of instruments to raise money, rather than just one. The name given to the balance of those instruments is structure. Structure can refer to the balance of debt to share capital and equity. Structure can also refer to the dates by which and on which loans have to paid back.

The financial structure chosen has to reflect each of the following points:

- Everything that you build into every company or organisation you have to pay for out of sales of products and services.
- Everything that you commit to, you have to pay for on the due date.
- Everything that you do has to have a fundamental financial strength and integrity.

So there are some very clear rules that you need to follow when you are determining the financial structure that is going to suit your purposes.

If you're preaching perfection, your whole financial structure should be based on selling sufficient share capital, plus retained profits. This way, you don't have any liabilities or repayments to make, whatever the state of your business.

Using loan capital

In reality, most companies have to take out loan capital at some stage. They must factor in the loan repayments as a commitment (a liability). The critical factors are the following:

- ✔ Your ability to make the repayments when demanded
- ✔ The purpose for which you've taken out the loan
- ✔ The amount of the loan

The relationship between share and loan capital is called *gearing*. Companies that are highly geared have a high percentage of loan capital; companies with low gearing have a high volume of share capital.

Financial structures that have a high percentage of loans are fine as long as you're in a rising or at least buoyant market, with high levels of regular income so you can make the repayments when demanded. Financial structures that include a high percentage of loans where income is irregular (for example, in project and capital goods work) have to factor in their ability to make the repayments even though they don't have the regular income.

Drilling down to the core: Strength and integrity

From your financial structure, you're seeking financial strength and integrity. *Financial strength* means that you can meet all your obligations, as well as invest whatever is required for the future. *Financial integrity* means that everything is honest and above board – you can clearly explain to stakeholders why you've chosen the particular structure over others.

Whichever structure you choose, be honest with yourself about the commitments involved and the obligations it brings. This way, you've a clear insight into what you have to do when things go wrong.

Financial strength and integrity additionally and crucially means that at no stage do you find yourself working from hand to mouth, taking long-term finance to pay for daily activities, fobbing off or delaying payments to suppliers – or worst of all, delaying wage and salary payments to staff.

Understanding assets and liabilities

All financial structures are founded on assets and liabilities, which I cover in detail in the following sections.

In practice, the relationship between assets and liabilities is complex. Something that is bought as an asset can quickly turn into a liability. Production, service and information technology bought as a long-term investment may be rendered obsolete at any time by new inventions. Building companies that buy land banks find that these banks become a liability if the demand for houses dries up or if the price of land falls. Projects for which capital goods have been bought may be cancelled if other costs or unforeseen problems make the venture no longer worthwhile.

Assets

Assets are the capital goods, technology, staff expertise and equipment in which you invest in order to carry out your activities. You need assets to support and facilitate everything that takes place in the organisation. The types of assets an organisation may have fall into two main categories:

- **Tangible assets:** These consist of your physical premises, as well as the technology, equipment, expertise and machinery you use in the production of the organisation's products and services. Tangible assets are sometimes referred to as *fixed assets*. Acquisition of assets is a combination of what the organisation can afford, the projected length of the asset's useful life and the uses to which they're best suited. Tangible asset expenditure also includes supplies and suppliers, the means of distribution, vehicle fleets, containers, retail and other points of outlet, including websites.

- **Intangible assets:** These assets consist of your reputation, goodwill, confidence, identity, brand and expectations. Intangible assets are therefore a major foundation of the basis on which people come to do business with your organisation. Goodwill and high expectations translate into repeat business, a better reputation, and greater customer demands and customer bases.

Somewhere in the asset base, you need to take account of the contribution of key figures. For example, the 'value' of Richard Branson to the Virgin Group is clearly considerable, but putting a precise figure on it would be difficult. Other examples of key figures who carry an asset value are Alex Ferguson at Manchester United, Michael O'Leary at Ryanair and Mark Zuckerberg at Facebook. In each of these cases, true 'value' is uncertain. What *is* certain is that the value of each of these companies takes a hit when these individuals leave.

Brand names and images are assets. Strong brand names (for example, Coca-Cola, Nescafé and Barbie) carry high and continuing levels of value. These brands also have a commercial value in their own right, and the companies that own them can (if they want to) put them up for sale.

Sales of assets

On corporate balance sheets and profit-and-loss statements, you often see 'sale of assets' listed. Organisations sell assets for one of two reasons:

✔ The assets being sold are genuinely assets, but an overriding organisational reason exists for selling them – normally, to get over a short-term crisis.

✔ The sale of assets is actually a sale of liabilities – the organisation is getting rid of things that it no longer wants.

When assets are being sold off, the value of these assets on the market nearly always declines. Those in other organisations know that the items have to be sold, so they're prepared to wait for the price to drop or name their own lower price in order to secure the particular item at a discount.

If you do sell assets, you have to be prepared to replace them at some stage in the future (and pay to do so) or go on without them in the future and do something else. And if someone else makes a success of something that you sold to them, never look back!

Assets have different lifespans. *Short-term assets* have a value for you now but will finish their useful life soon. Examples are project management expertise hired to get a particular project installed and up and running, and the acquisition of volumes of hotel rooms for the coming season by travel companies. *Long-term assets* support your activities for an extended period of time. Examples include company IT systems, manufacturing equipment, and lorries, ships and aircraft acquired by transport companies.

Some assets are *company specific* – they've a value to one organisation, but not to others. Examples include buying a competitor to secure its client base or buying a supplier of specialist technology or equipment in order to control it yourself.

Liabilities

Liabilities are the obligations and charges that you incur or that are present as the result of the company's current activities. Liabilities may be *tangible* (a piece of technology or equipment that is no longer cost-effective or doing the job that you need it to do) or *intangible* (for example, a loss of reputation or loss of shareholder or customer confidence). And, similar to assets, liabilities may be short term or long term. *Short-term liabilities* are ones that you have to deal with now; *long-term liabilities* are ones that you have for an extended period of time.

Long or short term, tangible or intangible, here are the kinds of liabilities an organisation may have:

✔ **Regular and continuing costs and obligations:** The most regular and continuing of these is staff – all staff incur costs in terms of premises and accommodation – and also they have to be paid. Other regular liabilities include capital repayments, interest charges, fuel, electricity, rent, property taxes (in the UK, rates), heating, lighting, communications, and supply, production and distribution costs.

✔ **Activity-related charges:** These vary according to the nature of the organisation, but they always include marketing activities, maintenance and upgrade charges, research and development, and pioneering and market development work.

✔ **Sudden liabilities:** Sudden liabilities occur as the result of a crisis or emergency that needs to be fixed instantly; for example, the sudden obsolescence of products and services, and production, service and information technology. A case in point was Boeing in 2012 and 2013, when it had a sudden liability in the battery systems of the 787 Dreamliner airplane, causing the plane to be taken out of service until the fault was found and remedied.

Allocating Resources

Any organisation has a limited amount of resources, so *allocating* those resources (deciding how much you're going to spend on *x* versus *y*) is essential. You need to ensure that you're allocating your money effectively. If you don't give your staff, departments, divisions, functions and activities enough in the way of resources, eventually the quality of their output declines – which can only be bad for your business.

Look at resource allocation in terms of the following:

✔ **Returns:** Your own desired levels of returns, the time period over which the returns are to be made and the performance of production and service delivery activities to the standard required by customers.

✔ **Timescales and deadlines:** See all financial performance in terms of how long it takes to achieve particular aims, objectives, goals and targets. So when you're allocating resources, how long it's going to take to reach a particular goal matters.

✔ **Wider expectations and perceptions of satisfaction:** You need to allocate resources so that shareholders, staff and customers are all satisfied.

You allocate resources to ensure high and improving levels of departmental, divisional, functional and sectional performance based on needs, wants and demands. From a financial management point of view, you need to make sure that every activity is adequately resourced.

Be especially concerned when it becomes evident that support functions are consuming larger volumes of resources in relation to primary activities. This situation is especially critical when the primary activities are declining as a result. When it occurs, you need to go back to the drawing board and commit yourself to restructuring so that primary activities get the resources they require in order to be effective.

Budgeting

A *budget* is nothing more than a written estimate of how an organisation – or a particular project, department, or business unit – will perform financially.

One of the keys to running a successful business is the ability for owners and managers to predict how a business is going to perform financially. If they can accurately predict a firm's performance, they can be certain that resources such as money, people, equipment, manufacturing plants and the like are deployed appropriately and effectively.

The real value in budgets comes when you compare estimates of expected performance to actual performance. When the figures match, you've a quick way of knowing that your organisation is performing just as it should. When the figures between your budgeted performance and actual performance differ markedly, you know that you need to take a close look at what's going on. The process of comparing expected financial results with actual financial results is called *variance analysis* (see 'Keeping your eye on the figures' later in this chapter).

Knowing why budgets matter

With the speed of business increasing all the time, and with raging change all around us, why bother doing budgets at all? Well, budgets offer the following benefits to organisations that use them:

✔ **Budgets are milestones on the road to your goals.** Every organisation has (or at least should have) goals. Budgets are a quick and easy way to see whether your organisation is on track to meet its financial goals. If, for example, you've already spent half your travel budget, but you're only one-quarter of the way through the year, you know that you've potentially got an overspending problem.

✔ **Budgets make decisions easier.** When you budget a project, new initiative or business activity, you quickly have a picture of what it will cost. Armed with that information, you can decide whether the costs you'll incur make good business sense. Will you make money or lose money as a result? How much money? For how long? The answers to these questions are important elements in the decision-making process, and you can find them in the budgeting process.

✔ **Budgets can be fast.** A budget can be as simple as a few figures scribbled onto the back of an envelope. A budget also can be a simple, one-page spreadsheet. Not every budget has to be complicated. With simple budgets, you can make changes quickly, in near real-time, and print them out or email them right away.

✔ **Budgets can be flexible.** You need to be able to make changes according to circumstances. If you need to take on extra staff to handle an unexpected order, doing so should be no problem – your budget can accommodate the change and create an up-to-date picture of how your organisation is performing. Or you can simply freeze your budget to see the variance between what your budget predicted and what really happened. No matter how fast your markets are moving, you can always keep up.

✔ **Budgets are positive.** Budgets are there to guide you and to help you predict what's going to happen. Creating a budget in which the actual results match your expectations is a real thrill. The only thing that's a bigger thrill is when your results are even *better* than you expected!

Although extensive, long-range ('strategic') planning seems increasingly less valuable to most organisations today, near-term ('tactical') planning is incredibly valuable. Budgets are a necessary part of the tactical planning process.

Looking at different kinds of budgets

When it comes right down to it, you can budget any activity in your organisation that has a financial impact. If you want a budget for self-managing work teams, research and development projects or office refurbishments, producing one should be no problem at all. Here are two of the most common budgets people use in business today:

✔ **Cash budgets:** A cash budget is an estimate of a company's cash position for a particular period of time. By using your current cash position as a baseline, you can estimate all cash inflows (sales) and outflows (expenses) during whatever time period you specify – say, a month – to determine a projected cash position at the end of the period.

✔ **Operating budgets:** The operating budget shows a business's forecasted revenues along with forecasted expenses, usually for a period of one year or less. The operating budget is a top-level budget; the following budgets are line items in the operating budget:

- **Staff budget:** A staff budget takes every person in an organisation, department or project and multiplies the number of hours they're expected to work by their wage rates. The result is the total staff cost that an organisation will expend for a set period of time.

- **Sales budget:** This budget is an estimate of the quantity of goods and services that an organisation will sell during a specific period of time. In the case of products, you can determine total revenue by multiplying the total number of units projected to be sold by the price per unit.

- **Production budget:** The production budget starts with the sales budget and its estimates of the total number of units projected to be sold. This budget then translates this information into estimates of the cost of staff, materials and other expenses required to produce these units.

- **Expense budget:** Every business – from a one-person home business to a huge multinational corporation with tens of thousands of employees – incurs a variety of expenses during the course of normal operations. The business prepares expense budgets for travel, utilities, office supplies, telephone and many other common and not-so-common expenses.

- **Capital budget:** If you plan to buy fixed assets with a long, useful lifespan (many organisations consider this lifespan to mean a year or more), then this is the place to budget for them. Items in your capital budget may include buildings, production machinery, computers, copiers, furniture and anything else that will still be in your office long after you're gone.

Some type of budget is available to you for almost any occasion. To see what a real operating budget looks like, have a look at the sample budget in Figure 11-1.

Small operating units or departments prepare budgets. These budgets roll up into larger budgets – for divisions or groups – which the organisation then combines into its overall budget. In this way, managers at all levels of an organisation can play a role in an organisation's financial health and well-being.

Spacely Sprocket Company

Revenue	Monthly Budget
Product sales	£81,250
Royalties	£1,000
Website ads	£8,500
Other income	£100
Total revenue	**£90,850**

Expenses	
Rent	£1,403
Wages	£10,000
Taxes	£1,235
Licences and permits	£100
Insurance (public liability)	£1,000
Insurance (other)	£500
Advertising and promotions	£5,000
Dues and subscriptions	£300
Training	£400
Micellaneous	£100
Office supplies	£2,000
Outside services	£2,000
Postage and delivery	£2,500
Printing	£2,500
Telephone	£1,000
Entertainment	£50
Gifts	£50
Meals	£500
Travel	£5,000
Commission	£2,000
Cost of goods sold	£5,000
Interest	£100
Total expenses	**£42,828**
Profit (Loss)	**£48,022**

Figure 11-1: A sample budget.

Developing a budget

Three key approaches to developing a budget that works come to mind – top down, bottom up and zero-based. Each has its advantages and disadvantages, and each approach can work well, although the pendulum swings in favour of the bottom-up approach.

Top down

In this approach, top management prepare budgets and impose them on the lower layers of the organisation, generally without any consultation or involvement on the part of those outside top management. Top-down budgets clearly express the performance goals and expectations of top management.

These budgets can be unrealistic because they don't incorporate the input of the very people who implement them.

Bottom up

In bottom-up budgeting, supervisors and middle managers prepare the budgets for their section/division/responsibility area, and then forward them up the chain of command for review and approval. These middle managers have the benefit of a close working knowledge of their part of the organisation and its financial performance. As a result, bottom-up budgets tend to be more accurate than top-down budgets. In addition, bottom-up budgets can have a positive impact on employee morale because employees assume an active role in providing financial input to the budgeting process. If you do the budgeting this way, however, you do need to ensure that everyone knows who is in ultimate control. You don't want any uncertainties arising from a known or perceived lack of control.

Zero-based

Zero-based budgeting is a process in which each manager prepares estimates of his proposed expenses for a specific period of time as though they were being performed for the first time. In other words, each activity starts from a budget base of zero. By starting from scratch at each budget cycle, managers are required to take a close look at all their expenses and justify them to top management, thereby minimising waste.

Keeping your eye on the figures

The classic role of managers is to control, and one aspect of controlling is regularly reviewing and analysing accounting reports to determine the financial health of the organisation and make better, more informed decisions.

One of the simplest ways to use a budget to keep your eye on the figures is through the use of *variance analysis* – in simple terms, a comparison of the financial estimates that you budgeted for a particular period with your firm's actual financial results. The variance is the difference between budget and actual, and it can be a positive or negative figure, or zero.

TIP

Getting back on track

Budgets provide a kind of early warning system that, when compared to actual results, can inform you when something is going wrong that needs your immediate attention. When your expenditures exceed your budget, you can do several things to get back on track:

✔ **Review your budget.** Before you do anything else, take a close look at your budget and make sure that the assumptions on which you've based it are accurate and make sense in your changing market. If your market is growing quickly, you may need to adjust your estimates. Sometimes, the budget – not the spending – is out of line.

✔ **Implement a spending freeze.** One of the quickest and most effective ways to bring spending back in line with a budget is to freeze spending. For example, you can freeze expenses such as pay increases, new staff and bonuses.

✔ **Postpone new projects.** New projects – including new product development, acquisition of new facilities, and research and development – can eat up a lot of money. If spending is over-budget, a common solution is to postpone new projects until you've enough revenue to support them. However, be sure to carefully balance your desire to bring spending back into line with the need to develop new products and services. If you're overzealous in this area, the result can be disastrous for the future growth and prosperity of the company.

✔ **Lay off employees and close facilities.** When you're trying to cut expenses, the last resort is to lay off employee and close facilities. Although these actions result in an immediate and lasting decrease in expenses, they also bring about an immediate and lasting decrease in the talent available to your organisation. In addition, the morale of those employees who survive the budget cut can suffer.

In the monthly expenses in Table 11-1, look at the variance between the budget and the actual figures. (Parentheses around a figure mean that the figure is negative.) This method gives you an immediate picture of financial issues that may require a closer look on your part.

Table 11-1	Variance Analysis		
Expenses	*Budget (£)*	*Actual (£)*	*Variance (£)*
Rent	1,403	1,403	0
Wages	10,000	12,500	2,500
Taxes	1,325	1,500	175
Internet access	60	0	(60)

Expenses	Budget (£)	Actual (£)	Variance (£)
Licences and permits	50	50	0
Courier service charge	25	100	75
Telephone system	200	200	0
Insurance (public liability)	1,000	1,500	500
Insurance (other)	500	500	0
Total expenses	**14,563**	**17,753**	**3,190**

In this example, fixed expenses were originally budgeted at £14,563 for the month. However, when the month ended, the accounting system reflected actual fixed expenses of £17,753. This figure resulted in a total variance – in this case, overspending – of £3,190.

After you've determined that you've a budget variance for the period in question, the next step is to decide whether the variance is significant and, if so, to figure out why it occurred. In Table 11-1, a variance of £3,190, which is 22 per cent of the original budget of £14,563, is definitely significant and warrants a closer look by the manager who's responsible.

Apportioning Costs

When it comes to costs, you need to be able to distinguish between the following:

- ✔ **Fixed costs (FC):** Incurred by companies and organisations regardless of whether any business is conducted. Fixed costs consist of capital charges, the costs of premises and staff, and administrative, managerial and support function overheads.

Many people would tell you that staff are not a fixed cost, but a variable cost. However, your life will be much easier if you regard staff as a fixed cost. After all, you can't change staff quickly or easily. And even if you need to lay people off, in the short term you're paying for people to leave your organisation rather than to continue working for it. And if you only employ subcontractors, then the price for the contracts is itself fixed. So get into the habit of looking at staffing costs as fixed.

- ✔ **Variable costs (VC):** Incurred as the result of conducting activities. Variable costs consist of raw materials costs, packaging and distribution costs, and the frequency and density of usage of equipment (for example, production technology, telephone systems and information systems).

- **Marginal costs (MC):** Incurred by the production of one extra item of output. They reflect the extent to which production capacity may be extended without incurring additional fixed costs in the form of investment in new staff, equipment and technology. The marginal cost tells you how close you are to operating at 100 per cent of capacity.

- **Opportunity costs (OC):** These costs relate to the opportunities you've passed up as a result of committing resources in one area instead of others.

  The option not taken by a business is also a cost, though it is used for comparison with what you actually did, rather than being an actual cost incurred. So the representation of the opportunity cost looks like: 'We did this and it cost us $x; we could have done y and it would have cost us $2x.'

- **Sunk costs (SC):** Incurred costs on which you've no reasonable prospect of any return at all.

  Increasingly, you should come to see production, technology and IT costs as sunk costs. Systems and the technology that drives them develop so quickly that you often have to replace them at short notice, and before your current systems and technology have been fully depreciated or utilised.

- **Consequential costs (CC):** Costs that occur as a direct consequence of making a particular decision.

- **Switching costs (SWC):** Incurred as the direct consequence of switching from one set of activities to others. Switching costs are incurred when, for example, production is relocated elsewhere; old products and services are discontinued, and new ones are brought in; and new production, service and information technology are installed.

All these costs add up to total cost (TC). *Total cost* is the sum of all costs that the organisation incurs under each of these categories as the result of being involved in its sector, making particular decisions, implementing initiatives and working in the locations that it chooses.

Clearly, organisations have a fair amount of flexibility in apportioning costs to particular activities, even if the total represents enduring financial obligation and commitment. Here are a few different approaches that organisations may take:

- Divide all costs between the range and volume of activities that you carry out, and then allocate a proportion of costs to each of those activities.

- Discount the fixed cost. Include every other cost in your financial assessments and then, as long as sales of products and services are more than covering every other cost, you're making what is known as a 'contribution' to the fixed cost base.

✔ Keep your cost bases and revenue streams entirely separate. Take the view that as long as income from sales more than exceeds the costs and other obligations, all is well with the world.

Keeping cost bases and revenue streams entirely separate is particularly risky. It can work as long as you keep a close eye on every cost, and constantly measure the revenue that is coming in. If you do take this approach, you need to assess products, services and revenue streams in terms of:

- Those that make money

- Those that lose money

- Those that you aren't sure about

For those you aren't sure about, you need to find a basis for calculating the effectiveness of their contribution on the double!

Chapter 12

Structuring Accounts

*I*f you've ever played in, or watched, a competitive sporting match – whether football, cricket, baseball, tennis, badminton or hockey – you know the importance of keeping score. An individual or team score instantly tells you three things:

✔ During the course of competition, who's ahead and by how much

✔ At the end of competition, who won and by how much

✔ How well the competitors did in relation to everyone else

Business works in much the same way. However, instead of recording the number of goals, points or runs scored, business tracks money. *Accounting* is the science of tracking money in a company.

An accounting system shows how much money has come into a company and how much has gone out – if you want to 'win', your company must have more coming in than going out. An accounting system also shows how much cash you have in your bank account, how much money you owe and how much money others owe you. An accounting system shows the value of the products that you keep on hand to sell to customers, as well as the money that you pay to employees in the form of salary and benefits. Finally, it shows the money that's left over at the end of each month – your company's profit.

In this chapter, I walk you through the basics of accounting, introduce you to a variety of financial statements and take the fear out of audits.

For a much more complete discussion on accounting, have a look at *Mastering Accounts* by Geoffrey Knott (Palgrave). This book is a clear and concise guide to everything you need to know about accounting.

Getting to Grips with the Basics of Accounting

In business, as in sports, winners and losers emerge. Some businesses make lots of money and thrive, and others lose lots of money and die.

In recent years, you may have heard about a third kind of business: a company that loses lots of money for years, but for some crazy reason, still has a stock market value of billions of pounds. Usually, such companies are Internet start-ups. Although this situation does occur, don't count on it for your business!

For the most part, winning and losing in the world of business is determined on the basis of financial measures. The most important financial measures are undoubtedly sales and profit. *Sales* represents the total amount of money that flows into a company as a result of selling that company's goods and services. *Profit* represents the money that's left over after you subtract a company's expenses from its revenues and income.

Before I get too deep into the nuts and bolts of accounting systems, I start at the beginning with the accounting cycle.

The accounting cycle

The entire accounting process – from beginning to end – is called the *accounting cycle*. The accounting cycle has three parts:

- ✔ **Transaction:** A *transaction* is something your business does that generates a financial impact that's recorded in the accounting system. For example, if a member of your sales staff sells one of your widgets to a customer who then deposits the cheque for £110 in the company's bank account, that's a transaction. Similarly, when your company makes a £150 payment to Joe's House of Cheese for supplying food for a company party, that's also a transaction.

- ✔ **Cash book:** As each transaction occurs, it goes into a cash book. A *cash book* is nothing more than a general file that temporarily holds transactions.

> ✔ **Ledger:** On a regular basis – daily, weekly, monthly or another frequency – transactions in the cash book are classified by type and moved into individual accounts, called *ledgers*. Individual ledgers include such accounts as payroll, travel and sales.

After transactions are put into their ledgers, managers have access to a wide variety of reports that summarise transactions and their effect on the business. I discuss these reports – which include the profit-and-loss account, balance sheet and cash flow statement – in the 'Understanding Financial Statements' section, later in this chapter.

The accounting equation

The accounting equation is the foundation of the science of accounting. According to the accounting equation

> Assets = Liabilities + Share Capital

Here's a look at each part of the accounting equation and how it affects an organisation's finances.

Assets

Assets are generally anything in a business that has some sort of financial value and can be converted to cash. The products you have stocked in your warehouse are assets, as is the cash in your till.

Assets come in two different forms: current and fixed. These forms represent how quickly you can convert the assets into cash:

> ✔ **Current assets:** Assets that you can convert into cash within one year. These assets can include money that arrived in the post today, invoices for a month's worth of consulting services and the computers for sale on your showroom floor. Assets that you can quickly convert into cash are also known as *liquid assets*; the speed by which you can convert assets into cash is called *liquidity*.

> ✔ **Fixed assets:** Assets that take more than a year to convert into cash. These assets can include the custom-built industrial milling machine that only three companies in the world have any use for, the building that houses your headquarters and even your old photocopier.

Here are the most common kinds of business assets – both current and fixed:

- ✔ **Cash:** Includes good old-fashioned money and money equivalents such as cheques, money orders, marketable securities, bank deposits and foreign currency (if applicable).

- ✔ **Accounts receivable:** Represents the money that your clients and customers owe you for purchasing your products or services. When you allow a customer to buy your goods today and pay for them later, you're creating a receivable. If you work strictly on a cash basis (hot-dog stand, ticket agency, e-commerce site), you won't have any receivables, and this item is zero.

- ✔ **Stock:** Comprises the finished products that you purchase or manufacture to sell to customers, as well as raw materials, work in process and supplies used in operations. If you run a grocery shop, your stock is everything on display for sale in your shop – the carrots, the tubs of margarine and the boxes of doughnuts.

- ✔ **Pre-paid expenses:** When you pay for a product or service in advance, you create a *pre-paid expense*. Examples of pre-paid expenses include a pre-paid maintenance contract on a car, an insurance policy with a one-year term paid in advance and an agreement for security alarm monitoring paid in advance on a quarterly basis.

- ✔ **Equipment:** The wide variety of property that your organisation purchases to carry out its operations. Examples include desks, chairs, computers, electronic testing gear, forklifts and security equipment.

- ✔ **Property:** Includes assets such as the land, buildings and facilities that a company owns and occupies. Some companies have little or no property assets, but others have huge property portfolios.

Liabilities

Liabilities are money owed to others outside your organisation. They're things like the bills you owe to the company that delivers your office supplies, the payments you owe on the construction loan that financed your warehouse expansion and the mortgage on your corporate headquarters building.

Like assets, liabilities also come in two forms – current and long-term – each representing the amount of time to repay the obligation:

- ✔ **Current liabilities:** Liabilities that you repay within one year. These liabilities include the money for next month's salaries, other short-term bill payments and short-term loans from the bank.

- ✔ **Long-term liabilities:** Liabilities that you repay in a period longer than one year. These liabilities include the payments, for example, on the company delivery van, the mortgage on the company's depot in Leeds and dividends to preference shareholders.

Just as many different kinds of business assets exist, you also have many different kinds of business liabilities. Here's a list of the most common:

- **Accounts payable:** The obligations owed to the individuals and organisations that have provided goods and services to your company. Examples include money owed to your computer network consultant, your local utility company and an advertising agency that your marketing department uses for advertising campaigns.

- **Loan notes and debentures:** Loans made to your company by individuals or by organisations such as banks. They could be anything from an IOU to a multi-million-pound loan secured from a large bank.

- **Accrued expenses:** Sometimes a company incurs an expense but has no immediate plans to reimburse individuals and organisations that are owed the money. Examples include future wages to be paid to employees, or interest due on loans and utility bills.

- **Bonds payable:** When companies issue bonds to raise money to finance large projects, they incur obligations to pay back the individuals and organisations that purchase those bonds.

- **Mortgages payable:** When companies purchase property, they often do so by taking out a *mortgage* (a long-term loan secured by the property itself). Mortgages payable represent the mortgages that an organisation has on all its properties.

Share capital

Share capital is the money that's left over when you add up all a company's assets and subtract all its liabilities. Share capital represents the owner's direct investment in the firm, or the owner's claims on the company's assets. Another way of expressing a company's share capital is its net worth. *Net worth* is simply a snapshot of your company's financial health for a particular period of time.

Here are the two types of share capital:

- **Paid-up shares:** Paid-up shares represent the money that people invest in a company. When companies such as BA, BT or Google offer to sell shares to investors, the investors are providing paid-up shareholdings to the companies.

- **Retained earnings and profits:** These are a company's earnings and profits that are held within the company to be re-invested and not paid out to shareholders as dividends. A dividend is a payment per share made to investors.

Double-entry bookkeeping

The accounting equation (see the preceding section) is like any other equation – a change to one side of the equation results in a change to the other. Therefore, every financial transaction results in not one but two entries to your accounting records.

The accounting equation– the basis of the entire science of accounting – was made around five centuries ago, in 1494, by Luca Pacioli, an Italian mathematician and Franciscan monk.

Say, for example, Aberdeen Steakhouses buys a large volume of beef to serve to its customers. Aberdeen Steakhouses starts with assets (stock) of £1,000, liabilities (accounts payable) of £500 and share capital of £500, so:

Assets = Liabilities + Share Capital

£1,000 = £500 + £500

When Aberdeen Steakhouses purchases its beef from the meat market for £100 and the meat market agrees to invoice Aberdeen for it, Aberdeen acquires an asset (stock – literally, raw material). It also takes on a liability of £100, the money owed to the meat market (accounts payable). After this transaction, the accounting equation looks like this:

Assets = Liabilities + Share Capital

£1100 = £600 + £500

As you can see, Aberdeen Steakhouses added £100 worth of stock to its assets, but it simultaneously added a payable of £100 to its liabilities. The share capital didn't change. Every transaction on one side of the accounting equation results in a transaction on the other side of the accounting equation.

A small business may process relatively few transactions per day, making its accounting system relatively simple. An accounting system for a particularly large business, one that does millions of pounds of business a day, is quite complex. In both cases, accounting systems – and the computers that run them, and the people who run the computers – are always important, regardless of the size of the business.

Depreciating your assets

Fixed assets have finite lifetimes. No asset lasts forever, especially if it has anything to do with technology – whereas a computer may have a useful lifetime of only 4 or 5 years, a steel mill may have a lifetime of 50 or 60 years. As assets are used over the course of their lifetimes, they gradually wear out or become obsolete. So, in the case of a steel mill with a 60-year lifetime, the mill doesn't retain 100 per cent of its value through year 59 and then suddenly lose all its value on the first day of its 60th year. Instead, this fixed asset steadily loses value as it experiences normal wear and tear over time.

Depreciation is this loss of value of a fixed asset, a method of allocating the cost of the asset over its useful lifetime.

Looking at various depreciation methods

You can choose from many different methods for calculating depreciation, some better than others. In this section, I offer a look at a few of the most common depreciation methods.

Straight-line depreciation

Straight-line depreciation is the simplest method of depreciating an asset. In the straight-line method, you simply divide the cost of the asset by its expected lifetime in years. Table 12-1 shows the straight-line depreciation of a £2,500 computer that has an expected lifetime of five years.

Table 12-1	Straight-Line Depreciation	
Year	*Depreciation Expense*	*Cumulative Depreciation*
1	£500	£500
2	£500	£1,000
3	£500	£1,500
4	£500	£2,000
5	£500	£2,500

As you can see, the amount of the asset depreciated each year is exactly the same: £500. At the end of the five-year life of the asset, the computer's original cost of £2,500 has been fully depreciated. Nothing could be easier or more straightforward than that.

Double-declining balance depreciation

The *double-declining balance* method of depreciation is what's known as an accelerated method of depreciation because it pushes the majority of the total depreciation amount into the early years of ownership. You calculate the double-declining balance by multiplying the *book value* (the original cost of a fixed asset, less cumulative depreciation) by double its straight-line rate. So, in the example of a computer valued at £2,500, with a straight-line rate of 20 per cent per year, the double-declining balance method allows a rate of 40 per cent per year of the asset's book value.

Table 12-2 shows the results of applying the double-declining balance method to a computer valued at £2,500.

Table 12-2	Double-Declining Balance Depreciation		
Year	Book Value	Depreciation Expense	Cumulative Depreciation
1	£2,500	£1,000	£1,000
2	£1,500	£600	£1,600
3	£900	£360	£1,960
4	£540	£216	£2,176
5	£324	£130	£2,306

So why would anyone want to accelerate the depreciation of an asset? The main reason is that doing so reflects the real world. Think of how quickly your new car depreciates after you've driven it off the forecourt (or away from the dealership) for the first time. As soon as you put anything to use, it loses its resale value, and double-declining balance depreciation reflects this loss of value much more accurately than straight-line depreciation. It also underlines the fact that however you depreciate, eventually you must pay for the particular piece of equipment in full, and normally write it off altogether.

Sum of the years' digits depreciation

In the *sum of the years' digits* method of depreciation, you first determine how many years of life an asset's going to have. Then you add the digits together to create the denominator of a fraction, with the year of depreciation as the numerator. You multiply the fraction by the asset's original cost to determine the depreciated value.

Lost? Don't worry – an example should help. For a £2,500 computer with an effective life of five years, first find the sum of the digits of its life: 1 + 2 + 3 + 4 + 5 = 15. This figure is your denominator. 5 is then your numerator. Table 12-3 shows the calculation involved to determine depreciation of the computer over its useful life.

Table 12-3		Sum of the Years' Digits Depreciation		
Year	Original Cost	Fraction	Depreciation Expense	Cumulative Depreciation
1	£2,500	$^5/_{15}$	£833	£833
2	£2,500	$^4/_{15}$	£667	£1,500
3	£2,500	$^3/_{15}$	£500	£2,000
4	£2,500	$^2/_{15}$	£333	£2,333
5	£2,500	$^1/_{15}$	£167	£2,500

As with the double-declining balance method of depreciation, the sum of the years' digits method pushes depreciation into the early years of an asset's life. This reflects the real world in a much more genuine way than straight-line depreciation.

Choosing the right depreciation method for you

You choose the method of depreciation that's right for each asset. This decision is influenced by your financial strategies and structures, and what your auditors and accountants advise. For example:

- ✔ You probably choose to depreciate transport equipment (such as cars) using double-declining balance depreciation.

- ✔ You depreciate production technology as quickly as possible – using the double-declining balance depreciation or sum of the years' digits depreciation – because you often have to replace such technology after a year or two.

- ✔ You probably choose to depreciate IT and support systems using the straight-line depreciation method, because these items have a much longer useful life (though they usually have little resale value).

When in doubt about which depreciation method to use, talk with your accountant. Accountants live for this kind of stuff!

Understanding Financial Statements

In business, everyone receives a variety of financial and project reports that are tailored to their exact needs. For instance, a software engineer may receive a weekly staff report that shows her exactly who worked on each of the team's software projects, how many hours each employee worked, the cost of those hours and a variance above or below budget. An accounts receivable manager may get a 'blacklist' of receivables that shows who owes money to the company, how much and for how long. And members of a production team may receive regular reports on the cost of products returned to the company because of quality problems.

However, when it comes to assessing the overall financial health of an organisation, people use three key financial reports universally throughout the business world. These reports – known more exactly as financial statements – are

- ✔ The balance sheet
- ✔ The profit-and-loss account
- ✔ The cash flow statement

Each of these reports offers a unique perspective for looking at a company's financial health – no one financial report tells the full story. You can understand the complete picture only by reviewing all the financial statements and sometimes by digging even deeper for more information.

In this section, I give you the lowdown on each of the statements. First, though, I kick off by looking at who reads them and why.

Gathering the important financial statements

Who reads financial statements? If you're a manager or business owner, you're probably already familiar with them. Your job is to keep close tabs on your organisation's performance and to make changes in the allocation of company resources to maintain a high level of financial return. If you're part of a self-managing work team, or if you work for an *open-book organisation* (one that shares financial and other performance data with all employees; see the later sidebar 'An open book'), you too are familiar with financial statements and the information they provide.

Banks need financial statements to make judgements on whether to extend loans or lines of credit. Accountants need the information to assess the health of the organisation. And investors and financial analysts also need the information provided within financial statements to determine the attractiveness of a particular organisation when compared with a wide range of other investment opportunities.

Financial statements tell readers the following important information:

- ✔ **Liquidity:** The company's ability to quickly convert assets into cash to pay expenses such as payroll, supplier invoices, creditors and others.

- ✔ **General financial condition:** The long-term balance between debt and equity (the assets left after liabilities are deducted).

- ✔ **Share capital:** The periodic increases and decreases in the company's net worth.

- ✔ **Profitability:** The ability of the company to earn profits, and to earn them consistently over an extended period of time.

- ✔ **Performance:** The company's performance against the financial plans developed by its management team or employees.

There's no such thing as a good figure or a bad figure. If a particular figure isn't what you expect it to be, that's your cue to research *why* the figure is different from what you expect. For example, the fact that profit declined from one period to the next may seem at first glance to be a bad thing. But the decline may be a result of your finance director's decision to sometimes *reapportion profits* (reducing profits and investing them elsewhere in the company, perhaps in equipment or research and development) to minimise the impact of income taxes on the company.

Reviewing financial statements is a great way to get started in the analysis of a company's financial health and its long-term outlook. However, to get the most mileage out of these reports, you need to undertake another, deeper level of analysis. You must apply financial ratios to the figures contained in the balance sheet and profit-and-loss account, and do financial forecasting (for more on this, turn to Chapter 13).

Taking a snapshot: The balance sheet

The *balance sheet* is a snapshot of the financial health of an organisation at a particular point in time. The famous tagline on the heading of any good balance sheet is likely to be something like 'As of 31 December 2013' or 'At 31 December 2013'. The balance sheet reveals the financial picture not for a period of time, but for that exact date only. The company's financial picture could be vastly different on 1 January 2014 (for example, if a large capital payment is due on that date).

A typical balance sheet looks something like Figure 12-1.

XYZ Company
Consolidated Balance Sheet - As of December 31, 2013
(In Millions)

ASSETS

Current Assets

Cash and cash equivalents	£25
Accounts receivable	150
Stocks	50

Total Current Assets	225

Fixed Assets

Equipment	200
Furniture, fixtures, and improvements	150
Allowance for depreciation and write-off	(20)

Total Fixed Assets	330
Total Assets	**£555**

LIABILITIES AND SHARE CAPITAL
LIABILITIES

Current Liabilities

Repayments to bank	10
Accounts payable	50
Wages and salaries	75
Taxes payable	20
Deferred taxes	10
Current portion of long-term debt	5

Total Current Liabilities	170

Long-Term Debt	100
Deferred Rent Expense	50
Deferred Taxes	50

Total Liabilities	**370**

SHARE CAPITAL

Ordinary shares	100
Additional paid-in capital	60
Retained earnings	25

Total Share Capital	**185**
Total Liabilities and Share Capital	**£555**

Figure 12-1:
A balance
sheet.

As you can see, the value of XYZ Company's assets is exactly balanced by its liabilities and share capital. Because of the accounting equation, no other option exists. The balance sheet demonstrates the fact that assets are paid for by a company's liabilities and share capital. Conversely, the assets are used to generate cash to pay off the company's liabilities. Any excess cash after liabilities are paid off is added to share capital as profit.

In the balance sheet, you list assets in order from the most *liquid* (readily convertible to cash) to the least liquid, and you list liabilities and share capital in the order in which they're scheduled to be paid. And don't forget: you can convert current assets into cash within a year; current liabilities are scheduled to be paid within a year.

By reviewing changes in a company's balance sheet over time, managers, bankers, investors and others can pick up on trends that may affect the long-term viability of the firm and that may positively or negatively impact the value of its shares.

Making money: The profit-and-loss account

The reason that businesses exist is to make money, pure and simple. Because making money is such an incredibly important part of the day-to-day focus of any business, companies need a quick and easy way of figuring out how much money the business is making. You do have such a tool, and the tool is called the *profit-and-loss account.* It is also called the P&L statement, or the income statement.

A profit-and-loss account is more than a snapshot of a business's financial position on one particular date, like the balance sheet. The profit-and-loss account tells its readers three key pieces of information:

- ✔ The business's sales volume during the period of the report

- ✔ The business's expenses during the period of the report

- ✔ The difference between the business's sales and its expenses (in other words, its profit or loss) during the period of the report

Figure 12-2 shows what a typical profit-and-loss account looks like. You can see that XYZ Company had £49,000 of net sales revenue (net is sales revenue after sales expenses are deducted) and a cost of goods sold of £10,000, leaving the company with a gross profit of £39,000 (before other expenses and tax liabilities are deducted). However, this gross profit was further reduced by the expenses of selling products and running the company (advertising, printing, rent, salaries, bonuses and so forth) and by income taxes. The result is a net income of $9,000. Divided by 250,000 shares of stock in the hands of investors and the company, this works out to an earning per share of $0.036.

XYZ Company
Profit and Loss Account - Twelve Months Ended December 31, 2012
(In thousands)

REVENUES

Gross sales	50
Less: Returns	(1)
Net Sales	49

COST OF GOODS SOLD

Beginning stocks	50
Purchases	10
Less: Purchase discounts	(2)
Net purchases	8
Cost of goods available for sale	58
Less: Ending stocks	48
Cost of Goods Sold	10

GROSS PROFIT 39

OPERATING EXPENSES

Total selling expenses	5
Total general expenses	10
Total operating expenses	15
Operating income	24

Other income and expenses

Interest expense (income)	5
Total Other Income and Expense	5

Income before taxes	19
Less: Taxes	(10)
Net Income/Profit	9
Average Number of Shares	250,000
Earnings Per Share	£0.036

Figure 12-2:
A profit-and-loss account.

Keeping more money than you spend: The cash flow statement

Have you ever heard the phrase 'Cash is king'? For any business, cash truly is king. It takes cash to pay employees, to purchase supplies and to pay bills. Most employees have their own obligations to meet – buying groceries, paying rent, bankrolling childcare expenses and much more – and they need cash to meet them. Paying employees with other assets such as long-term bonds or plant equipment just doesn't work. And you certainly can't pay employees with profit.

The *cash flow statement* (also called a *statement of cash flow*)is a specialised report that tracks the sources of cash in a company, as well as its *inflows* (money coming into a business) and *outflows* (money going out of a business). The cash flow statement is an extremely valuable tool for ensuring that a company has the cash it needs to meet its obligations when it needs to.

A number of different kinds of cash flow statements exist, each suited to a particular business need. Some are used strictly inside a business, and others are used outside a business (for investors, creditors and other interested parties). Here are a few of the most common types of cash flow statements:

- ✔ **Simple cash flow statement:** Also called a cash budget; it arranges all items into one or two categories, most often cash inflows and cash outflows.

- ✔ **Operating cash flow statement:** Limits analysis of cash flows to those items having to do with the operations of a business, and not its financing.

- ✔ **Financing cash flow statement:** Includes cash raised by issuing new debt or equity capital, as well as the expenses incurred for repaying debt or paying dividends on shares.

- ✔ **General cash flow statement:** Typically, an external statement that depicts the period-to-period changes in balance sheet items and the actual money amount for the period in question for profit-and-loss account items. This statement shows the following categories:

    - • Operating cash inflows

    - • Operating cash outflows

    - • Priority outflows, such as interest expense and current debt payments

    - • Discretionary outflows, such as equipment charges

    - • Financial flows, which are amounts you borrow and have to repay

You can find plenty of different kinds of cash flow statements to meet your every mood, whatever you do or wherever you are. But don't forget the first rule of cash management: happiness is a positive cash flow.

Table 12-4 shows a sample cash flow statement – one that's meant for internal rather than external use. (**Note:** Numbers in parentheses are negative numbers.)

Table 12-4	A Sample Cash Flow Statement		
Cash Flows (Fourth Quarter)	*October*	*November*	*December*
Cash inflow	£5,000,000	£7,500,000	£6,500,000
Cash outflow	£4,500,000	£8,000,000	£7,000,000
Cash surplus (need) this month	£500,000	(£500,000)	(£500,000)
Cash surplus (need) last month	£0	£500,000	(£500.000)
Cumulative cash flow	£500,000	£0	(£500,000)

An open book

In recent years, many organisations have taken a much more open approach in their dealings with employees when it comes to the financial aspects of the business. In part, this situation has been driven by managerial expertise. It has also been reinforced by UK and EU legislation requiring organisations to open up information to employees and to consult them on business decisions, as well as matters of employee relations policy.

Traditionally, the production and analysis of financial statements was a managerial prerogative. Not only did non-management employees have no need to see these statements (as far as most managers were concerned at least), but managers also generally assumed that employees wouldn't understand the statements anyway.

Fans of open-book management believe that all workers should have access to a company's financial statements. They also believe that all workers should be trained in what these statements mean, and in how the work they do impacts both the company and themselves as employees. Here are the characteristics of an open-book organisation:

✔ Every employee sees – and is trained to understand – the company's finances, along with all the other figures that are critical to tracking a company's performance.

✔ Employees discover that, whatever else they do, part of their job is to move those figures in the right direction.

✔ Employees have a direct stake in the company's success.

To make open-book management work, managers must be able to identify the critical figures that make their businesses work, whether those figures are occupancy rates in the hotel business or number of defects in a manufacturing process. Every business has multiple critical figures for the various functions inside the business. These figures directly affect their profits – and they're the figures that employees need to understand and against which employee performance is judged. In a well-executed open-book plan, a portion of every employee's pay is based on reaching agreed-upon targets for these critical figures, and the company pays profit-based bonuses when targets are exceeded. This system is a win-win situation for everyone. Knowledgeable employees like the open-book system because, after they understand it, they actually earn more than under more traditional systems.

If you're in any doubt over the value of open-book approaches to finances in particular, and management in general, learn a lesson from the Japanese manufacturing companies presently operating in the UK. Sharp, Sony, Nissan, Sanyo and others have all made a practice, right from the start, of opening up all information to their employees. Employees are consulted on and are expected to contribute to every aspect of financial performance, business decision making and the establishment of production and service delivery schedules and volumes. These companies have been among the most successful in the UK for over 30 years. Despite downturns in some of their markets, they remain enduringly viable.

Audits: The Key to Accuracy

The accuracy of accounting records and reports is incredibly important, especially to two groups of people:

✔ **The people within the organisation:** They rely on accounting information to make informed business decisions.

✔ **The investors and lenders outside the organisation:** They rely on accounting information to make informed decisions on the use of their funds.

For these reasons, organisations conduct regular audits of their accounting systems to ensure that results are accurate and that the system treats all financial information fairly and honestly.

You have two key kinds of audits:

- ✔ **Internal audits:** These audits are conducted by employees of an organisation as an internal check to ensure the integrity of accounting information and the reports that are generated from this information. Many large companies have entire departments devoted to this task, and they make auditing an annual event.

- ✔ **External audits:** External audits involve examination of a company's accounting system by an unbiased, outside individual or organisation – an accountancy practice or a chartered accountant. External audits are typically conducted on an annual basis, after the end of a company's financial year. Companies use these audits to ensure the integrity of the numbers that go into annual reports and financial statements, and to guard against fraud.

Chapter 13

Investing in the Present and in the Future

*I*nvestment is anything on which you anticipate or seek returns. Investments aren't limited to money – they can include time, energy and resources, as well as personal interest and commitment. Organisations invest in new business ventures, reputation, market share, market dominance and new product development, but regardless of what they're investing in, the goal is the same: to make returns. If organisations don't make returns on their investments, sooner or later they go out of business.

Nothing is certain in investment. You aren't guaranteed to get the returns that you seek or anticipate. If you don't know the purpose, context and risks involved in a particular investment, odds are you will fail.

In this chapter, I fill you in on how investment works. I explain what investment is and when and where it occurs. I walk you through forecasting so that you can assess the likely outcomes of a proposed investment. I explain how to analyse finances using ratios. And I outline what company annual reports tell you, and what to look out for when you read them. (If you need a grounding in the basics of company finances, please read Chapters 11 and 12 before this one.)

What constitutes success or failure in investment is a matter of perception. The questions that matter are: What did you set out to do? What returns did you need, want and anticipate? Did you achieve your purposes and gain the returns that you desired? And were the returns you desired feasible? (If you seek 30 per cent returns on your investment, you have to invest in industries and sectors where this level of return is possible.)

Understanding the Purpose of Investment

The purpose of investment is to gain returns. Returns on investment are normally stated in financial terms, but organisations sometimes make investments to gain non-financial returns as well. Here are some non-financial returns that your organisation may seek:

- **Reputation:** You may invest to enhance your existing reputation, to gain a broader reputation, to change your reputation or to rebuild your reputation after a crisis.

- **Footholds:** You may invest to gain or consolidate a foothold in a new or existing market.

- **Location:** You may invest to establish a presence in new locations and markets, to find new markets for existing products or to find and develop new products for existing markets.

- **Prestige:** You may invest to garner prestige for your organisation – for example, to build the biggest buildings, tallest towers, largest ships or fastest airplanes.

- **Command of resources:** You may invest in a scarce or valuable resource, commodity, expertise or technology, because you need it for your organisation or because you can buy it up and then ration it and sell it at higher prices to others who need it.

The first hedge funds

If anything should cause you to question the certainties of returns on investment, and the assuredness and predictability of financial returns, the story of the first modern hedge fund should do so.

The first hedge fund was called Long-Term Capital Management (LTCM), and it was founded by two economics and finance experts, Robert Merton of Harvard University and Myron Scholes of Stanford University.

Because of the complicated economic and mathematical formulae they used to produce the structure for the fund and because they were able to demonstrate that following these formulae would guarantee returns, Merton and Scholes won the Nobel Prize for Economics in 1997. Their work was described by *The Economist* as: 'some of the most useful work that economics has produced. The work of Merton and Scholes on how to price financial options turned risk management from a guessing game into a science.'

LTCM went bankrupt in ten months. *The Economist* somewhat changed its view: 'Like the *Titanic*, Long-Term Capital Management was supposed to be unsinkable. The hedge fund's dramatic downfall and bailout was the stuff of Hollywood disaster movies: fortunes laid waste, proud men cut down to size, giant tidal waves threatening to drown some of Wall Street's snootiest institutions. At the very least, the financial industry's finest were blinded by the reputation of LTCM and its founders, who last year shared the Nobel Prize for economics for their contributions to the understanding of financial risk.'

The lesson: investment has no certainties. You have to know what you stand to gain or lose.

Doing Your Due Diligence

When you're considering an investment, you have to perform what's known as *due diligence* (basically, detailed scrutiny to make sure that the investment is sound). You also have to understand:

- ✔ The range of returns possible – both positive and negative – in financial as well as non-financial terms
- ✔ The direction and deadlines for the particular investment that you have in mind
- ✔ The risks involved in the investment
- ✔ The level of returns that you can tolerate (the worst set of circumstances under which you're actually going to go ahead) and those you seek (the best-case scenario)
- ✔ The consequences of success
- ✔ The consequences of failure

When you're faced with making investment and financial choices on behalf of your organisation, ask yourself, 'Would I invest my personal money? If so, why? If not, why not?' If you'd be prepared to commit your own resources to a particular investment, that's a good sign – and if you wouldn't, that's a red flag.

Before making an investment, you need to consider:

- ✔ The cost of capital
- ✔ The ways in which you'll calculate returns
- ✔ The effects that this particular proposal will have on your organisation's activities in the future

---

Tuning out the noise

Stockbrokers, shareholders and their representatives, and financial advisers invariably push for organisations to go ahead with investments because of the short-term gains they may make. This situation especially applies to mergers and takeovers. In these cases, stockbrokers gain their immediate rewards as share prices rise (at least in the short term). Shareholders benefit as the value of their investment rises. And financial advisers receive their fees upon completion of the merger or takeover.

The thing is, none of these people has to manage and make effective the newly merged organisation. None of them is concerned with any restructuring or cost-cutting that has to take place. If you cave in to pressure from these people, you may make them happy . . . but the people who depend on the *long-term* success of your organisation (like managers and staff) may be left out in the cold.

The cost of capital

Commercial organisations draw their financial resources from capital shares, loans and retained profits (refer to Chapter 11). When you're considering an investment, you have to decide whether you need to raise additional share capital to cover the investment, take out loans or use retained profits.

Each resource has implications. If you use share capital, you forfeit some control to the shareholders. If you use loan capital, and this capital isn't enough, the costs of getting top-ups or additional loans may rise. If you use retained profits, you can't use them for anything else.

Don't forget to consider costs that you may incur due to inflation or changes (especially increases) in interest rates.

Returns on investment

Before you invest, you need to know the returns that you seek and all the things that could conceivably go wrong along the way. To further inform your decision as to whether to proceed, you can take one of the following approaches.

The net present value approach

The *net present value* of an investment is the value today of the surplus that the company makes over the future period of time that the surplus is made.

The net present value is based on two considerations:

- ✔ You've assessed the lowest acceptable rate of return.

- ✔ The investment has a better-than-even chance of achieving the returns that you require than the next most overtly profitable proposal available.

As long as the information you feed into the proposal is based on real research and venture assessment, and you've taken into account everything that could go wrong, you have a useful indication of likely rates of return.

If you calculate the best, medium and worst outcomes, and determine that the worst outcome is acceptable, you're making an informed decision.

The make/lease/buy decision approach

In the *make/lease/buy decision* approach, you decide whether you'd be wiser to:

- ✔ Make or produce something

- ✔ Lease something

- ✔ Buy something

For example, if it would cost you £50,000 to buy your own IT system or £5,000 to lease such a system for a year, which is better? Your decision needs to be based on the following:

- ✔ **The pure financial calculations:** In this case, you can see that you'll get ten years' leasing for the price of buying and installing your own system.

- ✔ **The amount of control that you want over the system:** If you lease, you have less control than you do if you buy.

- ✔ **The levels of service:** If you buy the system, what levels of service will the suppliers provide, under what conditions and at what cost? If you lease the system, the same questions apply.

- ✔ **Your own personal preference:** You may just prefer one over the other, and that personal preference factors in to your decision.

Ideally, you make decisions rationally, based on research and data. Irrationally, all people make choices based on their own preferences. When making investment decisions, odds are you choose what you want to do and then find reasons that support your choice.

The multiplier approach

The *multiplier* approach (see Figure 13-1) assumes that when you invest in one activity, beneficiaries of that investment spend a certain amount of what they receive. It also assumes that they won't spend it all.

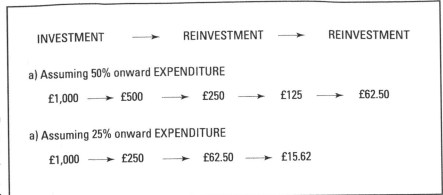

Figure 13-1:
The mul-
tiplier
approach.

The multiplier approach is used especially as the basis for public capital projects to generate employment, prosperity and further commercial areas in regions where unemployment is high.

The multiplier approach is used by all organisations as the basis for generating new activities, products and services. Companies use it to kick-start activities in their own markets, through the introduction of new products and services that, hopefully, attract buyer interest.

As Figure 13-1 shows, you can calculate the likely effect of multiplier activity by factoring in high and low percentages of onward expenditure. You can then arrive at the worst possible outcome. This information helps to inform the decision as to whether an investment is worth proceeding with.

Future effects

Any investment you make affects the future of your company. For this reason, you need to consider:

- ✔ Where investments and ventures are certain and *likely* to lead, and whether this direction fits in with your strategic approach

- ✔ Where investments and ventures *could conceivably* lead, and what other possible opportunities may present themselves in the future

By considering the likely and possible effects for the future, you're giving yourself the best chance of choosing ventures for maximum impact and positive influence for the company. If you only see the venture in isolation or purely in terms of what it costs now, you're limiting the basis of the judgement on which you're making the decision.

REAL WORLD EXAMPLE

Getting left out in the cold in Iceland

In the late 20th century, Iceland set itself up as 'the new financial centre of the world'. Iceland's national banks started offering high rates of return to investors who were prepared to place funds with them. Many organisations and institutions in the UK and elsewhere accordingly placed large sums of money with these banks. They then sat back and waited for the returns to roll in.

It quickly became apparent that these returns were, in fact, not available. The banking industry in Iceland simply wasn't big enough to accommodate the amounts of money that had been deposited and the returns that were being demanded. Accordingly, the banks defaulted.

As you can imagine, this situation turned into a major economic and political scandal. Questions were asked of the Icelandic government concerning its financial viability. In turn, the Icelandic government was forced to admit that it had established Iceland as a financial centre without considering the full implications, and without also having the funds available to sustain this in the long term.

More seriously, questions were asked of all the companies, organisations and public sector institutions that had placed funds in Iceland and its banks without conducting the proper investigations. Most were forced to admit that they hadn't investigated at all – they'd simply taken the returns on offer at face value. The experience of one UK county council sums up the entire position:

'We took the view that the returns on offer were simply too good to be true. Accordingly, we placed £50 million worth of investments in Iceland. This would have represented an excellent return on the council taxes raised for the people who paid them. And because it was a country, underwritten by the government, we never considered that things could go wrong in any way.'

And the lesson? A world of difference exists between the returns that something *could* provide and that something *will* provide. If something sounds too good to be true, it probably is!

You also need to look at the future from the point of view of choosing ventures. Invariably, you're going to be working with limited resources. If you have a choice of three possible ventures, but you only have the resources to carry out one of them, one of the critical factors in your decision is the assessment of the likely and possible future benefits that each can bring.

Focusing on Financial Forecasting

One thing you can always count on in business – nothing stays the same for long. In business today, change is a constant. But you try to anticipate, forecast and predict change before it occurs. Because financial considerations can mean the difference between life and death to a company, financial forecasts and projections are a cornerstone of proactive business management practice.

Ask questions like the following if you want to prepare accurate financial forecasts:

- How many employees do we have on board this year, and do we have the money to pay them when we need to?

- Do we have enough money to invest in new manufacturing equipment that will improve the productivity of our workers while increasing output and lowering rejects?

- How much money do we need in order to have enough stock in time for the holiday season, and will the money be available when we need it?

- By what amount can we expect revenues and profit to grow (or, heaven forbid, shrink) over the next year?

- What's the timing of payments from our major customers, and how will they affect our cash flow?

These questions, and others like them, are constantly on the minds of financial directors, managers and others who are responsible for ensuring that a business can meet all its financial obligations. Exactly for this reason, managers conduct regular financial planning and forecasting exercises.

Two key kinds of financial forecasts and projections exist:

- **Short-term financial forecasts:** If a financial forecast is for a period of one year or less, you can consider it a *short-term* forecast. Many firms use a variety of short-term financial forecasts and informal financial statements to manage day-to-day operations. Every organisation has its own version of these forecasts and statements, and you need to know what your organisation's methods are and keep as up-to-date as you possibly can on the daily financial performance of your company.

  Using cash forecasts just like this, companies can determine when they'll be taking in more money than they pay out to meet their obligations. They can then use this knowledge to guide decisions on when and how much to pay suppliers, the levels of supplies that they can comfortably keep in stock, the timing of investments in capital equipment and much more.

- **Long-term financial forecasts:** If you need to plan for a period that extends more than a year into the future, you need a *long-term* financial forecast. Given how fast the business environment is changing, why would you want to make plans for more than a year into the future? Aren't things sure to change at least five or ten times before then? Of course they will. But part of financial planning is planning for change.

Long-range planning has fallen out of favour in many businesses, especially those that realised that months of hard work often led to elaborate, beautifully bound documents that were promptly filed away and forgotten as soon as they were published. But done right, these plans can provide your business with a definite competitive advantage. How? By giving your business focus and direction.

Long-range plans require long-term financial forecasts to support them. Just as in short-term financial forecasts, you can forecast all kinds of financial data with a reasonable degree of accuracy. Here are a few of the most popular kinds of financial data subject to a long-term look:

- ✔ Assets, liabilities and net worth (balance sheet)
- ✔ Cash
- ✔ Profit-and-loss account
- ✔ Sales or revenues

The old acronym RIRO (rubbish in, rubbish out) definitely applies here. Financial forecasts of any sort are only as good as the data on which they're based. As the horizon for your forecasts extends farther out into the future, the reliability of those forecasts naturally declines and they become less dependable. Many companies in fast-moving industries are happy to forecast a year into the future with any degree of accuracy. Companies in more stable industries, however, can more safely and accurately forecast for periods of up to five years.

Long-term financial forecasts are built in much the same way as short-term forecasts, just with much longer horizons. These longer horizons require careful attention to long-range trends in markets and technology, and they assume the possibility of greater swings than do short-term financial forecasts.

Here are a few tips for putting together accurate long-term financial forecasts:

- ✔ **Look for long-term trends in revenues and expenses.** Are revenues and expenses gradually trending up or down over a period of five years or longer? Chart these trends out as graphs and make an educated guess as to where the trends are going to lead in the future.

- ✔ **Consider the natural business cycles.** Are the natural business cycles regular, and what is their frequency? Many businesses and markets go through regular business cycles. By looking at the big picture, you should be able to pick out the cycles and factor them in to your long-term financial forecasts.

✔ **Think about random events that are most likely to disturb the long-term trends in revenues and expenses.** What would happen if your company buys out a key competitor? How would that affect revenues and expenses? What if a competitor develops a new process that cuts its cost of production in half? Random events are just that – random. By nature, they're hard to predict, but the more you can factor them into your long-term financial forecasts, the more accurate your forecasts will be.

Long-term financial forecasts are an important part of the long-range planning process. Although they can never be as accurate as short-term forecasts, they're often better than nothing.

The whole point of preparing financial forecasts and budgets is to attempt to predict future performance while creating baselines by which you can compare actual results. If results are as predicted, terrific – you're right on track toward your goals. If actual results are significantly less or significantly more than predicted, managers know where to begin looking for sources of these variances.

Analysing Performance

You need to analyse the performance of all your investment decisions so that you know what went well and why, and what went badly and why. By doing this, you and your whole organisation can learn and become better at making effective and successful investment decisions. In particular, you can build on the factors that contributed to your successes and see what went wrong when things didn't work out as you'd planned.

Most companies and their managers analyse failures. However, many companies and their managers don't pay attention when things go well. They figure that they've been successful because they were experts, without ever working out what the expertise actually was. Be sure to evaluate all your successes, so that you can understand what your expertise actually is and where your strengths truly lie. That way, not only do you gain the fullest possible understanding, you also never become complacent!

You can analyse a company's performance in several ways. In this section, I cover three of them: variance analysis, ratio analysis and cost/volume/profit analysis.

Variance analysis

By comparing an organisation's actual results with its budgeted results (for example, its actual revenues versus its budgeted revenues), you get a quick picture of whether a company is on or off track, and by how much.

Ratio analysis

By comparing certain financial results within a company's financial statements (particularly the profit-and-loss account and balance sheet), you can quickly determine whether the company is operating within the normal limits for its industry. For example, dividing a company's current assets by its current liabilities results in a ratio (the *quick ratio*) that tells you whether the company is solvent and can meet its financial obligations to its lenders.

 In this section, I cover certain ratios that are common to all businesses. As you read through these financial ratios, be sure to keep in mind that they can vary considerably for companies in different industries. Manufacturing companies as a group have different ratios than consulting firms or utilities. Be sure that when you compare one company's figures with the figures from another company, you're comparing apples with apples and oranges with oranges.

Liquidity ratios

Liquidity ratios are a group of ratios that measure the *solvency* of a business – its ability to generate the cash necessary to pay its bills and other short-term financial obligations. Here are two liquidity ratios:

- ✔ **Current ratio:** The ability of a business to pay its current liabilities out of its current assets. For example, the 2.5 ratio says that a company has £2.50 in assets for every £1 in liabilities. In general, a ratio of 2 or better is judged to be good, and in fact many banks require that their borrowers maintain a current ratio of 2 or higher as a condition of their loans.

    Here's how the current ratio works (along with an example):

    $$\text{Current Ratio} = \text{Current Assets} \div \text{Current Liabilities}$$
    $$= \text{£250 million} \div \text{£100 million}$$
    $$= 2.5$$

- ✔ **Quick ratio:** A measure of a business's ability to pay its current liabilities out of its current assets. The quick ratio subtracts stock from current assets, providing a rigorous test of a firm's ability to pay its current liabilities quickly. Stock is often difficult to convert to cash because it may be obsolete, or simply not be easily or quickly sold on. A ratio of 1.1 or higher is considered to be acceptable.

    Here's how the quick ratio works (along with an example):

    $$\text{Quick Ratio} = (\text{Current Assets} - \text{Stock}) \div \text{Current Liabilities}$$
    $$= (\text{£250 million} - \text{£20 million}) \div \text{£100 million}$$
    $$= 2.3$$

Activity ratios

Activity ratios are an indication of how efficient your company is at using its resources to generate income. The faster and more efficiently your firm can generate cash, the stronger it is financially and the more attractive it is to investors and lenders.

Here are a few activity ratios:

- ✔ **Receivables turnover ratio:** Tells you the average amount of time that your company takes to convert its *receivables* (payments made by cheque, credit card, or transfer) into cash. The ratio is a function of how quickly your company's customers and clients pay their bills and points out problems that your company may be having in the collections process. The higher the ratio, the better.

  Here's how the receivables turnover ratio works (along with an example):

$$\text{Receivables Turnover Ratio} = \text{Net Sales} \div \text{Accounts Receivable}$$

$$= \text{\$100 million} \div \text{\$15 million}$$

$$= 6.67$$

  You can get another interesting piece of information by using your receivables turnover ratio. By dividing 365 days by the receivables turnover ratio, you find out the average number of days that your company takes to turn over its accounts receivable. This result is also known as the *average collection period*. In this case, the lower the number, the better, because it indicates that customers are paying their bills quickly. Here's how it works:

$$\text{Average Collection Period} = 365 \text{ days} \div \text{Receivables Turnover Ratio}$$

$$= 365 \text{ days} \div 6.67$$

$$= 54.7 \text{ days}$$

- ✔ **Stock turnover ratio:** Provides an idea of how quickly stock is turned over (sold off and replaced with new stock) during a specific period of time. This information represents the ability of your firm to convert its stock into cash. The higher the number, the more often stock is turned over – a good thing.

  Here's how the stock turnover ratio works (along with an example):

$$\text{Stock Turnover} = \text{Cost of Sales/Average Stock Held}$$

So, for example:

	Year 1 £ 000	Year 2 £ 000
Cost of sales	10,000	12,000
Average stock	1,000	600
Stock turnover	10 times	20 times

In the second year the stock is turning over much more quickly, and this either means that you are holding less in the first place (and so tying up less capital in stock), or that you are moving things much more quickly than in the past. However, the cost of sales has also gone up. So it is complex! And from this data you would need to ascertain whether or not you were improving the overall efficiency of your operations.

Debt ratios

For most organisations, going into debt is a normal part of doing business. Debt can plug the holes when cash flows can't cover all necessary operating expenses for short periods of time. Debt also allows companies that are growing quickly to finance their expansion. However, too much debt becomes a financial burden on any organisation. *Debt ratios* are a measure of how much debt a company is carrying and who's financing the debt.

Here are some debt ratios:

✔ **Debt-to-equity ratio:** Measures the extent to which a company is financed by outside creditors versus shareholders and owners. A high ratio (anything over 1) is considered bad because it indicates that a company may have difficulty paying back its creditors.

Here's how the debt-to-equity ratio works (along with an example):

$$\text{Debt-to-Equity Ratio} = \text{Total Liabilities} \div \text{Share Capital}$$

$$= \pounds100 \text{ million} \div \pounds150 \text{ million}$$

$$= 0.66$$

✔ **Debt-to-assets ratio:** A measure of how much outside creditors finance a company's assets versus the percentage that's covered by the owners. Ratios of up to 0.5 are considered acceptable; anything more may be a sign of trouble. (Note, however, that most manufacturing firms have debt-to-asset ratios between 0.30 and 0.70.)

Here's how the debt-to-assets ratio works (along with an example):

$$\text{Debt-to-Assets Ratio} = \text{Long-Term Liabilities} \div \text{Total Assets}$$

$$= \pounds50 \text{ million} \div \pounds500 \text{ million}$$

$$= 0.1$$

Profitability ratios

Profitability ratios indicate the effectiveness of management in controlling expenses and earning a reasonable return for shareholders and owners.

Here are some profitability ratios:

- **Profit ratio:** A measure of how much profit your company generates for each pound of revenue after you've accounted for all costs of normal operations. The inverse of this percentage (100 per cent profit ratio) equals the expense ratio or the portion of each sales pound that's accounted for by expenses from normal operations. The higher the ratio, the better.

  However, the expected ratio can vary considerably from industry to industry. For example, although grocery shops – which make money by turning over high volumes of stock quickly – are generally satisfied with profit ratios of just around two per cent, many software developers have profit ratios of 30 per cent to 40 per cent or more.

  Here's how to calculate a company's profit ratio (along with an example):

  $$\text{Profit Ratio} = \text{Net Income} \div \text{Net Sales}$$

  $$= \pounds 50 \text{ million} \div \pounds 100 \text{ million}$$

  $$= 0.5$$

- **Gross margin ratio:** An indication of the profitability of a firm. To determine gross margin, you use your *gross profit*, which is what's left over after you subtract *cost of goods sold* (the direct costs of making a product) from revenues. Gross profit tells you how much you have left to pay overheads and make a net profit. In this example, the company's cost of goods sold is £25 million, which leaves £75 million (which is extraordinarily high) to pay overheads.

  Here's the way to calculate the gross margin ratio (along with an example):

  $$\text{Gross Margin Ratio} = \text{Gross Profit} \div \text{Sales Revenues}$$

  $$= \pounds 75 \text{ million} \div \pounds 100 \text{ million}$$

  $$= 0.75$$

- **Return on investment (ROI) ratio:** One of the keys concepts in the world of financial tools, ROI measures the ability of a company to create profits for its owners. It gives a percentage that represents the amount of pounds of net income earned per pound of invested capital. As such, ROI is of great interest to investors, shareholders and others with a financial stake in the company. Quite simply, people investing in your company want to know how much money they're making, whether this amount is satisfactory, and why.

Here's the way to calculate the ROI ratio (along with an example):

$$\text{Return on Investment Ratio} = \text{Net Income} \div \text{Share Capital}$$

$$= £50 \text{ million} \div £150 \text{ million}$$

$$= 0.33$$

✔ **Return on assets (ROA) ratio:** Measures earnings before interest and tax that a company earns from the total capital employed. In this sense, ROA indicates the effectiveness of a company's utilisation of capital. A low ROA ratio should cause managers to investigate whether a company is using its assets as effectively as possible, and a high ROA ratio may mean that activities are fully effective, or it may mean that the company could use assets to work harder elsewhere.

Here's the way to calculate the ROA ratio (along with an example):

$$\text{Return on Assets Ratio} = \text{Earnings before Interest and Tax} \div \text{Net Operating Assets}$$

$$= £75 \text{ million} \div £300 \text{ million}$$

$$= 0.25$$

Cost/volume/profit analysis

By determining what products are the most and the least profitable for a company, you can make decisions about where to invest your company's time and resources. These are the key approaches to cost/volume/profit analysis:

✔ **Break-even analysis:** Allows you to determine at what sales volume your profitability will break even with the cost to produce it. Using electronic spreadsheets, you can run all sorts of what-if scenarios with a variety of different cost and price assumptions. In its simplest form, the break-even point is arrived at when:

$$\text{Sales Revenues} = \text{Fixed Costs} + \text{Variable Costs}$$

The complexities arise as the result of deciding which costs are directly related to sales and which are not.

✔ **Contribution/margin analysis:** Compares the profitability of each of a company's products or services, as well as its relative contribution to the company's bottom line. This analysis quickly points out underperforming products and services that your company should restructure or terminate.

If your company is underperforming, you can redirect resources to boost performance, or you can change plans to bring expectations in line with reality. If the company is performing better than planned, you can identify the reasons why, and do more of the same. At the same time, you can modify budgets upward to accommodate the improved performance.

Reading an Annual Report

Without a doubt, annual reports are at the pinnacle of corporate communication. With their glowing, future-looking words, their evocative photographs and their lovely, full-colour graphs, they can make for compelling reading. The point of the annual report is to provide a summary of exactly how a company has performed in the preceding year and to provide a glimpse of the future. Building a compelling annual report is both an art and a science, and more than a few consulting firms are doing well by hiring themselves out to create reports for all kinds of companies.

For many corporations both small and large – especially banks – the annual report doubles as a promotional and public relations tool. While the financial reports and discussions are clearly the main reason for the document, management also see it as the key communications tool representing their organisation. While huge amounts of money have in past years been set aside for annual report production (usually a printed piece), the trend more recently has been to put most of the information online and print fewer hard copies, in the interest of the environment and, of course, costs.

Annual reports are generally written for shareholders and other investors, but they're also required reading for lenders, banks, potential employees and MBA students working their way through gruelling accounting and finance classes. For the most part, publicly held, not privately held, companies produce annual reports. Almost certainly, you won't see a private company's annual financial statement unless you're an owner. For most of the public, the annual report contains the only financial documents they have ready access to; therefore, the annual report is the best source of information for most people to determine the financial health of a company and to find out about any potential problems or opportunities.

Reading an annual report can be a daunting prospect if you don't know exactly what you're looking for and where to find it. The good news, however, is that most reports are now standardised around a common model of nine key parts, making it easy to review any company's annual report when you get the hang of it.

The final format of the annual report depends on the needs of a company, its industry and any legal disclosure requirements. Regardless, an annual report contains a selection of the following nine parts:

- **Statement from the chairman:** This section is the traditional place for a company's top management team to tell you what a great job it did during the preceding year and to lay out the company's goals and strategies for the future. This statement is also a great place to find apologies for problems that occurred during the year, which may or may not have been solved.

- **Sales and marketing:** This section contains complete information about a company's products and services, as well as descriptions of its major divisions and groups and what they do. By reading this section, you should be able to work out which products are most important to a company and which divisions or groups are most critical to a company's success.

- **Ten-year summary of financial results:** Assuming that a company is at least ten years old, many annual reports contain a presentation of financial results over that period of time. This is a terrific place to look for trends in growth (or non-growth) of revenue and profit and other leading indicators of a company's financial success.

- **Management discussion and analysis:** This section is the place where a company's management has the opportunity to present a candid discussion of significant financial trends within the company over the past couple of years.

- **Signed by the auditors:** To be considered reliable, true and fair, company auditors have to sign off a company's financial statements. Look especially at any caveats or qualifications that the auditors have added to their statement.

- **Financial statements:** These statements are the bread and butter of the annual report. This is where a company presents its financial performance data for all to see. At the very least, expect to see a profit-and-loss account, a balance sheet and a cash-flow statement. Be sure to watch for footnotes to the financial statements and read them carefully.

In the financial statements, you can often find valuable information about an organisation's structure and financial status that hasn't been publicised elsewhere in the report. For example, you may notice information on a management reorganisation or details on a bad debt that the company wrote off. Also look at the 'notes to the accounts', which tell you how the company calculated the accounts and which elements it placed where.

✔ **Subsidiaries, brands and addresses:** Here you find listings of company locations – domestic and foreign – and contact information, as well as brand names and product lines.

✔ **List of directors and officers:** Public companies are required to list the names of their directors and officers, and the nature and level of remuneration (including share options) that they've received.

✔ **Share price history:** This section gives a brief overview of recent share prices, dividends paid, shares and rights issues, and other matters to do with share management. It also states the names of the stock exchanges on which the company's shares are listed.

Annual reports are the best tool that the public has for reviewing the performance of companies. And most annual reports contain lots of useful information that you can analyse to get a sense of the near- and long-term health of the firm. The more often you read annual reports, the better you get at it.

So now that you've got this wealth of information, what should you do with it? Here are a few definite musts when it comes to reading an annual report:

✔ **Review the company's financial statements and look for trends in profitability, growth, stability and dividends.** Refer to the 'Ratio analysis' section, earlier in this chapter, for information on checking the most common financial ratios.

✔ **Read the report thoroughly to pick out hints that the company is poised for explosive growth – or on the brink of disaster.** Places to look closely for such hints include the statement from the chairman and the sales and marketing section of the annual report. Of course, it also pays to keep an eye on the company through the business press or analyst reports.

✔ **Carefully read any footnotes to the financial statements.** These footnotes often contain information about company assumptions that can be critical to a full understanding of the financial statements.

To the unwary, annual reports are concocted of marketing glitz, feel-good platitudes and financial data presented to the best possible advantage. In order to make use of an annual report, you have to move past all the hype and get to the meat of what's actually being said. As you read the report, stay on the lookout for the following warning signs:

✔ **Turnover stagnant or falling:** There may be a variety of reasons for this situation – changes in customer and client behaviour, entry of new competitors into the market and so forth. What you really want to know is what the company is going to do to address these problems. Look for precise proposals. If the company has none, the chances are that it still doesn't see the problem.

✔ **Blaming external conditions:** All companies have to operate within the opportunities and constraints of their environment. External trading conditions become difficult in all sectors from time to time. So companies drawing your attention to these conditions isn't an issue, but a serious problem exists when companies have no direct and precise proposals to tackle the difficult trading conditions head on. Companies that put the blame for poor performance on the external environment normally continue their decline.

✔ **Large bonus payments to directors and top managers in times of difficulty:** These kind of payments are an almost sure-fire indicator that the company is in difficulty and that directors and top managers are insulating themselves against future losses. Anyone who has an interest in the future of the company should question the reasons for these bonus payments as closely as possible.

✔ **Employee relations' difficulties:** In the UK, the level of strikes and collective disputes is at an all-time low. With few exceptions, becoming engaged in lengthy and protracted disputes takes great ineptitude on the part of management, employees and their representatives. So examine closely the reasons for these disputes where they do occur, and pay attention to the effectiveness of any action that management is taking in order to resolve the matter.

✔ **Declining profit margins:** Good reasons may exist for declining profit margins – rising energy costs especially are a matter of present and enduring concern. It may be that the industry has had to restructure simply in order to retain existing levels of customers and clients. Examine the figures as closely as you can to see whether any of these factors are, indeed, the case, or whether other expenses are rising.

✔ **The precision of future plans:** The more precisely the chairman and other top managers have laid out plans for the future, the greater the confidence you can have in the company (on the face of it). The greater the clarity, the greater the capability to see in the future whether the company will be able to fulfil its plans. If, on the other hand, the company is simply making bland statements about its future prospects, be sure to question closely what it actually intends to do.

✔ **Lack of relationship between the chairman's statement, other statements and the figures:** Overwhelmingly, this situation arises when the chairman makes generally positive statements about the future while the figures show all sorts of crises and difficulties. There may be a case for commercial confidentiality – the chairman and top management may know exactly what to do but need to keep their plans a secret. If you have any doubt, concentrate on the lessons that the figures are delivering, instead of the written words.

Chapter 14

Using Numbers in Business

*N*umbers are a key part of any business. You're bombarded with data, and part of your job is to make sense of all that data and use it for the benefit of your organisation. In this chapter, I walk you through finding and using data, making sense of statistics, using business analytics to your advantage and calculating risk.

Delving into Data

Data is produced by every business activity and it allows you to quantify everything you do. For example, with data at your fingertips, you know:

- How many products you've produced, how long it took to produce them and the costs of production

- How many products you sold, how long it took to sell them and the income generated

- The number of applicants you get for particular jobs and the best media for recruiting potential staff

- Where customer complaints are coming from, how often and what the complaints are about

- When your IT system crashes, why it crashes and what effect those crashes have on your business

No matter which part of the business you're involved in, be sure to gather as much data as you can. Data helps to inform you about what's actually going on. It shows where you're making progress and where holdups are occurring.

Data also forms the basis for assessing, addressing and managing perceptions. If your department has 'received wisdom' about things that work and things that don't, gather as much data as you can on the issue. Test what you've discovered against what people believe to be true. If the preconceptions match the facts supported by the data, that's all well and good. If not, then you have to begin to manage people's perceptions and get them in line with what's actually going on.

Finding the data you need

Data and information come in the following forms:

- **Primary data:** Data you obtain yourself through observation, surveys, interviews and samples.

- **Secondary data:** Data from other sources, including official statistics and information provided by trade unions, professional bodies and employers' federations.

- **Government data:** Data from the government, providing overall national, regional and local pictures and information on a variety of issues.

Use primary data as much as you possibly can. Of course, gathering your own data takes time, so you may need to rely on secondary or government data. You always have to balance your ability to gather and use data with the time you have available.

You can find secondary data everywhere – but what matters is who gathered the data, and why. If you're using data gathered by someone else, make sure that you know why that person gathered it in the first place. Almost certainly, you'll be using it for a different purpose, so keep this difference in mind when using data to support your point of view.

If you need data quickly, consult the following:

- Information available through annual reports from competitors

- Information available through your own contacts

- Market research organisations

  ✔ Product and service performance data

  ✔ Trade federations, employers' associations and professional bodies

None of these sources is perfect or totally reliable, but you have to start somewhere. Then, after you've made a start, other sources of data should become apparent. If you don't have time to gather more data, make it clear in your reporting of the data that you were limited by time in producing your point of view.

Making use of the data

How you use data is up to you. You can use it to:

  ✔ Underline arguments and produce a basis for your proposals

  ✔ Indicate the next courses of action

  ✔ Support several different proposals so that people can make up their own minds

  ✔ Develop new products and services

  ✔ Evaluate where the organisation's problems and issues are occurring in terms of customer complaints, discipline, grievances and disputes among the staff, finance and administration

Whatever you use the data for, people won't listen if you just reel off a list of numbers in support of your point of view. You have to structure your presentation of data so as to show what you mean. You can then hand out the actual figures for people to read in detail later on. Figure 14-1 shows a variety of ways you might present data. Each of these methods is better than simply reeling off numbers or describing in detail the data you've gathered.

Never present vast arrays of numbers on a PowerPoint slide. People can't – and won't – read them from the audience. Instead, present the headlines pictorially. Then people can refer to the numbers later, in the detail that they need.

People tend to use data to advance their own points of view. For example, someone may have made up her mind to do something, so she produces a narrow data stream that supports her point of view.

(a) Tabulation

Year	Year	Profit £
0000	3430	114
0001	3560	119
0002	4740	240
0003	5862	650
0004	4711	350

(b) Bar chart

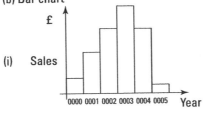

(i)   Sales

£

0000 0001 0002 0003 0004 0005   Year

(ii) Costs

£   Total

Other

Management

Marketing

Administration

Travel

(c) Line graph

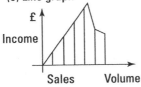

£

Income

Sales   Volume

(d) Scatter graph

Figure 14-1:
Data pre-
sentation
methods.

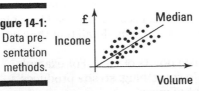

£
Income

Median

Volume

(e) Pie chart

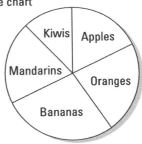

Kiwis   Apples

Mandarins

Oranges

Bananas

(f) Pictograms
Car sales

0000	0001	0002
⬤	⬤	⚬
40	100	25

Unemployment

0000	0001	0002
1%	2%	1.5%

£

Upper limit
A

Lower limit
B

Volume

The pasty tax

In 2011, the UK government decided to introduce 20 per cent VAT on take-away hot food. This VAT quickly became known as the 'pasty tax'. The government produced an impressive range of data that proved that this tax would raise £20 billion per annum. It would bring the take-away part of the restaurant and cooked food trade into line with the 'eat-in' sector, on which VAT was already charged.

Back came the critics with their own statistics. In particular, they pointed out that the government figures were predicated on the fact that there would be no loss of business if prices went up by 20 per cent. This was economically implausible at best! They also wanted to know what would happen to independent catering and take-away operations already operating on tight margins if a decline in business occurred alongside a 20 per cent price hike.

The government promised to consult more widely. In came more figures. One issue raised was how hot something had to be in order to be classified as 'hot'. Should they include warm croissants and cakes? Or pies and pasties (from where the tax got its name)? A set of data produced by the catering trade showed that in fact only 20 per cent of take-away food was indeed 'hot'. What about food that you could choose to have hot or cold (for example, certain sandwiches that the retail outlet would heat up for you if you chose)?

Faced with criticism of the proposals, the numbers produced as part of the counter-offensive by the catering trade and the ridicule brought on by adverse media coverage, the government dropped the idea in May 2012.

If you choose to go down a particular route and use data to support your proposal, make sure that the figures stand up to the most rigorous questioning and debate. In this case, the proposal was only valid or substantial in one set of circumstances.

If, as the result of using numbers, you get into the kind of debate illustrated here, you lay yourself open to ridicule. If you're going to do something based on flimsy data, back your own judgement and drive it through anyway or abandon the idea and think of something else.

Recognising what numbers tell you, and what they don't

Data has lots of uses, but it can't tell you everything. You often hear people in the business world say things like, 'The numbers speak for themselves.' But the fact is, numbers are just that – numbers. What you do with the numbers, and how you change (or don't change) your course of action in response to the numbers, is key – and the numbers don't do that work for you.

Numbers provide you with information on:

- ✔ Staff numbers by age, category and salary
- ✔ Staff numbers in terms of absenteeism and turnover

- Production, output and service delivery
- How many faults you have per product or service
- How many complaints you've received (which you can then break down into subcategories such as number of complaints per product, per member of staff or per outlet)
- How many customers you have (which you can then break down into number of customers per product, service, outlet or location)
- Spend per customer
- Costs and charges relating to every aspect of the business, enabling you to see where you can save
- Energy, premises and transport, and distribution costs and charges
- Costs and returns on marketing and advertising campaigns and activities

Numbers provide you with support and evidence. For this reason, they're a major contribution to the justification for decision making, such as in the following areas:

- Market, product and service development and expansion
- Withdrawal from markets, locations and particular product and service provision activities
- Organisational expansion and contraction
- Projections of returns on investment required when deciding which ventures to back and which not to back
- Increasing or decreasing staff numbers (which can be shown by age, occupation, location and activity)

Numbers provide you with the evidence that you need to decide whether to remedy or improve things – or not. For example:

- If you have staffing problems, you can use figures to support your understanding of where those problems lie and whether they're general or confined to specific occupations or locations.
- If you have customer complaints, you can use the numbers to support and inform your assessment of what the issues are, so that you can address your remedies in the correct place.
- If you have product quality issues, you can use the numbers to assess the volumes of those issues.
- If you have holdups in business processes (for example, the speed at which you process invoices), you can assess how many are being held up and for how long.

Numbers don't tell you what to do, why or how. The numbers only provide evidence and support for particular courses of action. On their own, numbers can't tell you what's going to happen in the future. (You can use forecasting and extrapolation techniques to try to make predictions, but predictions aren't certainties.)

You do have to use current and historic numbers (data you already have) as the basis for decisions that you haven't yet made or are about to make – this data is the only data you have. Just keep in mind the following:

- You can evaluate past and current data and evidence only to give an idea of what *may* happen in the future. Predicting what *will* happen is impossible.

- Past and current data and evidence needs to be fully up to date if you're to stand any chance of using it to try to predict future performance.

- You need expertise in data and statistical science if your projections and forecasts are to be of any value at all. Guessing at the future is no use – and guessing at the future based on incomplete data that hasn't been fully and accurately analysed by experts is especially risky.

Sidling Up to Statistics

Statistics is a branch of mathematics – the study of the collection, organisation, analysis, evaluation, interpretation and presentation of data in ways that are meaningful to those who use it. In addition to being a branch of mathematics, statistics are also business, management, professional and personal resources that inform people's views and opinions on every aspect of work and life. For example:

- All professional sports players have their own statistics (stats, for short) that indicate how many metres they cover in games, their ratios of goals per chances created, their assists, their tackles and so on.

- All movie stars have their own statistics in terms of the earnings that their films make.

- Statistics exist relating to the average length of time that it takes to drive five miles in the London rush hour, to take the kids on the school run, to make deliveries in different parts of the country and so on.

You can't escape statistics – they pervade and inform every part of people's lives! This section helps you get to grips with statistics in the business arena.

Knowing the statistics that are relevant to your business

The relationship between data and statistics is summed up better than most by the University of Michigan, as follows:

> 'What is the difference between Data and Statistics? In regular conversation, both words are often used interchangeably. There is an important distinction though: data is the raw information from which statistics are created. Put in the reverse, statistics provide an interpretation and summary of data.'

You need to be able to sort out the data and those statistics that are relevant to your business from the rest. Accessing and understanding all the statistics available in your company and its sector of operations is key. Here are some of the statistics you need to review:

- Production and sales figures for your own organisation, and for the sector as a whole
- Operational data relating to staff and technology performance
- Data relating to risks
- Data from which statistical probabilities can be assessed and calculated
- Market data, often produced by professional and trade bodies, relating to everything that's going on in the whole sector
- Data relating to production faults and errors
- Data relating to staff absence and turnover

In all cases, data is likely to be incomplete, even if it is very comprehensive. So you have to translate the data that you have into the statistics that you need. You do this translation by totalling up all of the data that you have on a given issue. Then you break it down in the ways that you need at the given time. You can use whatever you come up with to help, advise and support your judgement as to what's now to happen.

This task is trickier than it may appear. For example, if your organisation is going through a difficult time, that may not be reflected in sectoral statistics, or vice versa. The fact that you're having difficulty attracting staff may be a local rather than a sectoral issue, so you may have to gather data and statistics reflecting the overall local labour market and not just your own sector. Finally, if you're struggling to remedy product faults, that may not affect your standing in the market – you may be able to hold on to your present standing in spite of the faults of your products.

Think of the product faults and glitches that have accompanied many of Apple's products at their introduction. The iPod, iPhone, and iPad all had early glitches and teething troubles when first introduced. Did this affect the products' popularity or the reputation of Apple? Not at all! So make sure that you have statistics for the *real* problems – and if you find that you're working on your perceptions of what needs remedying, get data and statistics on these perceptions as well – get data on why people think like this, and what the sources are. It all helps to give the best possible picture.

Be sure to gather statistics on everything that's of conceivable value to your business. As you gather them, think about where and how you'll store them as well as how they may be retrieved, in what form, by whom and for what purpose. After you gather them, you then assemble them into whatever form you require. You can also make them accessible to everyone, or restrict access to those who need it.

So that you have the best possible data and statistical resources, ask every part of your company for information on each area that you have chosen. Ensure that all the IT systems and management information systems generate and produce data that you can use for all your stated purposes when required.

 Be sure that you have access to local and sectoral statistics for your own purposes. These statistics are likely to be available from your own trade associations and professional bodies. They're also likely to be available from chambers of trade and commerce in particular localities.

Assembling all these statistics sounds complex and expensive – and in truth, you can spend a lot of time and trouble on this. However, the outcome is that you have statistics drawn from each area of the business, available to support every decision you make. Additionally, when you're asked questions about specific activities or issues, not only can you respond expertly, but you also have statistics available to support your assertions.

Using statistics to your business's advantage

If you're going to use statistics to your business's best advantage, you need to know the areas in which you require full statistical support for your decisions. These areas vary between companies and organisations. However, most organisations need the following statistics:

- ✔ **Production and service output rates (per hour/day/week, per batch and per location):** Detailed statistics in these areas identify the frequency and nature of blockages and faults, as well as the maximum and minimum rates at which you can deliver products and services.

- ✔ **Sales statistics (per location and outlet, per customer or client, and per week/month/year):** You can also use sales statistics to identify correlations between purchase habits (for example, those who bought product X also bought product Y) and then use this information to inform promotions and sales campaigns.

- ✔ **Staff statistics (absence and turnover rates, by location or occupation):** Use these statistics to inform you of problems with specific occupations and professions. You can also establish whether particular locations or managers have problems. If your highest staff turnover comes from a single department, you can investigate to see what exactly the problems are.

- ✔ **Cost variations:** These statistics show you where, when and by how much your different costs are changing. You need to look at all variations – changes downward to see why things are becoming more cost effective, and especially changes upward because this means that your costs are increasing. You need to know the percentages by which costs are rising, so that you can find out why.

Statistics are used to underpin your business decisions. If you don't have the information on hand, you may come to the same conclusions, but you won't have anything to back up the moves you make.

Defining Business Analytics

If you study business, you're certain to come across *business analytics*, the practice of using all sources of data to inform corporate strategy, planning and decision making. Planning requires an understanding of every aspect of the business, what the business is capable of and how the business is performing today.

Analytics makes key references to the following areas of business practice:

- ✔ Relating expectations to outcomes based on historic analyses of similar events or circumstances.

- ✔ Relating statistical analyses of past events, so as to try and predict what might happen in the future in similar sets of circustances.

- ✔ Relating managerial expectations (in relation to particular courses of action) to the results produced by numerical analyses of data and statistics (in relation to the same courses of action), so that the likelihood of what managers expect to happen can be assessed as realistically as possible.

Analytics also contributes to developing the best possible basis for performance assessment. All businesses must be able to measure and manage their own performance. So business analytics identifies and considers factors and issues that relate especially to the following:

- Relating strategy to performance
- Relating objectives to outcomes
- Providing databases for monitoring, review and evaluation
- Informing the choices that are available, as a precursor to deciding what is to happen now and next

The overall purpose is to ensure that every aspect of situational analysis, decision making and performance assessment is supported as fully as possible by the best possible data and statistical evaluations:

- **Informing decision making:** The business analytics approach evaluates and provides data for every activity in the organisation. The line of reasoning is that when the point comes to make strategic and operational decisions, your decisions are informed by all the data that's available, rather than the bits and pieces that you choose, or the *headline data* (a summary of what people thought was at the back of the particular proposal).

  If you commit to business analytics, you can produce this data quickly and easily through the use of computer and IT systems. If your databases are secure and their management is effective, you can call up the data as and when you need it. It's all there – you just need to bring it out.

- **Assessing and evaluating situations:** Business analytics provides a solid and numerical basis for assessing and evaluating proposals, ventures, markets and locations. You have the full range of information at your disposal. So if an idea appears attractive, you can gather data about all aspects of the proposition – market data, costings, forecasts of market performance and management costs. As a result, you have a full set of data that informs you of:

  - The attractiveness of the thing being evaluated
  - The completeness of your evaluation to date
  - Where the gaps lie
  - Where further work is needed (if any)

Having data and statistics on which to support and base your decisions is vitally important. However, using analytical and mathematical-based approaches to decision making is often antagonistic to those in senior positions. In many cases, top and senior managers like quick decisions. If you tell them that arriving at the right decision takes time, you may develop a bad reputation – you become known as a stickler, not an adventurer; someone who doesn't have the right spirit or backbone!

Honest John

John Hargreaves worked for the Prudential Insurance company. He started out as a tax administrator, and rose to become the organisation's director of taxation affairs. After he had been in the post for three years, he started to notice tax irregularities and the misrepresentation of data. Thinking nothing of this, except that an error had been made, he raised this issue with the chief executive, who agreed that an error had been made and assured John that he would put it right next year.

Next year, the same thing happened. John Hargreaves raised the matter again. This time, he was summoned to the chief executive's office and summarily dismissed. John Hargreaves sued Prudential, winning over £300,000 in compensation.

He had found data irregularities and deliberate misrepresentation of profits, surpluses and tax liabilities. By taking time to do the job properly, he had produced results that the company didn't like and didn't particularly want. Nevertheless, the data proved him right. And the fact that he was correct was what led to the particularly high level of settlement that he was awarded.

Calculating Risk

You use numbers to calculate risk in many situations. Putting numerical values onto risk means that you lay out in front of you the probability of something occurring and the consequences if it does occur. You then use this information to decide whether to accept the risk and mitigate its effects should the need occur, or avoid the risk by doing something else.

Accepting and mitigating risk

If you're calculating risk, you ask the key question: 'What is the risk?' You factor in the following:

- The likelihood of failure
- The consequences of failure
- Any long-term lasting future effects of the failure

So you begin to break down the data that you have. For example, if you're calculating the risk of an airliner engine failure, you question:

✔ How far the particular engine has flown so far

✔ How far all engines like this one have to fly before they become unreliable

✔ How far along the maintenance schedules you are, as recommended by the manufacturers

✔ Whether any variance exists between the schedules recommended by the manufacturers and the maintenance schedules operated by the airlines

✔ The maintenance content and activities that are carried out in particular cases by individual airlines

✔ The maintenance content and activities that are carried out by the best performing airlines, and the worst performing airlines

Having assessed and evaluated all the information you have, you plot the risk as shown in Figure 14-2. You use your judgement, informed by the data you have, to determine in which part of the graph each element should go. You then have an overview of the risks that you have to accept, mitigate or avoid.

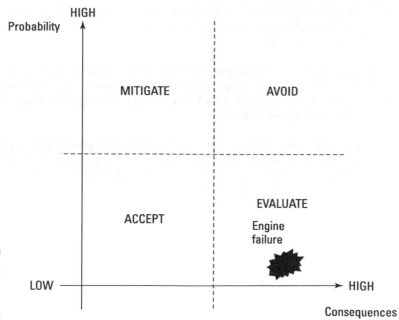

Figure 14-2: Calculating risk.

After you've plotted the risks, you have a basis for their consideration. Your risk will fall into one of the following four areas:

- **Low probability/low consequences:** Accept the risk and mitigate its effects.

- **Low probability/high consequences:** Evaluate each risk on an individual basis.

- **High probability/low consequences:** Take steps to mitigate the risk, and do your best to develop operational procedures to reduce the level of risk. You may also need to manage people's expectations: that things may go wrong from time to time, and that when they do, there is a pre-stated and known set of responses that quickly engage.

- **High probability/high consequences:** Avoid these situations if you possibly can.

Don't go there: Avoiding risk

Avoiding risk means you're choosing not to take certain courses of action because they're not worth it. If you calculate and plot risk (refer to Figure 14-2), the area of high probability/high consequences indicates the activities and locations to avoid.

Some people and some organisations go ahead anyway, even if the probability of an event happening is high and the consequences if it happens are severe as well. If you do go ahead and things go wrong, don't lose sight of the consequences of your actions.

If what you're being told to do comes out in the low probability/high consequences or high probability/high consequences areas of the graph, and if you're under pressure to go ahead, make sure that you have a contingency plan for the failures that are likely to arise.

Part V
The Awkward Bit: The People!

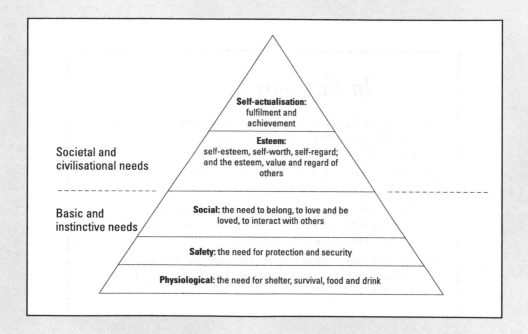

In this part . . .

- ✔ Recognise the differences between organisational, collective and individual behaviour and get the best out of the people in your business.

- ✔ Take a closer look at human resource management and learn how to attract, retain and motivate good staff.

- ✔ Get up to date on employee relations and regulating people's behavior in the work place in order to implement positive patterns of behaviour and performance.

- ✔ Optimise your problem-solving skills and your maintenance of discipline to promote people's productivity within your business.

Chapter 15

Knowing People

. . . .

In This Chapter

▶ Understanding how people behave and communicate

▶ Identifying an organisation's culture and values

▶ Looking at leadership

▶ Examining motivation and work ethics

▶ Working together as a team

▶ Managing across borders and frontiers

. . . .

All organisations are about people in one way or another, so you have to make an effort to understand how people work. Understanding people can be awkward and uncertain – everyone has unique ambitions, aspirations, hopes and fears, and reacts in different ways at different times. You may be able to quantify exactly what to expect from your product or service, but you can never be sure of anything where people are concerned, because people change, and sometimes for reasons that seem irrational. You can't just produce your product or offer your service – you have to understand human behaviour, and everything that goes along with it, in order to be a success.

In this chapter, I look at the key aspects of human behaviour as they apply to business. I fill you in on how people behave, cover the importance of communication, consider your organisation's cultures and values, and evaluate the critical areas of leadership, motivation, work ethics and teams. Finally, I let you know the main factors to consider in organisations that operate across borders and cultures.

Oh, Behave! (How People Behave)

By the time you've reached adulthood, you've likely experienced every conceivable pattern of behaviour in the people around you. Depending on how people have behaved toward you, you've come away:

▸ Happy and uplifted (if someone has been kind and polite)

▸ Angry and upset (if someone has been angry and upset with you)

- ✔ Frustrated (if someone won't see and accept your point of view)

- ✔ Sullen and angry (if the boss has pulled rank)

- ✔ Stressed (if someone hasn't done what he promised to do)

Whenever someone's behaviour has disappointed you, try to work out for yourself why he behaved that way. Consider the situation from the other person's point of view. For example, why did he break his promise? Was he, in turn, refused permission by his boss to take a day off? Did he forget? Was he ignoring you?

One of the greatest injuries you can do to anyone is to wound the person's pride. People will admit to all sorts of things quite readily if they have reasons. But if you're asking someone to admit to being silly, forgetting something or making a mistake, beware! You're affronting that person's pride and he's probably going to seek to protect it.

In a nutshell, considering situations from the other person's point of view is the foundation on which you begin to build your understanding of people and their behaviour.

If you treat people with dignity, respect their point of view (even if you don't agree with it) and draw a clear line between the right and wrong ways to behave toward other people, you lay the best possible foundation for effective interactions with others.

Communication Nation: Seeing the Importance of Communication

In the world of business, you have to be able to communicate, and that means understanding how communication works. Let me start with some basic assertions:

- ✔ If you want to know something, ask.

- ✔ If you want others to know something, tell them.

- ✔ Show rather than explain – explanation should come alongside the showing, not replace it.

- ✔ Use clear and direct language.

- ✔ Tell the truth. But if you can't tell the full truth, never lie.

In this section, I introduce the various channels of communication, types of communication and what can get in the way of communication.

Channels of communication

In businesses, as in every part of life, you have at your disposal many different channels of communication. Figure 15-1 illustrates these various channels, and in the following sections, I walk you through them.

Simple

Simple channels of communication can be centralised or decentralised:

- **Centralised:** Information flows to and from the central person. This channel of communication is effective because everyone has direct access. You do have to ensure, however, that the central person doesn't become overloaded with information.

- **Decentralised:** Information flows all around the network, as well as from the central figure. This channel of communication can be effective, but you have to watch out for the grapevine and for people misinterpreting the message if they relate only to their colleagues and not to the central figure.

With simple channels of communication, you're critically dependent on the central figure being fully informed and prepared to share what he knows with the group.

Complex

A variety of complex channels of communication exists, as follows:

- **Hierarchical:** Information travels up and down the ranking order of the company. In this channel of communication, information gets filtered and re-presented as it travels up and down the ranks.

- **Briefing:** Information tends to flow one way (although sometimes with the opportunity for question-and-answer sessions). Because of the size of the group, people tend not to get all the answers they seek.

- **Hourglass:** Information goes through a single source, leaving the communication open to interpretation (or corruption) by the key figure.

- **Chains:** Information is passed from person to person, in a chain. There is potential for each person in the chain to edit, skew or corrupt the message, based on their own perceptions or understanding. They may also use their position in the chain deliberately to corrupt what was originally said.

- **Cascade:** Information cascades down from group to group. The message tends to be diluted as it falls down through the different phases.

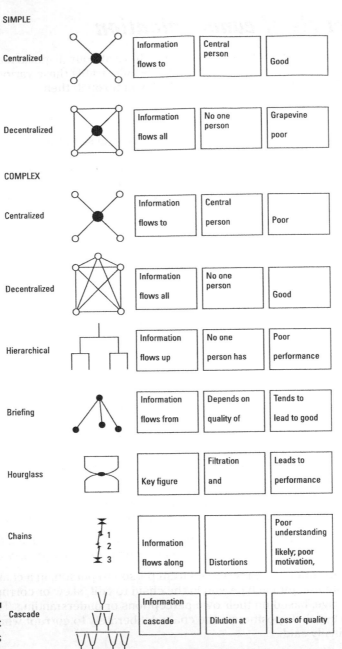

Figure 15-1:
Channels
of communi-
cation.

Note the comments in the right-hand column - and especially the fact that very few of the methods used lead to good communication performance.

The problem with these complex channels of communication is that they're largely ineffective – and yet some of these channels, such as briefing groups and cascades, are popular in organisations today. The single most effective method of communication is still one person speaking with a group of five or six others. If you have to use other methods, be aware of the possible and likely consequences.

Types of communication

Several types of communication exist: oral, written and non-verbal.

Oral communication

This communication is spoken – one person talking to another person or a group of people. It could be as simple as a conversation with an employee in the hallway or the CEO talking to thousands of employees around the world through videoconferencing.

Here are a few tips for effective oral communication:

- ✔ Use simple, clear and direct language.

- ✔ Be open and prepared to discuss anything at any time with anyone who works for you.

- ✔ Be clear with people about what you expect of them, why, when and how.

- ✔ Make sure that your people know how they should raise issues and problems with you – and when they do so, be clear about how you're going to respond and by when.

It's important to work at your oral communication skills. If you can become an open and honest communicator with the people around you, you quickly build a reputation as someone they can trust. In particular, when you have to deliver bad news (and you know that time is going to come sooner or later), your openness and honesty will garner respect in your organisation.

Written communication

Written communication is a key method of communication in business. Whether in the form of a memo or email, or a corporate report, writing is key to communicating your message.

In many cases, you find yourself having to say things to people (via oral communication) and then follow up with written statements and summaries. If you're in this position, always make sure that what you said and what you write agree. Make the message consistent across all methods of communication.

If your communication is inconsistent, you can quickly gain a reputation for dishonesty. When employees come out of a productive and positive meeting only to find that the written summary that follows has been distorted in some way, they feel frustrated. Lasting damage to your reputation – and that of the company or organisation – can then begin to build.

Non-verbal communication

Non-verbal communication is much more powerful than words alone. You communicate a powerful message through the expression on your face, your body language, how well you listen and so on. When the non-verbal message is out of kilter with the words you use, the non-verbal message is what leaves the lasting impression. It doesn't matter how often you tell employees that you care about what they have to say – if you're checking your mobile while they're talking to you, they get the real message loud and clear.

Non-verbal communication covers all aspects of business activities and human interaction. You need especially to be aware of the following:

- **Appearance:** The way you dress says something about how you feel about yourself and your job. If you show up to work looking like you just rolled out of bed, people may get the idea that you don't really care – no matter how well you perform at work.

- **Eye contact:** Maintaining eye contact with the person you're talking to demonstrates interest, trust, concern, affection, empathy and sympathy. If you avoid eye contact, you may be perceived as being untrustworthy, fearful or dishonest.

- **Touch:** People's perceptions of you are influenced by the firmness or otherwise of your handshake. In the business world, a firm handshake generates confidence.

- **Body language:** Note how people in authority use their physical presence to reinforce that authority. Note also how when their authority is questioned, they use arm movements, raise their voice, and if necessary stand up, advance towards you, and make other assertive or aggressive gestures to try and get their authority back.

What we have is a failure to communicate: Barriers to communication

Communication barriers arise by:

- **Accident:** Where the choice of language is wrong, even though people act with the best of intentions.
- **Negligence:** When barriers are allowed to arise by default.

✔ **Design:** Where people create barriers in order to further their own ends. For example, people use their information and expertise as a commodity to be bought and sold, and as a bargaining chip for getting their own way.

In the context of recognising where communication problems come from, the main barriers to identify are as follows:

✔ **Language:** People use bureaucratic phrases and jargon to edit others into and out of conversations.

✔ **Physical distance:** When people communicate with others only by email or telephone, the manner and frequency of communications creates barriers.

✔ **Trappings:** Some trappings exude power, authority and fear. For example, the person who has his own parking space, two personal assistants and a personal washroom puts up psychological barriers to communication with more junior staff. Junior staff, in turn, find themselves discouraged from approaching him.

✔ **Control mechanisms:** People make requests for specific information in forms that are inappropriate or dishonest.

✔ **Confidentiality:** This becomes a barrier when people use it as a means of managing and enhancing status.

People in authority use the 'need to know' barrier to reinforce their own position and status, as well as to downgrade the position and status of those who don't 'need to know'. Of course, you have to acknowledge matters of confidentiality. On the other hand, if you do ever use 'need to know', make sure that you can fully justify doing so.

✔ **Lack of visibility and access:** This lack leads to perceptions that you can't resolve problems quickly because you can't get at the person who needs to address them.

Culture Club: Considering Your Organisation's Culture and Values

The culture of an organisation is the basis of its management and operational style, as well as individual and collective attitudes, values, behaviours and beliefs. Here I take a look at what makes up culture, and how organisations create it.

Understanding the characteristics of culture

Culture is:

✔ **Learned:** People have to be taught how to behave. They need to be taught the correct attitudes and values when they come to work in the organisation.

✔ **Shared:** Everyone has to accept the attitudes and values of the organisation.

✔ **Continuous:** As new people come in, they have to accept the existing culture.

✔ **Adaptive:** People coming into the organisation clearly have to adopt (or at least acquiesce) to the prevailing attitudes and values. However, the culture is constantly adapting as new people come in and new ways of working and relationships develop.

✔ **Regular:** When people within the organisation communicate with each other, a common body of understanding evolves on which they base their transactions.

Out of all these characteristics, the following arise:

✔ **Norms:** Distinctive standards of behaviour; the ways in which people address each other; understanding of the relationships between ranks and hierarchies; understanding of general patterns of behaviour, habits, dress and speech.

✔ **Philosophy:** The policies concerning beliefs and standards of performance, attitudes, behaviours and conduct apply to everyone, regardless of their occupation.

✔ **Rules:** The formal rules, processes and procedures that underline the constitution of the organisation apply evenly to everyone when required.

✔ **Organisational body language:** Every aspect of organisational conduct reinforces the perceptions that everyone has about the organisation.

Seeing how culture evolves

Organisational culture is based on the following business and social issues:

- The history and tradition of the organisation
- The nature of the organisation's activities
- The technology that's present, and the people and expertise used to make it work
- The purposes, priorities and conduct of the business itself
- The size of the business and the organisational structures that are in place to make it manageable
- The leadership and management style of the organisation

An organisation's culture may be *designed* (in which you set the standards required and make sure that they're enforced and developed) or *emergent* (in which you allow standards of behaviour and performance to emerge, rather than structuring and implementing them). Those in senior positions need to design, shape and reinforce culture and ensure that it's accepted by everyone else. This job involves setting standards of attitudes, values, behaviours and performance to which everyone is required to subscribe as a condition of employment. If an organisation's culture is allowed to emerge, the result is that people think, believe, behave and act according to their own priorities rather than those of the organisation. Your organisation mustn't tolerate anything that's legally, socially or morally unacceptable.

Organisational culture is constantly evolving and developing. If you're aiming for a strong, positive and dynamic culture, the last thing you want is to be stagnant and inert. This process of evolution means that you can change your culture in ways that work for the organisation.

Here are some examples of organisational cultures that have evolved:

- Nissan UK transformed a population of former miners, shipbuilders and steelworkers into the most productive and effective car factory in the world by treating everyone who came to work for it with respect and by valuing their contributions.

- British Airways transformed a bureaucratic, nationalised monopoly into a customer-orientated multinational corporation through attending to the key values of customer service and commitment to the company itself.

- Ryanair transformed a loss-making luxury airline into a profitable low-cost mass-transit airline through transforming the attitudes of everyone (including the Ryan family, which owns the company) towards achieving profitability.

In order to change your organisation's culture, you have to demonstrate that change is in people's best interests. You have to make sure that they know why the change is necessary and what the path ahead entails. If you communicate your goals effectively, employees understand why you're making a change – and most of them will follow you.

Enron

A month before Enron collapsed, CEO Kenneth Lay said: 'We are moving from being the world's best energy company, to being the world's best company.'

Over the previous decade, Enron had transformed the energy market in North America. By turning electricity into a commodity, Enron found that it was able to buy up supplies wholesale and then sell on to regional electricity companies at assured prices, both for the present and the future.

All this success was reinforced by a strong inclusive and exclusive culture. The company's head office in Dallas, Texas, was known as the 'Death Star'. Everyone who worked at Enron felt privileged, exclusive and special. They enjoyed high salaries and looked forward to taking Enron's activities global and securing a permanent place in history.

They didn't quite expect to secure that permanent place as the largest ever corporate collapse and the largest ever corporate fraud!

Many of those working in the company used their own positions and the company's assets to secure large-scale cash advances, which were then paid out in the form of bonuses or syphoned off by staff. This practice had started for completely legitimate reasons: for a particular project, the company had needed short-term finance and had raised it against one of its projects. However, people quickly found out that they could turn to this practice at any time, and because the company was so well known and regarded, the funds would come pouring in.

When the company collapsed under the weight of losses incurred in these ways, trauma and disbelief abounded, especially among middle and junior members of staff. They simply could not believe that the collapse had happened! After all, Enron was 'the world's best company', and they were expecting to have long and prosperous futures there.

The lesson? If you've a strong and inclusive – and exclusive – culture, you still have responsibilities. You have to behave in an ethical and responsible manner, and you have to ensure that people can, indeed, have long and successful careers with your organisation.

Oh, Captain! My Captain! Looking at Leadership

The style, quality and expertise of leadership has a critical effect on people and how they behave. Leadership is a combination of:

- Giving vision and direction to everything that goes on
- Energising and galvanising people to behave and perform as you want them to
- Setting and enforcing absolute standards of behaviour, attitude, presentation and performance

Those in leadership positions have to concentrate on short-term activities, getting optimum performance from those carrying out the work. They also have to be able to adopt a macro-level, long-term perspective, without losing sight of the short term.

Leaders are also concerned with ensuring continuity, development and improvement. They're responsible for resource utilisation, business performance, success and failure. They're accountable to shareholders and stock markets, and ultimately to staff, customers and suppliers.

The key leadership roles include the following:

- **Figurehead:** The leader acts as the human face of the department, division or organisation to the rest of the world.

- **Ambassador:** The leader acts as an advocate, cheerleader and problem-solver on behalf of his department, division, organisation and people.

- **Servant:** The leader uses his position to go into areas and activities, and to meet people that the rest of his staff can't.

- **Maintenance:** The leader attends to problems and issues as they arise, takes steps to prevent problems arising in the first place and handles crises and blow-ups when they occur.

- **Role model:** The leader sets a style, standard, attitude and behaviour for others to follow. If you're in a leadership position and show qualities of commitment, enthusiasm, energy and honesty, you're entitled to expect these same attributes from the people who work for you. If you don't show any of these qualities, however, why should anyone else?

- **Ringmaster:** The leader brings all the preceding traits together, creating a productive and harmonious working environment and positive working relations with everyone.

The authority of the leader comes from a variety of sources. Some leaders are appointed; their authority is legitimised by virtue of the fact that they've gone through a selection process in order to get a leadership position. Other leaders are bureaucratic; their positions are legitimised by the rank they hold. This situation is common in corporate hierarchies and complex organisations. Functional and expert leaders command authority by virtue of their expertise. Finally, charismatic leaders command authority by virtue of their personalities; people are willing to follow them because of their charisma. Of course, many leaders' authority comes from more than one place – a leader may have great charisma and technical expertise, as well as be appointed via a selection process, for example.

Three main styles of leadership exist: autocratic (benevolent or tyrannical), consultative/participative and democratic/participative. Table 15-1 compares and contrasts these styles of leadership.

Table 15-1	Leadership Styles		
	Autocratic (Benevolent or Tyrannical)	**Consultative/ Participative**	**Democratic/ Participative**
How decisions are made	The leader makes all the decisions for the group.	The leader makes decisions after consulting with the group.	The group makes decisions, by consultation with the leader or by vote. Voting is based on the principle of 'one person, one vote', and the majority rules.
Individual and collective interests	Individual members' interests are subordinate to those of the organisation.	The leader respects and accommodates individual interests, if possible.	All members are bound by the group decision and support it.
Communication between the leader and group members	Leaders disregard group members' views.	The leader and members of the group communicate openly.	All members may contribute to the discussion.
Attitude toward questioning authority	The leader discourages questioning.	The leader encourages questioning.	Questioning is open, but the final decision rests with the group.
Extent of supervision	The leader closely supervises his subordinates.	The leader leaves individuals to work in their own ways and monitors only the final performance.	The group establishes norms.
Development of coalitions and cliques	The leader breaks up coalitions and cliques.	The leader recognises coalitions, and addresses their concerns.	Coalitions and cliques develop.

	Autocratic (Benevolent or Tyrannical)	Consultative/ Participative	Democratic/ Participative
Who assumes the leadership role	The power figure assumes the leadership role. Leadership is wielded through patronage, threat and coercion.	The power figure assumes the leadership role. Leadership is wielded through confidence and communication.	The chair assumes the leadership role.
Work environment	Conformist/ coercive.	Conformist/ engaged.	Conforms to group norms.
Accountability	The power figure takes credit for successes. The power figure takes responsibility for failures or finds scapegoats.	The leader retains responsibility for results.	The group retains responsibility for results.
Demands on staff	The leader places great demands on staff.	The leader places agreed-upon demands on staff.	The group places demands on individuals.
Organisation development	The staff develops as ordered or required.	The leader is supportive and developmental.	The organisation develops in accordance with collective norms and values.
Leadership	People respond to leadership demands.	The leader is accessible and discursive.	Leadership exists *de facto* in the group.
Ways of working	The leader prescribes ways of working.	The leader leaves ways of working largely unspecified.	The group agrees ways of working or they emerge from the group and its norms.

Motivation: Why People Do What They Do

Motivation is the reason behind behaviour. In the workplace, a key part of motivation is recognition, praising people for a job well done. People need to experience, and be associated with, success. They need rewards – both *extrinsic* (for example, money, benefits and promotions) and *intrinsic* (for example, a sense of self-worth and a sense of being valued). They need the chance to grow and improve in their jobs. Please also flip to Chapter 16, which shows the relationship between motivation and rewards.

If you're trying to get people to do something, you need to figure out what motivates them.

In this section, I fill you in on two theories to do with motivation. One is Maslow's hierarchy of needs; the other, Herzberg's two factors.

The hierarchy of needs

In 1943, American psychologist Abraham Maslow presented what he called a *hierarchy of needs* (see Figure 15-2), which explains different levels of motivation. Starting at the bottom, and working up to the top, the needs that Maslow identified are as follows:

Figure 15-2: Maslow's hierarchy of needs.

Societal and civilisational needs

Basic and instinctive needs

Self-actualisation: fulfilment and achievement

Esteem: self-esteem, self-worth, self-regard; and the esteem, value and regard of others

Social: the need to belong, to love and be loved, to interact with others

Safety: the need for protection and security

Physiological: the need for shelter, survival, food and drink

- **Physiological:** Food, drink, air, warmth, sleep and shelter.

- **Safety and security:** Protection from danger, threats and deprivation; the need for a stable environment.

- **Social:** A sense of belonging to society and the groups within it – for example, the family, the company and the work group.

- **Esteem:** Self-respect, self-esteem, appreciation, recognition and status, both individually and in relation to other people.

- **Self-actualisation or self-fulfilment and accomplishment:** Recognition for work well done, progress and development.

So what does Maslow's hierarchy of needs have to do with your workplace? Your organisation needs to ensure that it meets the needs of your employees, whether that's by making people feel confident that the company won't go broke, helping employees to feel part of the organisation, or recognising employees for good work or progress on the job.

When Maslow first published his work, people generally assumed that not everyone was capable of self-actualisation. But today, everyone aspires to self-actualisation – to being the best they can be. So, as an organisation, you need to do everything possible to help people do exactly that.

The two-factor theory

In 1959, American industrial psychologist Frederick Herzberg put forth the two-factor theory (see Figure 15-3), which defines two sets of factors affecting workplace motivation:

- **Those factors that, if wrong, lead to extreme dissatisfaction with the job and the organisation, such as:**

    - Adversarial policies, and supervisory and management styles

    - Low and declining levels of pay and salary

    - Bad relationships with peers and managers

    - Lack of status

    - Loss of job security

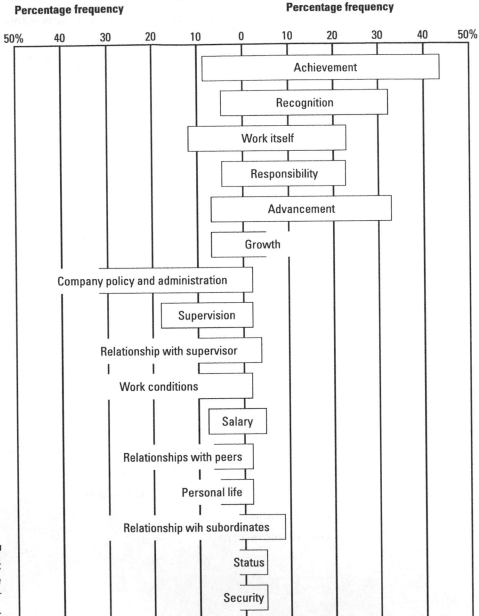

Factors on the job that led to extreme dissatisfaction but not satisfaction

Factors on the job that led to extreme dissatisfaction but not dissatisfaction

Figure 15-3: The two-factor theory.

✔ **Those factors that lead to extreme satisfaction with the job and the company, such as:**

- Achievements

- Recognition

- The nature of the work itself and the amount of control that the individual has over it

- Levels of responsibility

- Prospects for advancement and promotion

- Opportunities for personal growth and development

If you understand the two-factor approach – based on first, what motivates people and second, what doesn't – you can take action when a lack of motivation is apparent, as well as build on those things that do motivate people. Be sure to look at the following:

✔ Pay rates and the extent to which they're suitable for the work and can support life outside work for your staff

✔ Supervision and the extent to which this supervision is hostile or participative and supportive

✔ The working environment and the extent to which people have everything they need in order to carry out their work fully and effectively

By examining pay, supervision and the working environment, you're looking at all those things that, if wrong, demotivate people. By doing what you can to put them right, you're removing the reasons people *don't* want to come to work.

Top companies especially concentrate as much on removing de-motivators as they do on generating commitment and motivation actively. For example, Google pays high salaries, has a highly participative management style and provides an exceptional working environment that includes all technology and equipment on request, a high-quality restaurant and leisure facilities. The message that Google is communicating to its employees is: 'We've addressed and removed everything that gets in the way of progress, motivation and commitment. So now you've no reason not to deliver the highest quality work possible.'

Be sure to recognise people's achievements and progression. You have to build in opportunities for people to shine. This goal is the driving force behind such varied approaches as employee of the day/week/month/year, additional rewards and bonuses for specified extra achievement, and rewards attached to staff suggestion schemes.

Whatever you do, if you want to motivate your people and gain their commitment to you, you have to look at where you can demonstrate recognition. Then commit yourself to recognising everyone who achieves high standards.

Building the Work Ethic You Want

An organisation's *work ethic* is a combination of the standards set by leadership, the demands of the work, the identity and loyalty that people have with the organisation and their motivation and commitment. You need to modify and direct people's behaviour so that they accept the work ethic required and then work to the standards that you set.

How people work is as important as what they do. You don't want to be the next media story about bad working practices, corruption, mis-selling of products and services, or giving misleading figures about what something will actually cost. But all these events continue to happen in the business world, and they happen because people think that they're acceptable. They also think that such events are what their company expects of them – and in many cases, they expect praise for their efforts.

Mis-selling happens when something doesn't deliver the benefits that it claims that it will. The UK has seen great scandals with financial services mis-selling, especially selling hedge fund products to small depositors.

Evaluate your organisation's working practices, activities and methods. Which of these reflect your work ethic? Which don't? And what can you do to build on what works and reform what doesn't?

People's behaviour and the extent to which the organisation encourages or punishes it reinforces the work ethic. If people see their co-workers slacking off the last hour of every day and management does nothing about it, they'll think that slacking off is acceptable. Eventually, slacking off will be part of your organisation's work ethic – whether you want it to be or not.

If someone does something that you know is wrong and you do nothing about it, the action is effectively no longer wrong because you have *de facto* tolerated it. And then it's only a short step from being 'no longer wrong' to being 'right'.

Go, Team!

In every organisation, people work together, so they're part of a team (or multiple teams), whether you call them teams or not. Here are the most common types of teams:

- **Formal teams:** Constituted by the organisation for particular purposes.

- **Project teams:** Work on specific projects and ventures, such as technology installation, premises development and new product and service initiatives.

- **Work improvement and quality improvement teams:** Remedy particular problems.

- **Self-managing teams:** Management grants these teams the authority to manage themselves and get things done as they see fit.

To work effectively, all teams have to be free of the interference of supervisors and managers, except in ensuring that the teams meet the necessary standards, quality, costs and deadlines.

The best teams function when they've their own strong and distinctive culture, identity and cohesion. But the team's culture should always benefit the organisation as a whole. When teams begin to set their own standards and practices, managers need to step in and, if necessary, disband and reconstitute the team.

Teams aren't stagnant – they evolve and become more effective over time. You have to give teams the opportunity to experience the different stages of growth:

1. **Form.**

   Members get to know one another while cautiously testing the boundaries of the team and its leadership. People are usually energised and excited by the prospect of getting things done, but they still need to get to know each other.

2. **Storm.**

   A kind of panic sets in among team members as they begin to realise the difficulty of what they need to accomplish. At this stage, usually you see a great burst of energy and ideas as people turn their attention towards the team's goals.

3. **Norm.**

   Team members begin to establish roles and norms and support each other. The ground rules begin to emerge. The work ethic also begins to take shape.

4. **Perform.**

   Team members are fully comfortable in their relationships with each other. They know the capabilities and shortcomings of all team members. Each person plays to his own strengths and supports everyone else. The team pulls together to create an entity that can achieve more together than any one person could achieve on his own.

Managing across Cultures, Borders and Time Differences

Dealing with people is complex enough in simple organisations set in one location. But it becomes much more complex when you have to work in large and diverse organisations, with activities in many different parts of the world. On the one hand, you have to establish reporting relationships that build and develop a cohesive culture for the organisation as a whole. On the other hand, you have to recognise that people don't do things the same way everywhere – you have to relate what you do to local habits and norms.

Commit yourself to understanding local customs and patterns of behaviour wherever your organisation operates. If your organisation tries to impose its ways of working on another location, cultural and behavioural clashes are bound to occur. Breakdowns in communication will happen. Instead of fostering motivation and commitment, you may well encounter frustration and resistance. Work *within* the local customs and habits, and limit your activities and objectives to what's possible under those circumstances.

Here are a couple of key questions to answer when you're looking at managing across borders and cultures:

- ✔ Does this location actually need or want us? If so, why and under what conditions? If not, why not? Can we do anything to change this view?

- ✔ Where do the local sources of power and influence lie? What's the nature of the relationship that we should develop with those sources of power and influence? How can we relate what we want out of the particular location to what they want out of our involvement?

The answers to these questions should yield a detailed analysis of the ways in which you can develop your cultural knowledge and understanding.

Part of working around the world is knowing what motivates the people in diverse locations. Consider their drives and ambitions, and how they need and want recognition for a job well done. What motivates people in your home office may not matter to people in your office halfway around the world.

Also, learn to speak the local language – or at least understand how people use their own language in their own domains. Communicating effectively in your own language is hard enough, but when you throw in language differences, it gets even harder. Find out as much as you can about the most effective ways of communicating with your colleagues in remote parts of the world. Hire interpreters when necessary.

Even if you know the language, have someone who can help you with misunderstandings. For example, in the USA, someone may casually hand another person his business card, but in Japan, the exchange of business cards is much more formal, involving bowing and presenting the business card with the text facing up. Have a liaison in the local area who can educate you on the proper etiquette wherever you do business.

The people you work with in different parts of the world are your colleagues, just as much as the people down the hall from you are. Be sure to respect and value their contribution to your organisation, as well as the ways in which they do things. If you have problems working across cultures, distances, languages and time zones, take as much time as you need to understand why those problems have occurred so that you can remedy them to the satisfaction of everyone involved, including your long-distance colleagues.

Chapter 16

Managing Human Resources

. . . .

In This Chapter

▶ Recruiting and selecting new employees

▶ Investing in training and development

▶ Recognising the good work your employees do

▶ Keeping your employees safe and healthy

. . . .

*E*very organisation depends on people to make it run and flourish. Businesses need more than buildings and stock stacked up to the rafters in countless warehouses in endless cities. They also need more than computers humming away as they direct the flow of bits and bytes over worldwide telecommunications networks. Without people to help oversee the buildings, manage the stock and operate the computers, businesses wouldn't exist. And you won't find it a surprise that the better the quality of the people in your organisation, the better the quality of the organisation itself. Quality people result in better products and services.

In this chapter, I focus on managing people effectively. I walk you through recruiting new employees – from defining the job to setting the salary to interviewing candidates and checking references. Then I underline the importance of training and developing your current employees, and rewarding them for their successes. Finally, I cover the importance of creating a healthy and safe working environment.

Recruiting New Employees

Simply snapping your fingers to attract the best and brightest employees whenever you wanted them would be nice, but as you know, the process isn't quite that simple. In fact, if you're serious about attracting the best employees to work in your organisation, the recruitment process is a lot of work. But the good news is that the rewards of making a good choice are tremendous and long lasting. These rewards include:

- ✔ Better customer satisfaction

- ✔ Improved morale

- ✔ Increased productivity

- ✔ Increased profit

- ✔ Increased revenues

In this section, I cover the key steps in the recruitment process and offer advice on how to conduct them the right way, every time.

Defining the job

The first step in recruiting a new hire – something you need to do *before* you place an advertisement in a newspaper or post a job notice on the bulletin board at work – is to create a detailed job description. A *job description* explains the duties and responsibilities of a particular position and defines any special requirements or skills that the successful candidate needs.

Here are some specific elements that every job description should contain, regardless of the position:

- ✔ **Job title:** The name of the job – for example, 'programmer/analyst', 'accounts clerk' or 'personnel assistant'. Whatever you call the job, make sure that the job title gives a clear indication of the responsibilities and duties involved, and the qualifications required of any applicant.

- ✔ **Department or division:** The department or division in which the specific position is located – for example, the Accounting Department or the Operations Division.

- ✔ **Responsibilities:** Everything the person performing the job is responsible for. The list of responsibilities isn't just a one- or two-sentence summary of a job's most important duties – it includes every task of the position.

  Writing a complete description of a position's responsibilities isn't a simple task. Start by asking the employees currently performing this job exactly what they do – every little thing. Then compare your employees' lists against what you think they *should* be doing. You can compile your final list of responsibilities in a narrative/paragraph-type format or as a bulleted list, or a combination of the two.

- ✔ **Required skills or expertise:** The specific skills that a person needs in order to do this job. Perhaps the person doing the job must be able to type 80 words per minute or be able to build wooden forms for pouring concrete building foundations. This part of the job description includes the skills, expertise and number of years of experience required.

✔ **Desirable qualifications:** Additional qualifications that would be nice to have. For example, if you're hiring a secretary, maybe you need that person to be able to type 80 words per minute, but you'd also like the person to be familiar with Microsoft Office. In this section of your job description, list anything you'd like to have but that you can live without.

If you've never prepared job descriptions before, or if you just want an easier way to deal with them, get help. The Chartered Institute of Personnel and Development (CIPD; www.cipd.co.uk) provides all the help that you need. You may have to pay a small fee for this service if no one on your staff is a member of CIPD.

You must write job descriptions in ways that meet equal opportunities legislation and guidance. Unless specific qualities or qualifications are attached to the particular job (for example, having female staff to work as caregivers for female patients), you give everyone equal treatment when applying. If you want to limit the field in any way, you have to prove what's called a *genuine occupational qualification* (GOQ).

Setting a salary

Paying employees what they're worth is particularly important when the job market is tight and unemployment is low. But that doesn't mean that if unemployment is high, you should keep salaries unfairly low. Part of retaining good employees is making them feel valued, and compensation is one part of that equation.

If you aren't offering pay rates and salaries that are competitive with other companies, you'll have a tough time attracting the best employees to your firm. Other elements of an overall reward package – such as health benefits, retirement plans and share options – can also enter into a candidate's decision about whether to accept a job offer. Salary, however, is still the most important compensation consideration of all.

So how do you work out how much to offer for a particular job? The first step is to develop an overall reward philosophy for your organisation. This overall philosophy is the foundation that helps to guide pay and salary decisions for all your employees. Be clear about what you're paying for, and why you've arrived at the balance of pay and salary with other benefits. You need to be able to answer in detail the following questions:

✔ Will you make your basic salaries simply competitive with the going rate for employers in your area or higher?

✔ Will you establish a structured pay scale for specific jobs in your company, or will you set salaries on an individual basis, based on the qualities and potential of the person filling the job?

✔ To what extent will the monetary rewards that you offer your employees take the form of salary, performance bonuses or benefits?

✔ Will you base the salaries on how well people perform or on other factors, such as how long they stay with your organisation or what credentials they bring to the job?

✔ Will you award bonuses on the basis of individual performance, tie bonuses to company results or use a combination of the two?

✔ Will you take into account local factors (for example, the cost of living in the city where the job is located) and pay above or below the going rate for the particular job according to these factors?

✔ Will you balance the pay and reward aspects with the intrinsic interest (the actual personal commitment that you have) in the job?

✔ Will you offer a structured career progression – a way for people to advance within your organisation?

When you've decided on your strategic approach to pay, you're closer to setting the salary for a given position. For example, if you're going to base salaries on the going rates within your geographical area, your first step is to do a wage survey to determine exactly what those going rates are for each position within your organisation.

Wage information is available from a variety of sources, including the Internet, government employment offices, chambers of commerce, local business newspapers and magazines, and employment consulting firms.

No matter how you decide to pay your employees, keep in mind that wages, salaries, bonuses and benefits – and the fairness and consistency with which you determine them – have a direct and measurable effect on employee happiness and motivation. In turn, your employees' job satisfaction has a direct and measurable effect on customer satisfaction and, ultimately, revenues and profit. If your competitors are offering better salary packages for the same jobs, you can be certain that your employees are going to find out and be tempted to move to where the grass is greener.

Finding the cream of the crop

Where do you go to find the best employees? To some extent, the answer to that question depends on the kind of position you have to fill and the kind of people you're seeking. To increase the chances of getting your message in front of the right people, first decide what kind of person you're looking for and then decide the best method for communicating the opportunity to that person.

Show me the money!

Many organisations now offer complex reward packages to their staff, including company cars, further education, and nursery and crèche facilities. However, a survey carried out by the online recruitment agency Vault.com found that salary is still by far the most important consideration to the vast majority of people when considering whether to apply for a job.

The results of the survey question 'Which part of the reward package at your job needs the most improvement?' are as follows:

- Salary: 48.8 per cent
- Share options: 17.6 per cent
- Holidays: 12.6 per cent
- Medical benefits: 11.6 per cent
- Hours: 9.2 per cent

You can choose from a variety of ways to advertise a job opportunity to the best candidates. Here are some of the most commonly used methods:

- **Your own organisation:** One of the best sources of top-quality job candidates is within your own organisation! The beauty of internal candidates is that you can usually get candid references on their job performance from their colleagues and past and present supervisors. Another plus is that internal candidates are already familiar with company policies and procedures. As a result, they can move into their new positions more quickly than someone from outside your firm can. Don't overlook this rich resource of job candidates!

- **Business and personal networks:** Everyone has a network of contacts. Your personal friends and professional contacts can often be excellent sources of job candidates. People in your networks not only know about your business and the kind of people you're looking for, but also they aren't likely to send you candidates who'd reflect badly on them.

  If you offer a plum position to a friend, make sure that she's the best-qualified person for the job. Otherwise, at the very least, you're behaving unethically, and your colleagues will want to know what you think you're doing, and at the very worst, you may be breaking the law. If you've any questions about whether hiring a friend or relative is okay, talk with a lawyer.

- **Newspaper advertisements:** Newspaper ads are one of the first places that most employers think of looking for new employees. But is placing an advertisement in your local newspaper the best way to find the people you're looking for? Maybe not. The best candidate for the job may see your advertisement – but you may miss many other terrific candidates, both locally and outside your immediate geographic area. You may try a newspaper ad just to see which candidates turn up, but if it doesn't do the trick for you, quickly move on to another method.

✔ **The web:** In recent years, the web has exploded as a resource for employers and job seekers. Hundreds of different websites cater to those seeking jobs. Many such websites are specific to different kinds of opportunities – for example, information technology, purchasing or sales. To get an idea of what's out there, research a few job sites affiliated with your industry or the type of position you have open. You can soon discover which websites suit your needs best, and which don't.

In addition, many job sites are more all-purpose in nature – as opposed to catering to a specific industry. On sites such as Indeed (`www.indeed.co.uk`) or Totaljobs (`www.totaljobs.com`), potential candidates can post their CVs or résumés and organisations can post open jobs. On the upside, these all-purpose sites give you access to a huge field of candidates each time you have a vacancy. On the downside, when you post openings on these sites, you may be overwhelmed with responses that you have to spend time wading through.

✔ **Headhunters:** If you're targeting someone with a specific level of expertise or experience, one approach is to hire an executive search agency, commonly known as a *headhunter*, to produce a likely list of candidates and their profiles. Headhunters cost money, but you quickly get an idea of who's available, their experience and how much you may have to pay them.

✔ **Employment agencies:** Similar to headhunters, employment agencies (including temporary staffing agencies) can be terrific sources of job candidates. Especially in urban areas, employment agencies are always seeking to place job seekers, and a good agency can tell you quickly whether it can help you.

✔ **Universities, colleges and other schools:** Educational institutions are excellent sources of employees. Recent graduates are likely to have a high level of knowledge and (hopefully!) boundless enthusiasm, but they typically need a thorough orientation programme in order for you to be able to capitalise on their knowledge and energy.

Recruiting is an uncertain game, even at the best of times. On the one hand, the larger your pool of candidates, the greater your chance of finding someone who's just right for you. However, you can't spend time interviewing hundreds of candidates for every open position. Finding the best candidates takes trial and error.

Be sure to keep records on which methods you've used to find candidates, how many applications you received from each method and which methods produced the highest-quality candidates. Advertising online may elicit thousands of applications, but the percentage of those applicants that are perfect for your job opening may be low. On the other hand, mining your personal and

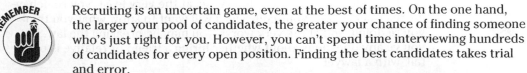

business networks or attending job fairs at universities in the area may result in fewer applications, but the percentage of high-quality applicants may be higher. Figuring out which methods work best for your organisation takes time.

When you arrive at something that works well for you, don't get stuck in a rut. Maybe colleges and universities are your best source of applicants today, but that may not be the case for every job, or five years down the road. Shake things up by trying alternative methods once in a while, particularly if the quality of applicants you're getting has slipped.

Sorting through the applications

After you've placed an advertisement or otherwise solicited interest in your position, the applications start rolling in. Now you need to sort through all the applications you receive. Depending on the position you're seeking to fill, you may have hundreds of applications to sort through.

You can reduce that stack of résumés by immediately rejecting any candidate who doesn't have the required qualifications. (You may get lots of applications that fall into this category – some job seekers seem to apply to every opening they find, whether they're qualified or not.)

You then go through what you have left to see how they match up against the job description and the qualities that you are seeking (refer to the section 'Defining the job' earlier in the chapter). You keep the close fits and these will be the people that you take on to the next stage – interviews and other selection activities.

If an application is incomplete but otherwise strong, consider contacting the candidate to get the necessary information. Narrow your selection to no more than five of the best candidates; these applicants are the people you invite to interview for the position.

Interviewing candidates

Interviews are one of the most critical – and often among the most dreaded – parts of the recruitment process. For job candidates, they're an opportunity to answer detailed questions about their experience and to give a potential employer an idea of what kind of employees they'll be. For employers, interviews are a unique opportunity to ask questions that go beyond the one-sided marketing pitch of most applications and to get a feel for how candidates will fit into their organisations.

Here are the main reasons for interviewing job candidates:

✔ **To get in-depth information about a candidate's work skills and experience, straight from the candidate's mouth:** The interview process lets you see whether what the candidate tells you is consistent with her application.

✔ **To assess the candidate's personality and to determine how that personality will fit into your existing work team:** On paper, dozens of candidates can look rather similar. But when you've a flesh-and-blood human being in front of you, you can gather all kinds of information about that person's personality.

✔ **To assess a candidate's enthusiasm, intelligence and poise:** A candidate may come across as enthusiastic on paper, but can she translate that enthusiasm into an in-person conversation? A job seeker may have loads of help writing a cover letter and résumé, but in person you can tell whether she can speak as intelligently as she writes. And poise is a reflection of confidence – interviews are nerve-wracking for job seekers, but if a candidate can answer your questions without breaking a sweat, you know that she can manage the toughest days on the job.

✔ **To test the candidate's ability to think and reason or anything else you need to assess:** In an interview, you can see how a variety of candidates respond to the same set of questions. For example, you may pose a question about a particular challenge the candidate may face on the job and ask how she would handle that problem.

No one can guarantee that someone who shines during an interview will work out as a new employee. Every manager has tales of ace interviewees who got the job but didn't last long. However, a well-conducted interview can greatly increase your chances of landing the best candidate for the job. First, find the right space. You're looking for a quiet office or conference room that's free of interruption from phones, computers and other employees. Then follow this process for interviewing:

1. **Welcome the applicant and put her at ease.**

   Most job applicants are more than a little bit nervous when interviewing for a job, and they've reason to be – job interviews often make or break candidates. Greet the candidate warmly, offer her something to drink (alcohol free, of course) and direct her to a seat.

   Instead of launching right into the interview, spend a couple of minutes breaking the ice and taking the edge off the interviewee's nervousness. Open the conversation by talking about a neutral topic such as the weather. Build as much rapport as you can in a few minutes. This small talk allows the candidate to focus more on your questions than on her nervousness.

2. **Summarise the position.**

   Take a minute or two to give the candidate a brief summary of the position. Include details of the job responsibilities, how the job fits into the organisation, who the person in the position reports to and expected customer interactions.

3. **Work through a structured set of questions that you ask of every candidate.**

Be sure to address the following:

- Why the candidate applied for the job

- What the candidate can add to your organisation

- What the candidate expects from your organisation

- What kind of person the candidate is

- How much the candidate expects to be paid

Ask questions that explore each of these areas, and carefully note the candidate's answers. If you don't get the answer you're looking for or if the candidate seems evasive on a particular point, don't hesitate to push until you get a satisfactory response.

Take plenty of notes. Better still, prepare an interview form in advance to guide you through your questions and to allow you to jot down notes on your candidate's responses. This advice is especially important if you've many candidates to interview or if you won't have a chance to review each candidate's performance immediately after the interviews.

4. **Probe the candidate's strengths and weaknesses.**

When you assessed the candidate's application before the interview, you probably picked up on these strengths and weaknesses. Now's the time to probe your candidate further about them, as well as any others that become apparent during the interview.

5. **Conclude the interview on an 'up' note.**

Ask your candidate whether she has any other information that you should consider in your decision-making process. Then give the candidate a chance to explain that information. Thank the candidate for her interest in the job (no matter how well or how poorly the interview went), and give her an idea of when you'll be making a decision or whether you'll be conducting an additional round of interviews.

Do *not* make any sort of promises such as, 'You're definitely the best candidate – we'll be making you an offer for sure.' Not only are you setting yourself up for real trouble if you don't follow through on your promises, but the next candidate you interview may be even better than the last.

For a terrific, in-depth discussion of how to interview employees (much more in-depth than I have the space to cover here), as well as sample questions, interview forms, interview evaluation forms and much, much more, be sure to check out Max Messmer's book, *Human Resources Kit For Dummies*, 3rd Edition (Wiley).

Never ask these questions in an interview

Equality of opportunity and equality of treatment legislation require that every candidate is given an equal chance during the interview and other parts of the selection process. In particular, you may not discriminate on any of the following grounds during the selection process unless a genuine occupational qualification (GOQ) permits you to target persons of a specific gender or ethnic origin. If you're in any doubt, get legal advice before you advertise the position. And when you interview candidates, never ask any questions that relate to any of the following:

✔ Age

✔ Arrest and conviction record

✔ Disability

✔ Gender or sexual preference

✔ Marital status

✔ Race or ethnic origin

✔ Religious beliefs

If you become aware of anyone in your organisation asking questions along these lines, put a stop to it immediately.

Checking references

Although many employers are understandably wary about providing reference information about former employees (many employers have been sued for giving bad references), checking an applicant's references is still worth your time. You never know what kind of information can turn up in your investigation.

Excellent past performance is no guarantee of excellent future performance, and poor past performance doesn't mean that the person will perform poorly for you. References are just one piece of information in the selection process.

Here are some of the best places to dig deeper to find out how your candidate may really work out in the new job:

✔ Colleges, universities and other schools

✔ Current and former customers and clients

✔ Current and former supervisors

✔ Networks of common acquaintances, such as industry associations or professional groups

✔ Public sources such as the Internet or local newspapers

Many companies now look at Facebook, Twitter and other social media sites for information on job candidates. By searching these sites, you're likely to dig up more details on candidates that may help you make up your mind as to their suitability for the position. When you look at a candidate's social-networking accounts, you're getting a peek into her personality and the way she talks with friends. But keep in mind that the way people conduct themselves on their personal Facebook pages or Twitter accounts isn't always an accurate reflection of how they conduct themselves at work.

Ranking your candidates

After you've completed your interviews and conducted your reference checks, it's time to rank each of your candidates against one another. The easiest way to rank them is to put the name of each candidate along the left side of a piece of paper and list your recruitment criteria along the top of the page. Create a grid like the one in Figure 16-1 for a hypothetical group of three candidates.

Figure 16-1: A candidate ranking worksheet.

	Customer Service Skills (A)	Help Desk Experience (B)	References (C)	Total Points (A+B+C)
Maria	1	2	1	4
Tom	3	1	2	6
Sally	2	3	3	8

Rank each employee from 1–5 on each of the recruitment criteria. In our example, Maria ranks first for customer service skills, Sally ranks second and Tom third. Go through each of your recruitment criteria (you may have many more items than this simple example does) and assign rankings in this way. Finally, after you've ranked all the candidates, add up the totals for each employee and note the figure on the worksheet. The candidate with the *lowest* score is the one you should employ. In this case, that candidate is Maria.

You can weight the criteria so as to emphasise the factors that are of greatest value to you. For example, maybe references don't matter as much to you as the candidate's help desk experience. If you want to weight the factors, be sure to weight them the same for each candidate, and make sure that the weighting makes sense – for example, if help desk experience is twice as important to you as references, you multiply all the help desk experience scores by 2 as you're coming up with the totals.

Now, at last, you can make your job offer. If, for some reason, your top candidate declines the offer, offer the job to your second-choice candidate. Or if you've reservations about your second choice, you can restart the whole recruitment process.

Don't allow desperation to rule your recruitment decisions. Leaving a position unfilled is usually better than taking on an inferior candidate. If your first round of recruiting and interviews doesn't bring you the right candidate for the job, by all means try again. Interviewing more candidates is far less painful than trying to dismiss someone who doesn't work out the way you hoped.

Welcome aboard! The first few days and weeks

The first few days and weeks of work for your new employee can be both exciting and disorientating. No matter how much experience a new employee may have, starting a new job means starting from scratch (at least in some ways). And when you add in a new office, new colleagues and entirely new relationships, policies and procedures to sort out, you've a recipe for instant confusion.

Fortunately, you can help make your new employee's transition into your organisation relatively quick and painless. Here are a few tips on how to make your new employee's first day at work productive:

✔ **Make the new hire feel welcome.** Set aside plenty of time for your new employee. Be sure that others who are to supervise or be supervised by the new employee also allot some time to talk with her. Nothing is worse for a new employee than being shoved alone into a cubicle for hours (or days or weeks) because no one can spare a few hours of time to help.

✔ **Provide a sense of place and belonging.** Be sure that the new employee's office or workstation is ready to move into right away. Stock it with office supplies (paper clips, pens, pencils, paper, stapler and so on), and make sure that the phone and computer are properly hooked up and immediately available.

✔ **Introduce your new employee to the team.** You can introduce the new hire by escorting her around your offices to meet people on an informal basis. Or you can schedule an informal get-together early in the day or over lunch so that your work unit or department can get to know the new employee.

✔ **Don't drown your new employee in forms and paperwork.** Although paperwork is a necessary evil when people are hired, avoid drowning your new hire in it on the first day. Take care of only the essentials. Give the new employee a week to complete the rest of the forms and turn them in.

✔ **Make the first day enjoyable.** Above all, make sure that your new employee's first day is enjoyable and positive – one that starts off on the right foot with your organisation. The employee will have plenty of time down the road for the job to get serious, so you don't need to rush her.

You've only one chance to make a first impression. Take the time to ensure that the new hire's first impression of your organisation is that you truly care about her well-being. But don't let that impression end after the first day of work – renew it every day with *all* your employees through your own thoughts and actions.

Training and Development: Helping Your Employees Learn and Grow

Business never stands still but is constantly evolving. Staff are a key part of any business, so it makes sense that training and development are critically important. But you don't just want to throw money at training seminars, you want the best possible return on your investment. And your employees want to get the most out of their training too – any training you provide your employees expands their skillset and makes them more valuable.

Some companies and organisations are afraid to train their staff – they worry that employees will become too powerful or leave to join a competitor. That's a losing strategy any way you look at it. If you're doing a good job of showing how much you value your people, they won't want to leave. And if someone does leave to join a competitor, it just creates another opening for fresh new talent and ideas to come forth within your organisation.

Developing at all levels

Training and development takes place at four levels:

- ✔ **Professional:** People commit themselves to developing their expertise as far as possible.

- ✔ **Occupational:** People develop the potential of the job that they're doing as far as possible.

- ✔ **Organisational:** People undertake training and development according to the direction, needs and wants of the organisation.

- ✔ **Personal:** People follow their own preferences.

These levels are all integrated. You must attend to each, though; otherwise, you'll have problems. If you offer professional development to the exclusion of the other types, you're simply sponsoring your employees' future career prospects. If you offer occupational development to the exclusion of the other types, your employees become experts in their present jobs but won't have much to offer for the future. If you offer organisational development to the exclusion of the other types, employees are valuable and effective only as long as they continue to work for you. And if you offer personal development to the exclusion of the other types, you're simply accommodating your employees' preferences without an eye on what matters to your organisation.

You've a variety of means of training and development at your disposal, and you should use it all. Most of the following should be available to most employees at least some of the time:

- **Project work and secondments,** so that people can push their own expertise into uncharted territory, as well as develop a wider perspective on the organisation.

- **Specific job and work training,** especially in technology and its uses and applications.

- **Self-development,** in which staff are given the space to explore what they see as the potential of the organisation, and their own potential within it. An increasing number of companies are demanding that their staff do take full initiative in growing their jobs, and therefore the organisation, by following up on work that they have generated through their own initiatives.

- **Working on joint ventures and pioneering initiatives,** to gain a broader perspective on how the organisation may be developed.

- **Periods of off-the-job training,** such as taking recognised qualifications or short courses that have particular aims and objectives.

Be sure that employees have opportunities whenever possible. If people come to you with proposals for training or development, try to accommodate them if you can.

Whatever the training and development, make sure that you can see tangible results and that people can use the new expertise that they've acquired in the development of their present jobs.

Using performance appraisal

The best approaches to training and development arise out of performance appraisal. As the result of effective performance appraisal, employees and their managers agree on immediate and longer-term training and development needs. These needs must be based on a combination of immediate performance requirements and the longer-term objectives of both the employee and the company.

You conduct performance appraisals for the benefit of the organisation and its departments, divisions and functions, as well as individuals. To be effective and successful, performance appraisals must be:

- ✔ Conducted with pre-set and agreed-upon objectives, priorities, targets and deadlines for achievement.

- ✔ A process of regularised formal reviews combined with a continuous and participative working relationship. The CIPD states that supervisors should formally appraise performance every three months but at least once a year.

- ✔ Concentrated on a combination of measuring and evaluating achievements, together with establishing what the employee needs to do for the future.

In addition to establishing training and development needs, effective organisational appraisal schemes may seek to:

- ✔ Identify potential

- ✔ Identify wider areas of concern in relation to collective and individual performance

- ✔ Identify mismatches between occupations and people

- ✔ Help to manage poor performance

Appraisal schemes fall into disrepute for the following reasons:

- ✔ Employees don't believe in or value them.

- ✔ The appraisal schemes don't contribute to the wider success of the organisation.

- ✔ The schemes are bureaucratic rather than productive.

- ✔ The company values the schemes and the accompanying paperwork, but not the outcomes.

- ✔ Reviews are too infrequent or missed altogether.

- ✔ The company doesn't deliver in practice what it promises at the point of appraisal.

Appraisal schemes also suffer from performance criteria identified in general terms only. This problem leads to an unevenness of application across the organisation.

Conducting performance appraisals is a key part of managing employees – and much more complex than I have room for in this book. For more information, check out *Human Resources Kit For Dummies* by Max Messmer, and *Performance Appraisals & Phrases For Dummies* by Ken Lloyd (both published by Wiley).

Atta Boy! Atta Girl! Rewarding Your Employees

If you've hired top-quality staff, they're already highly motivated – and your job is to keep them that way! A key way to keep your employees motivated is to reward them. In this section, I fill you in on the difference between intrinsic and extrinsic rewards, and tell you how to make rewards pay off.

Identifying the difference between intrinsic and extrinsic rewards

Extrinsic rewards relate to money and other tangible returns (for example, a company car, bonuses or longer holidays). Extrinsic rewards reflect the financial value that companies place on particular occupations. They indicate the levels of responsibility and accountability that individuals have in their jobs. For example:

- A marketing executive on £125,000 per annum is likely to have to meet some pretty demanding targets
- A marketing director on $32,000 per annum is likely not to have much overall responsibility or authority.

Extrinsic rewards acknowledge achievement and advancement in the form of salary increases and enhanced material returns. *Intrinsic rewards* are intangible or psychological, such as:

- A certain amount of autonomy for an employee in doing her job
- Certificates of achievement
- Praise for a job well done
- Project work and time-constrained tasks that give the employee not only variety but also more opportunities to shine
- Recognition for achievements outside the organisation (for example, the gaining of qualifications and the chance to do volunteer work in the community)
- Small gifts and gift certificates
- Training and development opportunities (see the preceding section)

If you deliver intrinsic rewards effectively, they greatly strengthen the bond between employer and employee, reinforcing staff loyalty. Plus, if you reward people intrinsically, you're much more likely to get a favourable response from staff when you demand overtime or when you need your people to get you out of a crisis.

Whenever you reward someone, you have to make sure that she knows what she's being rewarded for and why. Make sure that she understands that, at the core, the reward is about a job well done. Above all, make sure that you reward everyone who achieves anything positive; otherwise, you may get a reputation for having favourites.

Making rewards and incentives pay off

One of the truths of business is that you get what you reward. And you get what you *actually* reward, not what you *say* you reward or what you *think* you reward! So, for example, if you say you reward high performance, but you actually reward conformity, you get conformity, not performance. Similarly, if you say you reward everyone, but you actually reward only those who work at the head office, you're going to have a scrabble of people wanting to work at the head office.

Make sure that you're clear about what you actually reward and what people think you reward. Go to great lengths to publicise those who get rewarded and why. Make sure that the message is consistent. If you do so, you go a long way toward ensuring the levels of performance you want from your people.

If you offer incentives and bonuses, tie them into performance that an employee wouldn't otherwise deliver. Incentives work best when you need:

- ✔ Short-term extra efforts
- ✔ To get a particular product or service out on time
- ✔ To finish a project on time
- ✔ To get out of a crisis

Incentives work least effectively when they:

- ✔ Become a regular part of the pay and salary package (meaning that people find ways of working to gain the incentives and then do no more)
- ✔ Are paid for attendance rather than performance
- ✔ Become so regularised that people come to rely on them to support their quality of life (for example, staff who've enjoyed overtime at premium rates for years find their standard of living falls if you cut or cancel the overtime suddenly)

The luck of the Irish?

For many years, the Allied Irish Bank found itself having to manage absenteeism. Finally, it carried out a full survey to assess the extent of the problem. The company found that, on average, staff were taking 10 to 15 days per annum as self-certificated sick leave.

The top and senior management of the bank were determined to do something about it. They introduced a policy that stated:

- Anyone who took no self-certificated sickness absence would gain an extra fortnight's holiday per annum.

- Anyone who did take self-certificated absence would forego this holiday.

The initiative failed. Those who weren't in the habit of taking days off here and there gained an extra fortnight's holiday (so the bank incurred an additional expense). Those who were genuinely ill for a day or two simply made up the holiday that they'd now lost by ensuring that they took enough days off to compensate them anyway.

And the point of this story? If you are going to give out incentives, then make sure that you have thought them through in full before implementing them. Otherwise, as in this case, you just make the situation worse.

Feeling Good: Health and Safety

One of the best ways that you can show your staff you value them is by making your workplace safe. In the UK, under the Health and Safety at Work Act 1974, you've a statutory duty to provide a place of work that is both healthy and safe. You've specific obligations and responsibilities in the following areas:

- **Working time and hours:** You need to establish basic levels of hours that are normal and sensible for people to work.

- **Substances hazardous to health:** You must register, monitor and, when not in use, keep under lock and key these substances.

- **Computer equipment and screens:** Don't allow anyone to work more than 2½ hours without giving them at least 15 minutes away from the screen.

- **Breaks:** Everyone who works for a continuous period of 4 hours should get a break of at least 30 minutes.

- **Emergency procedures:** You must write down these procedures and make them known to all employees.

- **Waste and effluent management:** You dispose of all the waste you produce in a safe and healthy manner.

Additional features that you must attend to relate to the overall quality of the working environment:

- ✔ **Temperature:** There are rules that govern minimum and maximum temperatures on all work premises. In particular, you must provide proper training, equipment and clothing for those who have to work in extreme heat or cold.

- ✔ **Lighting:** Lighting must be adequate to work without strain on the eyes.

- ✔ **Ventilation:** All work premises must be properly ventilated where necessary, through air conditioning and filtration.

- ✔ **Toilets:** You provide separate facilities for each gender and the disabled.

- ✔ **Safety:** All machinery and equipment must have built-in guards and cut-outs. Everyone who uses and operates machinery must have training. In addition, you maintain offices and other premises in a safe way: for example, no trailing telephone and computer wires, no propped open or locked fire doors, and clear passages and corridors. All buildings must have at least two exits to maximise people's chances of getting out in an emergency. And those who lift heavy weights or work with toxic or dangerous substances or fumes get specific training.

Be sure to keep accurate records of all accidents. You must report to the Health and Safety Inspectorate any accident that results in fatality, loss of limb, other serious injury or absence from work for more than three days.

Additionally, organisations are increasingly assuming responsibility for the good health of their staff and taking positive steps to ensure that employees stay fit, healthy and productive. Employees who have persistent or regular time away from work may be assessed by company medical staff, as well as the employees' own doctors. Occupational health schemes and approaches also provide valuable general sources of medical knowledge by which you can assess the overall state of your workforce's health.

In particular, you need to be aware of the following:

- ✔ Alcohol and drug abuse

- ✔ Repetitive strain injuries that are caused by continuous use of certain muscles or the carrying out of certain activities – for example, continuous lifting or keyboard working

- ✔ Smoking, which is now banned from all public places and places of work

- ✔ The effects of computer screens on eyesight

- ✔ The levels of industrial and commercial heating and lighting, and the relationship between these factors and minor ailments such as eyestrain, coughs, and colds

Chapter 17

Handling Employee Relations

. . . .

In This Chapter

▶ Clarifying policies and procedures

▶ Coping with conflict and fostering participation

▶ Holding employees accountable for their actions

▶ Handling complaints from employees

▶ Working with trade unions

▶ Complying with the law

. . . .

*E*mployee relations are the relationships between individuals and groups of employees at work, and the relationships between staff and their employer. They affect everything that happens in your organisation – if employee relations are lousy, your business won't be able to thrive. In Chapter 15, I cover the main influences on collective and individual behaviour. In Chapter 16, I explain how you can recruit and retain employees. This chapter is about how to regulate what goes on during the working day and how to address the daily problems that arise.

Formal systems versus informal systems

Two systems are required for effective employee relations:

✔ **Formal systems:** Policies, procedures and staff handbooks.

✔ **Informal systems:** The relationships that exist among everyone in the organisation, especially among staff and their immediate managers.

Although the formal systems must be in place, ideally conflicts should be resolved through the informal systems.

If relationships are so bad that every conflict gets referred to the formal systems, a backlog of problems will occur. This situation leads to greater frustration and escalating conflict across the workplace.

Take a look at how the informal systems work in your organisation and how effective they are. Make a list of the problems that get referred through the formal systems. Note how long it takes to resolve these matters, the effects on behaviour, performance, motivation and morale, and how things could be resolved more speedily if only there were a collective corporate will.

Policies and Procedures: Putting Them on Paper

In part, employee relations deals with the formalities – written processes and procedures – that are required to ensure that management sets and maintains standards in the workplace.

Any organisation must comply with a range of employment laws. (I provide a summary of these laws at the end of this chapter.) Written policies and procedures spell out how the management will establish, maintain and implement legal aspects in your organisation.

Most organisations issue their policies and procedures in the form of a staff handbook. The policies and procedures cover:

- ✔ Consultation and negotiating
- ✔ Discipline and dismissal
- ✔ Health and safety, and sickness and absence management
- ✔ Pay, rewards and negotiation of pay raises
- ✔ Performance management and appraisal
- ✔ Recruitment, selection and promotion
- ✔ Redundancies and layoffs
- ✔ Working patterns and practices

Policies and processes carry the force of law. In other words, if you get sued by an employee or former employee, you have to be able to show that you followed your own policies and procedures. Failing that, you have to have good reasons for not following them.

Your policies and procedures must provide for the following:

- ✔ **Equality:** The company must treat every employee equally and fairly, regardless of gender, ethnicity, religious background, disability, membership of a trade union (or refusal to join a trade union) or location of origin.
- ✔ **Payment of wages and salaries:** You should typically issue wages and salaries monthly, sometimes bi-monthly, or weekly. Wages and salaries must conform to minimum-wage payment regulations.

✔ **Health and safety:** You must guarantee health and safety for all your employees. If some occupations need specialist training or equipment, you have to provide it.

✔ **Right to redress:** If you somehow wrong an employee, you have to put things right.

The policies and procedures apply to everyone in the workplace, regardless of occupation, length of service, location of work or hours worked.

Handling Conflict in the Workplace

Conflict is part of being human, which means that that conflict is part of any workplace as well. Your organisation should have a plan for managing and resolving conflicts when they occur – instead of waiting for a conflict to arise and then asking, 'Now what?' If you don't address problems quickly and effectively, they can only get worse.

Preparing for conflict means knowing the likely and possible sources of conflict:

✔ Giving certain people the 'worst' jobs to do at the expense of others

✔ Interpersonal and inter-group relations

✔ Over-burdening certain people with work, and under-burdening others

✔ Power struggles between powerful individuals and groups

✔ Relationships between different departments

✔ Relationships between different professions and occupations

✔ Resource struggles between different departments

You have two basic approaches to deal with conflict when it arises:

✔ Get everyone to agree that, regardless of the problem, they have to operate professionally and cooperate with one another while at work.

✔ Use discipline and grievance procedures to resolve conflicts formally.

Whatever approach you use (you may start by trying the former approach and then have to turn to the latter if the conflict isn't resolved), follow up to make sure that the conflict continues to be resolved.

Getting Employees Involved in the Organisation

When you build a positive, active and cohesive bond between the business and the staff, the result is participation. If people are actively involved in the company – they don't just turn up to work and go through the motions – they're much more likely to:

- Increase their productivity

- Raise problems and issues early

- Take an active interest in the company's future

- Take less time off work

- Work harder and smarter

So how do you get people to actively participate? You need to foster the attitude that 'we're all in it together'. Everyone at the company – from the top managers to the frontline and administrative staff, the security guards, the catering service and cleaning staff – has to feel like they're part of the team. They need to recognise that their own future well-being is tied up in the enduring viability and profitability of the company.

If you want genuine participation and involvement, you have to create the conditions in which they're possible:

- Treat people equally and with respect.

- Value the contribution of everyone, whatever people's jobs may be.

- Commit to training and development and providing opportunities for everyone, limited only by people's capabilities.

- Create a system of employee relations in which anyone can raise any issue at any time and get resolution quickly and completely.

Also think about *empowerment:* giving employees the maximum possible latitude in order to carry out their jobs to build effective and enduring employee relations. Depending on the individual and the nature of the work, empowerment may be simply about delegating tasks and authority, or it may require training and development. Either way, empowerment builds a much greater identity between company and employees. The more you empower your employees, the greater the contribution your employees can make, and the greater the potential for their own development becomes apparent.

Participation breeds success at Semco

Semco is a Brazilian manufacturing, engineering and Internet services company. Over the past 20 years, it has grown every venture that it has pursued, and it remains one of the most profitable companies in South America.

Semco has achieved its success through a strategic and fully integrated approach to participative management. Here's what Ricardo Semler, the company's chief executive and managing director, has to say:

> 'When I took over Semco from my father, it was a traditional company in every respect. With a pyramid structure and a rule for every contingency. Today, our factory workers set their own production quotas and come in their own time to meet them without prodding from management or overtime pay. They help redesign the products, they make and formulate the marketing plans. Their bosses for their part can run our business units with extraordinary freedom, determining business strategy from the top brass. They set their own salaries with no strings. Then again, everyone will know what the salaries are since all financial information is open, and openly discussed. Everyone has unlimited access to our books.

> We don't have clerical staff. Everyone at Semco fetches guests, stands over photocopiers, sends faxes and emails, and uses the phone. We have stripped away all the unnecessary perks and privileges that feed the ego but hurt the balance sheet, and distract everyone from the crucial corporate tasks of making, selling, invoicing, and collecting.

> We have done this through fully participative management as above. We are not the only company to do this. In so many other places however, it has just become a fad and hot air.

> For us, the rewards have already been substantial. We have taken a company that was moribund and made it thrive chiefly by refusing to squander our greatest resource, our people. Semco has grown six-fold despite withering recessions, staggering inflation, and chaotic national economic policy. Productivity has risen seven-fold. Profits have risen five-fold. We have had periods of up to 14 months in which not one person has left us. We have a backlog of more than 2,000 job applications from people who state that they would take any job just to be at Semco.'

The lesson? Simple: Semco shows what can be done with effective employee relations and a commitment to full participation. It also shines a clear and guiding light for anyone who wants to tackle and improve their own employee relations.

REAL WORLD EXAMPLE

Let me feel your forehead: Managing employee sick days

Managing absence due to sickness is an enduring problem for most organisations. People need to have time off work if they aren't well. Employees also ring in sick if they fancy a day off or can't quite be bothered to go in.

Here are a few statistics:

- If an employee has a 220-day working year, and he takes 2 days off sick, this rate of absence is more or less 1 per cent sickness absence.

- A company or organisation that has a sickness absence rate of 10 per cent is having to exist with every member of staff off sick, on average, for 22 days per year.

- For every percentage point of sickness absence, you're employing an additional member of staff. For example, a 1 per cent sickness absence rate means that you're employing 101 people to do the work of 100.

Absence due to sickness is expensive and you must tackle it. Every time someone returns to work after a sickness absence, interview him. Make sure that he's feeling well now. Make sure too that no serious problems exist that you

need to be aware of. Conduct this interview every time for every person. Take notes on what the employee says.

Some companies are more proactive than others in this area. For example:

- Toshiba's recruitment literature states: 'If you are the sort of person that has a lot of time off work then you should think seriously before coming to work for us. We need and want you here. We need your expertise on the premises.'

- Whenever a member of staff takes a day off work from Sanyo, a member of the management team goes round to his house carrying a bunch of flowers or a box of chocolates. When the member of staff opens the door, the management team member states: 'Please accept this gift with the compliments of the company. We do hope it will not be long before you are back at work and fully recovered.'

Both of these approaches have resulted in the companies having a sickness absence rate that's negligible.

Disciplining and Dismissing Employees

An unfortunate part of running any organisation is having to discipline and, from time to time, dismiss employees. This part of the job isn't why you went into business, but you can't ignore it.

REMEMBER

Dismissal should *always* be the last resort. Before you get to the point of having to dismiss an employee, do whatever you can to help the employee get back on track and become a productive member of your team. In some cases, disciplining the employee through written or spoken warnings is enough of a wake-up call to get the employee back on track. In other cases, you may be able to transfer the employee to another job or to another department where he may be more productive.

In the following sections, I take a close look at how to discipline and dismiss employees.

Discipline: Wearing the proverbial dunce cap

Why should you discipline employees? Wouldn't everyone be happier if you simply left well enough alone? Not exactly – well enough is often not good enough! If employees aren't performing up to the standards you've agreed to, you must take action and not ignore the problem.

Understanding why you discipline

Here are the two key reasons for disciplining employees:

✔ **Misconduct:** Every organisation has policies and procedures that employees are supposed to follow. Failure to follow certain policies and procedures (for example, taking two reams of paper from the supply cabinet when you're supposed to take only one ream at a time) may have only a minor impact on the organisation. But other infractions, including the following, are particularly serious:

- Assault

- Bullying

- Discrimination

- Fraud

- Harassment, including sexual harassment

- Theft

- Vandalism

- Victimisation

- Violence

You have to tackle serious problems such as the above the moment they come to your attention. Failure to do so can lead to your being named as part of the problem on the grounds that you knew about a problem but did nothing.

✔ **Performance:** You expect every employee to achieve a certain level of performance. Whether this level is producing 50 widgets an hour, selling $50,000 worth of products a month or answering the telephone before the third ring 90 per cent of the time, every job has minimum standards. An employee falling below these minimum standards repeatedly or for a prolonged period of time usually triggers the disciplinary process.

Knowing how to discipline

The term *discipline* applies to a wide range of activities meant to provide feedback to employees about deficiencies in their conduct or performance. Employers generally provide such feedback in the hopes that employees decide to change their behaviour so that a supervisor or manager doesn't need to take further action. The most commonly accepted discipline in use today is called *progressive discipline*, in which feedback becomes progressively more serious for repeated or major performance lapses or cases of misconduct.

All organisations must have disciplinary procedures, and these procedures must meet the minimum standards laid down by the Advisory, Conciliation and Arbitration Service (ACAS; www.acas.org.uk). Disciplinary procedures must:

✔ Be in writing

✔ Specify to whom they apply

✔ Be freely available to all staff

✔ State the conditions under which the company applies them

✔ Specify the penalties for serious and gross misconduct, and give examples of each

✔ Include a series of warnings (you give an employee at least two warnings before contemplating dismissal; many organisations allow for three warnings)

✔ Give the employee a chance to explain their conduct and/or performance

✔ Allow for employees facing discipline to be represented and/or accompanied by counsel

✔ Include provision for appeal at each stage

Of course, you hope it never comes to this situation – and in the vast majority of cases, a quick word in the employee's ear is enough to ensure that he remedies unacceptable behaviour or performance. However, when you do need to apply a disciplinary procedure, you must record the whole process. If you issue warnings to employees, retain a copy on file; such warnings must state what the disciplinary matter was, how the employee must remedy the issue and by when, and how long the warning is to remain in the individual's file before deletion. Review matters when the particular deadline arrives.

Where the case is complex, or where an individual is facing serious allegations, the employee is suspended from work – normally on full pay. The individual is innocent until proven or demonstrated guilty. When an employee is suspended, use the period of suspension to carry out a full and thorough investigation as quickly as possible so that the matter doesn't drag out. Then have the individual come in with his representative, tell the individual the case against him and ask for his explanation.

Treat all employees equally when facing the same or similar offences or issues, regardless of occupation, status, length of service or hours of work. Doing otherwise is unfair and illegal. The only exception is one in which a new employee is working a probationary period, but even in these cases you must give the employee the opportunity to state his case in advance of any decision to end employment after the probationary period finishes.

When disciplining employees – especially as the discipline escalates beyond a single warning – make sure that you notify both your own manager and the human resources department of the problem and the actions you're taking to solve it. Not only do they need to know what's going on, but they can also offer you their support and assistance throughout the process.

Dismissal: You're outta here!

Sometimes, no matter what you do to try to work with an employee or to help him achieve an acceptable standard, all your efforts fail. You may be left with no choice but to remove the employee from his job. Firing an employee is certainly the toughest job by far for any manager or supervisor – and one that no one looks forward to (with the exception, perhaps, of Donald Trump and Lord Sugar). The pain of dismissing an employee is felt not only by the employee but also by the entire organisation, especially by colleagues and the employee's supervisor or manager.

Defining grounds for dismissal

Dismissal occurs only after you give employees ample opportunities to improve their performance or behaviour and they fail to do so, or when an offence is so serious that it constitutes serious or gross misconduct and merits immediate or summary dismissal. Here are some examples of behaviour meriting summary dismissal when proven or demonstrated:

- ✔ Breaking confidentiality concerning the organisation and/or members of staff

- ✔ Bullying, victimising, discriminating or harassing other employees

- ✔ Committing fraud

- ✔ Committing vandalism or being violent

- ✔ Exhibiting *gross insubordination* (extreme bad, violent or abusive language toward superiors)

- ✔ Misrepresenting yourself on a job application

- ✔ Stealing from colleagues or from the organisation

- ✔ Using or selling illegal drugs at work

- ✔ Violating safety and security rules in an extreme way (for example, removing safety guards from production equipment or giving out security details for information systems)

You must allow employees facing such allegations to state their case and to respond to any allegations, to have representation and to appeal against any decision.

Taking the correct steps

Be sure that you follow all the proper procedures before you dismiss someone. Firing an employee is bound to unleash all kinds of hurt and resentment on the part of the dismissed employee and can even land you in court or a tribunal. The following criteria must be met before you dismiss an employee:

- ✔ **Documentation:** If you're planning to dismiss an employee for performance, have evidence (written proof) of any shortcomings. Documentation can be anything from a supervisor's written notes in a daily planner to time cards showing that an employee is habitually late, all the way up to falsified expense reports or other documents. When you make the decision as to what kind of documentation is most appropriate for a particular situation, ask yourself, 'Would the documentation convince a court or a tribunal that dismissing the employee was justified?'

- ✔ **Fair warning:** If you plan to dismiss an employee for performance shortcomings, be sure that you give the employee fair warning of the consequences of continued problems. Serious misconduct can be grounds for immediate dismissal and doesn't necessarily require advance warning – though you must still follow procedures when such a case arises.

- ✔ **Response time:** Give employees enough time to improve before firing them. You can reasonably expect an employee's performance to improve after a couple of weeks to a month.

✔ **Reasonableness:** Dismissal should be reasonable and appropriate for whatever offence led up to it. Firing an employee for being five minutes late to work once isn't reasonable. Firing an employee for being two hours late for several weeks or more – with no change in behaviour even after repeated oral and written warnings – is reasonable, provided you followed procedures and asked for an explanation.

✔ **Appeals:** All disciplinary and dismissal procedures must have an appeals process. When you make a particular decision, allow any appeal as quickly as possible so that the matter is resolved quickly and effectively. The appeals process is in everyone's best interests.

Dismissing an employee is one of the most unpleasant tasks you have to do, and when you have to do it, you want to be effective and professional. Here are the steps to take when dismissing an employee:

1. **Meet with the employee and his representative in a private location.**

   Bring a co-worker (another manager or your supervisor) with you to observe the proceedings. Lay down an agenda and structure in advance.

2. **Tell the employee that you're dismissing him.**

   Be straightforward and direct.

3. **Explain why you're dismissing the individual.**

   Give the reasons in concise and precise terms. Provide a written explanation as well – the written version must line up exactly with anything you state orally.

4. **State the date of departure.**

   Be sure to pay the employee in full, and give him any necessary documentation (whatever you give any employee who leaves your organisation). In particular, notify HR, payroll and your own manager.

5. **Make any final arrangements.**

   Make sure that the employee knows the procedures for clearing his desk and for removing personal effects. If the employee wants to say goodbye to co-workers, allow for that. If he wants to have a reference from you, make sure that you agree the terms of such a reference beforehand.

Addressing Employee Grievances

Any employee may raise a *grievance* (a complaint against your organisation) at any time. They typically happen when an employee believes that he's being bullied, victimised, discriminated against, harassed, scapegoated or blamed for things he didn't do. Grievances are individual and collective matters of concern. When they're first raised, many grievances are actually little more than requests. They become true grievances only when managers and supervisors fail to address the requests and matters become more serious.

You must address grievances fairly and swiftly. When it comes to grievances, your organisation should have in place the following:

- The means for any employee to raise a grievance whenever he feels necessary

- An informal means of resolving grievances (for example, having a pre-meeting to establish whether the matter can be resolved without formalities)

- A formal means of resolving grievances (based on a hearing, whereby the employee states the grievance and produces evidence, and then the organisation issues a response)

- A means for appeal for all parties

- Allowance for everyone involved to have legal representation, if desired

- A written statement of the eventual outcome that's agreed and accepted by all parties

Handling grievances, especially serious ones, is uncomfortable for everyone involved. Because of this, many organisations choose to move the accused person away from the scene of his wrongdoing, instead of disciplining or dismissing the person. Sometimes moving the person away comes in the form a promotion – anything to get the person out of that environment. Moving the person away isn't only ethically wrong, but it encourages other people to behave in the same way (especially if a promotion is involved).

You're in the Union, Jack: Appreciating the Role and Function of Trade Unions

Trade unions were originally constituted as a way for people to bond together to ask for higher wages and better working conditions. They took their lead from guilds, professions and craft trades, in which members of these bodies were able to demand higher pay and prescribed working conditions by virtue of their expertise.

In the UK, trade unions have always carried a socialist identity and heritage. This situation isn't the same elsewhere in the world. For example, Italy has Christian and conservative unions. France has communist and conservative unions. Germany has 11 large and powerful unions, representing almost 40 million workers and job holders. And in the United States, unions act as non-political and highly organised lobbies, campaigning for investment in industry, public services and infrastructure, as well as employee rights.

Whatever the approach and orientation, unions today provide a range of benefits to their members:

- ✔ General representation in collective and individual matters

- ✔ Health and social care plans and policies

- ✔ Legal services and court and tribunal representation

- ✔ Support for collective and individual disputes, grievances and other employment issues such as layoffs and redundancies

- ✔ Training and development

In the UK, trade unions chiefly work to support individual cases taken out against people's employers through employment tribunals and the court systems.

Companies and organisations have different approaches to trade unions. For example:

- ✔ The Body Shop has never wanted trade unions on the premises, so it removed any reason any employee would want to join a trade union in the first place. In other words, it made the working conditions and pay good enough that employees didn't feel the need to unionise.

- ✔ Sony took the view that by recognising a single trade union, it simplified the formal systems of employee relations. It also ensured that the trade union acted as a monitor of the company's own high standards of employee relations.

- ✔ London Regional Transport recognises 11 different trade unions, taking the view that different categories of staff require different representation.

Whatever your preferred approach, if more than 30 per cent of your staff want to join a trade union, you must accept that they do and recognise the union. You then need to agree with your staff on the extent to which the union can have influence. You have to decide whether the union represents the staff on all employee relations matters or is recognised only for a limited range of activities (for example, maybe you consult the union on pay and working hours but not other benefits, such as cars and healthcare).

In times of disputes, grievance or disciplinary issues, you must allow employees to have union representation.

Consulting and Negotiating with Your Staff

Most organisations consult and negotiate issues with their staff because doing so makes solid business sense. Regular and substantial consultation means fuller participation and involvement. Employees come to understand the business, its strengths and weaknesses, and the opportunities and threats that face it. They understand the company's finances. They gain proper knowledge of product and service performance, and of the company position overall. All this consultation helps to drive the business forward and enables you to identify problems and issues early, and you foster mutual understanding and respect with staff.

When it comes to negotiating, you must:

- ✔ Clearly state the substance of the matter under negotiation
- ✔ Establish the process for the negotiation
- ✔ Have the authority to make and deliver the agreement
- ✔ Cover every detail
- ✔ Have the resources to deliver and implement the agreement

Decide in advance whether what you're arriving at is:

- ✔ **Distributive:** You're going to settle one issue at the expense of others.
- ✔ **Integrative:** You're going to settle everything to the satisfaction of everyone involved.

The value of negotiation

Any organisation has room for negotiation.

Imagine that you're a staff representative, and you've just asked for a 30 per cent pay rise and an extra five days of holiday a year. The company has said yes! Are you really happy? Or do you come away thinking you should have asked for more?

Now imagine that you're the managing director. You've offered a 1 per cent pay raise, phased in over three years, and you want people to give up two days of holiday per year. The employees have said yes! Again, are you happy? Or could you have forced further additional burdens?

The lesson is that you never accept the first position – you always enter negotiations to agree the best possible results for all.

Also, are you going to use the process to try to influence attitudes for the future, or will it be a stand-alone activity?

Flex Those Muscles! Flexible Working Conditions

In today's working environment, all organisations have to be prepared to accept and offer flexible working practices. Here's why:

- Companies need work 'when it's required', not just Monday through Friday from 9 a.m. to 5 p.m.

- Technology means that people can work wherever – they don't have to come to the office to get work done.

- In the UK, there is a legal requirement to offer flexible working to parents of dependent children. It is likely that this provision will be extended to everyone with any dependents, for example, elderly parents and relatives, a spouse who is ill.

- Flexible approaches mean that people can fit other commitments around their work responsibilities without loss of effectiveness or performance.

Of course, flexible and non-standard patterns of work aren't new. Energy, transport, distribution, telecommunications and healthcare, among other industries, have always depended on non-standard patterns of work. In these industries and many others, people are used to night and weekend working. Flexible work approaches simply ensure that non-standard patterns of work are open to many others.

You need to manage those working flexible and non-standard patterns, or work in remote locations. Ensure that you:

- Include flexible arrangements and on-standard patterns of work in as many organisational activities as possible.

- Revisit the policies for flexible and non-standard work patterns as regularly as possible.

- Open up opportunities for progression and advancement to everyone, including those on flexible and non-standard patterns of work or working in remote locations.

Following the Letter of the Law

Business must comply with a huge range of UK and EU laws in terms of employment practice.

Be closely familiar with the key employment laws that affect the way you run or manage your business. If you don't comply with the law on any matter to do with employment, you can be prosecuted, taken to tribunal or have to answer to the offices of ACAS. Larger organisations have human resources departments and experts to deal with these matters; however, that's no excuse for ignorance on the part of other managers and supervisors. You must know what you can and can't do, and make sure that others stick within these boundaries too.

The following areas are of particular importance:

- **Equal pay:** Everyone has the right to receive the same pay and other terms of employment, regardless of gender, ethnic origin, disability or age, when working on the same or similar work or carrying out equivalent work of equal value.

- **Minimum wages:** The government lays down minimum levels of pay and reviews them every year. Employees must receive at least the minimum wage, regardless of occupation, status, length of service or hours worked. Specific provisions exist for those who are 16 to 18 years old.

- **Discrimination:** You mustn't discriminate against anyone on the grounds of sex, race or ethnicity, religion, membership in a trade union (or refusal to join a trade union), age or registered disability. It's also illegal to discriminate against people on the grounds of spent convictions for offences previously committed (although many exceptions exist, and you should deal with each case on its merits).

Employers who face allegations of discrimination normally have to answer the case in full and prove that they didn't discriminate. So make sure that your employment practices preclude the possibility of these kind of allegations happening under any circumstances.

- **Trade union membership:** Anyone may belong to the trade union of his choice, or refuse to belong to a trade union at all. However, organisations and employers can state clearly the particular trade unions that they recognise and under which conditions and limitations. Some employers take the view that recognising trade unions makes for simplified and effective employee relations; others take the opposite view. Whichever view your organisation takes, it should be an active management decision. Especially when you *don't* recognise trade unions, managers should remove all the reasons employees would want to join a trade union. (Refer to 'You're in the Union, Jack: Appreciating the Role and Function of Trade Unions', earlier in this chapter, for more information.)

✔ **Transfers of undertakings:** If your business is bought, sold or acquired, or if it changes its status or activities, all those employed must be transferred to the new ownership or directorate on their existing terms of employment. In particular, you may not conduct redundancies and lay-offs with a view to making one part of your business more attractive to potential buyers or acquirers.

✔ **Redundancy:** Redundancies occur when employees have no work to carry out. Redundancy procedures must be in place, and these procedures must show who's at risk of redundancy and the circumstances in which the organisation conducts redundancies. The guiding principle is 'last in, first out' – and if you don't want to follow this principle, you must produce alternative criteria that are equally fair.

✔ **Working hours:** You can't ask an employee to work more than 48 hours a week, except with his actively expressed consent. If someone refuses to work more than 48 hours a week, he may not be victimised or discriminated against on any grounds whatsoever.

✔ **Right to consultation:** The EU Acquired Rights Directive states that a company must consult and inform employees of any business decision that actively affects their future. All organisations with 500 employees or more must have a forum for consultation; all organisations with 1,000 employees or more must have a European Works Council at which employee representatives may raise any matter at all for debate and discussion. In particular, a company must consult all employees on

- Changes in technology usage

- Changes in working hours

- Changes in working times and practices

- Material changes in occupation

- The possibility or threat of redundancies

All these situations may arise as the result of legitimate and essential business decisions; nevertheless, you must consult employees.

✔ **Pregnancy and maternity:** All employees who are pregnant must have full statutory rights to attend medical institutions in any matter regarding their pregnancy, regardless of length of service or hours worked. Employees who give birth within one year of commencement of employment get maternity leave of six months; maternity leave is extended up to one year after 52 weeks or more of continuous service. The father may also take paternity leave of up to four weeks at any time during the first year of a child's life.

✔ **Contracts of employment:** All employees must receive contracts that state the main conditions under which they are to work. Where a company doesn't issue a contract, a contract *de facto* is deemed to exist after 13 weeks of continuous employment. Contracts specify:

- Duties carried out
- Hours worked
- Wages and salary
- Other benefits, including, for example, healthcare, bonuses, expenses, company cars and season ticket loans
- The boundaries of discipline
- The conditions under which the management may change the contract (for example, pay rises)

This list is by no means comprehensive, nor is it an in-depth guide to employment law. It does give the main areas of concern, however – those that all managers should be clear on. Additional guidance is available on each area from ACAS, and employer associations and trade federations are excellent sources of information. Many large organisations have expert employee relations departments, including legal experts; most smaller organisations have an employment lawyer available at the end of the phone.

European Union employment law

EU employment law is broadly superior to that of the UK; any case that goes through the UK tribunal and court system and reaches the European Court of Justice will be judged by European standards as the final conclusion to the matter in hand. The particular priority of EU employment law is strengthening and upholding individual and collective rights in all aspects of life – including employment. Here are the main areas of concern:

✔ Adequate and continual vocational training

✔ Equal treatment for everyone regardless of gender, race, ethnic origin or nationality

✔ Freedom of association, especially the right to join (or not join) trade unions and associations

✔ Freedom of movement for workers and self-employed persons across the European Union

✔ Improving health and safety at work

✔ Information, consultation and participation for employees on all major workplace issues

✔ Protection of employment and remuneration

✔ Specific protection for stated groups of employees, especially children and young people, the elderly and people with disabilities

The general principle is that UK legislation reflects the demands of EU law and standards. Note that those who judge a case that reaches the European Court of Justice are duty-bound to take a European perspective.

Part VI
Putting It All Together

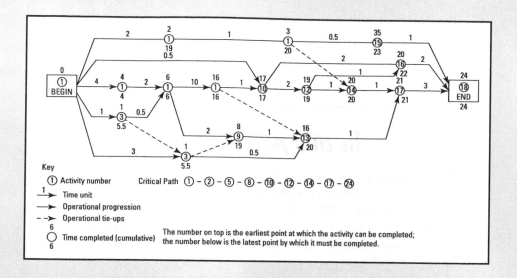

In this part . . .

✔ Gain an overview of absolutely everything that goes on inside a business, company or organisation and ensure that you run yours as smoothly as possible.

✔ Explore the nature of production and service delivery and prepare yourself and your business for the demands associated with this.

✔ Fine-tune your project management skills by identifying projects and examining the most effective ways of implementing them.

✔ Consider the critical contribution that technology makes to business and find out how you can utilize technology to ensure enduring viability and profitability for your business.

Chapter 18

Examining Operations

In This Chapter

▶ Understanding the nature of production and service operations

▶ Ensuring integration in operations

▶ Determining the scales of production and service delivery you can support

▶ Assuring the quality of products and services

▶ Creating the conditions in which effective operations can take place

▶ Seeking opportunities for growth and diversification

*O*perations are the steady-state activities of business – the things you do day in and day out. They comprise the following:

✔ Primary production and service functions – the production, delivery, selling and invoicing of what you're in business to do

✔ Customer service functions, including after-sales and maintenance

✔ Support functions, including managing the supply side, administration, finance, HR, security and catering

✔ Directional functions, relating to how the company or organisation is run and managed

Whatever the balance of these functions, you have to pay for all customer service, support and directional functions out of the sales of your products and services. So as you structure your operations, make sure that you can afford them.

In this chapter, I cover the main areas you need to be aware of when studying and evaluating production and service activities. I look at scales of production and service delivery, define the quality of operational activities necessary and explore the need for support functions, balancing their demands against the primary activities. I also fill you in on how to grow and develop your operations so that you manage and optimise the return on your capital, your expertise and your success to date.

Identifying the Nature of Production and Service Activities

Production and service activities are what you're in business for. You need to gear up everything about your organisation – staff, technology, equipment and processes – to ensure that you get the best possible product and service delivery volumes from your organisation.

Like every other part of business, operations is a process. Operations depend on continuous integration of marketing, sales, new product and service development, finance and investment. As marketing and sales drive up demands for products and services, you ensure the efficiency of everything you do. As you produce the products and services, you're depending on marketing and sales to attract customers to pay the prices that ensure that you do, indeed, remain profitable.

Go jump in the Lake(r)

For many years, Laker Ltd was a profitable travel company. Its core products were sales of package holidays, car hires and air, sea and rail tickets. Frustrated by the prices that airlines were demanding for ticket sales and by reduced commissions, Freddie Laker, the company's chief executive, decided to open his own airline.

This move seemed logical. After all, Laker would now be selling its own tickets, as well as those of other airlines. Laker would now be using its own planes, which meant that it had complete flexibility over how much to charge.

To gain an identity and attract customers, Laker launched a publicity campaign offering return tickets from Great Britain to the United States for £50. There was a rush to buy the tickets, but Laker quickly found that it couldn't satisfy the demand. The result: people were frustrated. Asked to wait for several weeks for a plane ticket, potential customers went back to using their previous airlines or abandoned their plans altogether.

Laker found that delivering and servicing the 'good idea' was expensive. Having bought the planes, the company now had to make repayments on them. The company had to pay for fuel, staff, landing slots and maintenance.

The position quickly became untenable. The company was forced to close. In the weeks before closure, Laker's credit ratings had been reduced to 'cash only', which meant that pilots were having to carry around many thousands of pounds to pay for fuel and landing slots each time they used them.

The lesson? Your operations have to be viable, sustainable and profitable. And if you develop your operations in ways that look rational or logical, test every part of your line of reasoning to destruction. In this case, Laker was overtly extending its core business. It moved away from what it knew – and at which it excelled – into something it knew nothing about (the airline industry).

Operational activities always relate to strategy, policy, direction and priorities to ensure that everything you produce contributes to the overall direction of the organisation.

Your organisation must be clear on the following:

- ✔ The core business on which you depend for your immediate and enduring viability and profitability

- ✔ The peripheral business, which provides additional useful streams of income but will never become part of the core business unless you can grow it alongside your existing mainstream activities

- ✔ Pioneering and prospecting work, in which you're constantly on the lookout for new markets and opportunities to grow alongside your core

You have to know the capabilities of your staff and the equipment and technology they use. You need to know how much productive activity you have to undertake to remain viable. You also need to know both the opportunities and consequences that your levels of activity bring with them.

Integrating the Efforts of Your Employees

All operations require staff. Except for one or two standardised production and service delivery processes, you integrate the staff so that their activities take place in harmony with each other. For example:

- ✔ The work of those engaged in the production of dolls integrates with that of those who produce the boxes and who operate the packing processes.

- ✔ The work of those engaged in travel updates integrates with that of the staff providing travel information.

- ✔ The work of those producing restaurant meals integrates with that of those buying the food and ingredients.

The combined effort is only as good as the integration. To do this, you need departmental and divisional managers who meet on a regular basis to ensure that all of their efforts are coordinated. These managers additionally need excellent communications between them all, so that each and every problem is raised and addressed as early as possible.

It's also important for these managers to be expert and effective in harmonising the work of their own departments and divisions. No matter how expert the staff who work in their own particular fields are, effective operations require harmonisation if their efforts are to be enduringly effective.

If you don't harmonise your employees' efforts, the following may occur:

- **People do an excellent job individually, but the organisation suffers.** This problem was one of the main triggers of the banking crisis in 2008. Commodities traders working in the banks did record volumes of business and received large bonuses for doing so without knowing whether the banks could support their activities and trades. When it turned out that the banks could *not* support these activities, you had, in practice, excellent staff producing excellent work . . . but at the same time destroying their organisations.

- **People start to cut corners.** If industrial production is driven purely and narrowly by volume output, those involved start to reduce or cut out downtime and maintenance schedules. In the short term, production goes up. In the long term, when machines do break down, they require more extensive servicing than would otherwise have been the case.

- **Call centre work that's driven purely by call volume leads to an increase in customer complaints if each call centre worker doesn't adequately or comprehensively address each enquiry.** At the same time as meeting their volume demands, the call centre staff are increasing volumes of work for customer complaints staff.

- **Sales staff operating in isolation from their colleagues become tempted to promise offers, discounts and advantages that the company can't or won't deliver.** Sales staff make these kind of promises to meet and, if possible, exceed their targets. By the time the customer takes delivery of the product or service, the salesperson is long gone. Other parts of the organisation now have to clean up the mess.

The greater your ability to integrate, the greater your chance of developing:

- A positive, strong and inclusive culture

- Collective cohesion

- Mutual understanding and respect across the organisation

- Teamwork and inter-occupational and inter-departmental harmony

This, in turn, makes the organisation a happier and more productive place to work. Then you can begin to improve your overall organisational and staff effort. When people in your organisation understand what everyone else does, they see any training that they receive not just in terms of enhancing their own knowledge and expertise, but also in its widest possible context. And that can only benefit the organisation.

Considering the Scales of Production and Service Delivery

This section helps you get to know the scales of production and service delivery that your organisation can support.

Classifying production and service delivery

Scales of production and service delivery are classified as follows:

- ✔ **Jobbing or unit production:** The manufacture of single, unique or specialist items. In many cases, a company makes and delivers each of these items to order. People who are specialists or experts in the particular field carry out a lot of unit production. In many cases, small organisations and sole traders are the ones who carry out unit production. However, many larger organisations also operate small specialist functions to produce unique goods and services.

- ✔ **Mass production:** The manufacture of identical items on a grand scale. Mass production techniques and activities require investment in technology and skilled and semi-skilled staff in order to become and remain effective. Companies use mass production to produce high volumes of standard quality products and services. Traditionally, mass production has been the cornerstone of all consumer goods. The principles of mass production apply to the output of consumer services too (for example, holidays, travel and transport, and banking and financial services).

- ✔ **Batch production:** The manufacture of medium volumes of products and services. Batch production activities are often labour and resource (especially technology) intensive. Batch production activities consist of short-term runs of high-volume products and services. For effective batch production, you need technology and expertise, which:

  - Has specific capabilities

  - Can be re-jigged according to the nature of the batch demanded

  - Is fully flexible in its operation

Drug and pharmaceutical manufacturers use batch production as standard. Batch production is also common in the package holiday sector, where travel companies buy up volumes of hotel rooms, airline seats and other facilities in advance and combine them into distinctive 'batches' to sell to the public.

✔ **Flow production:** The manufacture of products in a continuous flow. Flow production is capital intensive and demands the employment of highly qualified experts to ensure that it works to its maximum capacity. Flow production is traditionally applied to oil, petrol, chemicals, plastics, steel and paper manufacturing. In each of these cases, the output is produced in a continuous flow.

Seeing how technology helps

Technology has brought additional features to the production and service delivery process. The process can now customise jobbing, batch and mass production much more easily and quickly, which means, for example:

✔ Individual wedding dresses are made by haute couturiers to the highest specifications, but they can make a dress quickly . . . for a price (jobbing or unit production). Such high-end clothiers can agree to precise specifications, timescales and quality targets for the delivery of their products and services.

✔ Those who are engaged in the production of seasonal goods (mass and batch production) can gear up much more quickly when it becomes apparent that demand will increase.

✔ Those who sell tickets and holidays online (mass and batch service delivery) can offer mass reductions to generate demand. The Internet is a much more immediate way of generating these activities and sales than putting up posters in travel agents' windows.

✔ Those who want their clothing to have a more distinctive appearance can order it and have it tailored to their own requirements. Levi Strauss offers fully customised jeans and shirts (batch production). LightInTheBox offers made-to-measure wedding and formal clothing tailored to individual shapes and sizes (batch production).

✔ Primark and Matalan are able to offer shorter runs of their clothes if, for example, a particular colour or design suddenly becomes fashionable (mass production).

✔ Car companies are now able to offer limited editions of particular models with high-value features without breaking into the continuous production line activities (mass production). They set aside a particular timeframe to produce the limited edition, and after they produce them, the production line returns to normal.

> ## Stemming the flow in commercial and public services
>
> The delivery of commercial and public services uses a form of flow production – for example, banking, where the maintenance of individual accounts, mortgages and other financial products is a continuous process, and health services, where hospitals see a constant flow of patients at hospitals, each of whom needs treating according to her illness, injury or symptoms.
>
> Problems arise with 'flow' in commercial and public services when you try to modify one part of the process.
>
> One retail bank went through a process of closing branches based purely on the average volume of money held in current accounts. Then it wondered why a more fundamental decline in business volumes occurred. The bank failed to consider the knock-on effect of asking people to take their continuous volumes of business elsewhere.
>
> A National Health Service (NHS) trust 'managed' the cost-effectiveness of its ward operations by the single criteria of frequency of bed usage. Any wards that fell below a certain frequency were simply closed down. Both the hospital and the trust then faced increased numbers of patients for whom they couldn't provide a full service, which led to additional expenses because they had to provide transport for urgent patients and those with serious injuries to move them elsewhere upon demand.

Flow production technology is normally expensive, requiring expert staff to operate and maintain it. When the opportunity arises to produce new chemicals, oil and plastic products, you have a clear decision: whether to use the technology you already have (in which case you need to shut down, clean, reset and restart it) or commission a new flow production facility (which is certain to be expensive upfront, and which requires that you hire more expert and expensive staff).

Technology means that companies can achieve all scales of production and service delivery to a much greater standard of quality, conformity and assurance. Whatever the scale of production, you're entitled to expect quicker work and higher volumes.

Making Quality Your Top Priority

All operations need quality assurance and standards – for example, your finance department needs to be quick and accurate. And, of course, the products and services that you make and sell must have clear quality assurance.

Analysing blockages

Your operations form the basis of the overall reputation of the organisation and the confidence held by customers, as well as the organisation's enduring viability and profitability. All activities within the company exist to enhance the actual and perceived quality and value that you deliver.

In addition to high-quality production and service delivery technology, everything else must be right. You need good and highly motivated staff to deliver the products and services. You need good and highly motivated staff also in everything else that you do – HR, finance, administration, sales and after-sales, maintenance and IT.

Any flaw or gap detracts from your organisation as a whole. If you spot an area where the organisation is underperforming, you must remedy the situation. Sometimes, you can do so by attending to a member of staff who isn't clear on her responsibilities. On other occasions, the gap is symptomatic of a deeper problem – for example, obsolete technology, lack of training, computer glitches, under-paying your staff or the inability to attract or retain good people.

One way of looking at underperformance is to carry out a blockage or obstacle analysis. Blockages occur

✔ Because the organisation progresses overall at the speed of its lowest operation

✔ When people aren't given proper training in the use of IT or production technology and methods

✔ When people are resisting change – for example, when they don't like changes in work patterns, tasks or new working hours

You need to tackle blockages and obstacles if you can. Otherwise, you have to be prepared for holdups until you can find other ways around the blockage.

Whenever you're examining blockages and obstacles, do so without preconceptions. For example, if 'everyone says' that something is going wrong, do a full investigation, which doesn't have to take long. If you investigate without prejudging the issue, you come to your own *informed* judgement.

When it comes to assuring quality, you can take one or more of several approaches:

✔ Establish a quality assurance department.

✔ Sample products as they come off the production line.

✔ Perform service walk-throughs (go through the process as a customer and see how everything is working).

✔ Use anonymous customers (mystery shoppers) to report back to you on how they viewed what you're offering.

✔ Respond to customer complaints.

Whichever approach you use (and you may use them all), you need service standards and service-level agreements. You must remedy the fault, problem or complaint within a certain period of time.

Always set the service standards from the customer's point of view. Use as the basis the speed and remedy you'd want if you'd found the fault or were making the complaint.

Many companies and organisations offer 'no quibble guarantees' and returns policies. On the face of it, these policies can appear expensive and cumbersome. However, if these policies did *not* exist, the companies would quickly lose their reputations for top-quality service. And the loss of reputation would cause customers to go elsewhere.

In the following sections, I cover three key aspects of quality assurance that are essential if you're to deliver products and services of the highest order: uniformity, differentiation, and access and convenience.

Quality assurance and consequences

The key competitive position for car manufacturers is reliability. If your mass market models come to be known as unreliable, customers have plenty of options elsewhere.

For the past 30 years, since Japanese manufacturers first gained a reputation for producing good-value, reliable cars, every other car company has had to address this issue. Companies have made improvements all around. They now offer service, exchange and replacement plans as part of the overall purchase. Most offer courtesy cars if your vehicle is off the road for any reason. At the manufacturer's end, technology drives every component and assembly. Today, technology is far more accurate and exact than was possible when everything was done by hand. In the event of customer complaints, manufacturers log every issue and use this data to make improvements.

Nissan has done away with its customer complaint function altogether. Customers now refer their complaints directly to the factory and production crew that actually produced the car. The production crew have to answer the customer, address the issue and put the matter right.

At the core is the drive to satisfy ever-increasing customer demands for reliability and satisfaction. Failure to concentrate on these points and to address issues when they do become apparent is certain to mean loss of business.

Uniformity

Uniformity gives structure and order to all activities and operations. You need to standardise and make uniform as much as you possibly can. You create this uniformity from the point of view that:

- ✔ All employees need specific ways of working to give structure to their jobs.
- ✔ Organisations need to conduct every operation in ways that are more or less assured and predictable.

The goal is to form effective relationships and patterns of behaviour. You need these relationships and patterns of behaviour in order to create the basis for stable, effective and improving performance.

 Much of the time, resistance to change comes from radical alterations to working relations and behaviour. People who've become comfortable and effective in what's gone before find both their comfort and their effectiveness challenged. If you need to change behaviour and relations, always tell people why. They're much more likely to go along with you if you're not asking them to take a leap into the unknown.

Differentiation

Differentiation means giving people both a comprehensive structure for their work and also the opportunity to grow and develop themselves in terms of their own interests and also those of the organisation (flip to Chapter 17 for more on getting employees actively involved within the organisation). Differentiation means giving people:

- ✔ The chance to shine and to make a name for themselves
- ✔ A certain amount of freedom, trust and autonomy to produce and deliver their work as they see fit
- ✔ The space to develop their jobs and interests as far as possible

 You need structures to be able to get the work out as you need it, and also to ensure that people do grow and develop. Getting the balance right works in everyone's interests: you get the best out of your people, and they deliver the highest possible quality of work.

You have to structure and implement both steady-state and development activities. You offer or allocate development opportunities to people to give them the chance to demonstrate their potential. When you do this, you get from employees ever increasing volumes and quality of work in the majority of cases.

High and increasing levels of job and work satisfaction are key points of differentiation, setting some employees apart from others who just turn up and work. When structuring and implementing development activities, you need a clear view of what job satisfaction means to each person. Here are some examples:

- To progress as far as possible
- To achieve something every day
- To gain promotion
- To feed the family
- To turn up, do the job and then go home

All these examples are legitimate definitions of job satisfaction. So you have to recognise what is important to each member of staff, and tailor your efforts to developing people accordingly.

You still need to get high and increasing levels of performance from the person who just wants to turn up, work and go home – she's committed to work for you for a specified number of hours each week – but you also need to recognise and respect her goals. Get everything that you need from her during her working hours. Make clear the standards that you expect. In addition to getting the results of her hard work, you're likely to find that you begin to develop her identity and commitment to your organisation.

Access and convenience

In today's business world, access is no longer simply about being able to get into work. Technology means that people can access work at any time and do work when you need it done. You don't have to wait for the office to open. As soon as you need something, you can notify your people and they can get on with it. If you have operations and partners halfway around the world, you can be in contact with them at any time on any issue at all. If you need problems solving, you can get the expertise that you require; you don't have to use someone just because she lives near where you're located.

Physical locations of work have to become more flexible in their opening hours and in allowing access to staff. Staff now come to the workplace at nonstandard times. In addition to having specific appointments to call people elsewhere in the world, many people find that they can get much more done when they come into the office if they can come in early and/or stay late. And that's only good for business! (For more on flexible working, refer to Chapter 17.)

Greater access and convenience enhances the quality of:

✔ Work

✔ The working environment

✔ Your reputation for the speed and effectiveness of your operations

✔ The service that underpins the products and services that you deliver

When you up the expectations you place on your people for high-quality work, invariably they respond fully in meeting these expectations – and encouraging flexible working makes it easier for employees to achieve these goals.

Tackling Organisational Issues

Places of work have to be comfortable and convenient. If you need people to use technology, make sure that the technology is as convenient as possible and that the workstation itself is comfortable. If you need people to work on a computer for most of the day, make sure that the furniture is comfortable (and that you give the breaks that the law demands). If you need people to work in remote locations, make sure that the technology you give them is reliable.

Whatever the nature of your operations and the products and services delivered, you have to recognise some critical and key organisational issues. In the following sections, I cover these issues and give tips on how to address them.

Managing alienation

If you don't pay attention to your work environment, you cause alienation among your people. *Alienation* comprises the following:

✔ General rejection based on the lack of value placed by the organisation on the individual and reinforced where adversarial management and supervisory styles exist

✔ Isolation, which may be physical (if workstations are far apart from each other) or psychological (if staff form no affinity with the organisation and just turn up to do as little as possible in return for their salary)

✔ Lack of prospects or advancement, leading to feelings of being stuck in a rut and trapped

✔ Lack of empathy with the organisation and its work

> ✔ Low feelings of self-esteem and self-worth, arising from the lack of value placed on staff
>
> ✔ Meaninglessness, in which people come to see themselves as purely cogs in a machine or process
>
> ✔ Powerlessness, or the inability to influence work and work conditions through being given repetitive and low-skilled jobs all of the time with no prospects for advancement

Alienation is a major cause of people failing to stay in particular jobs and occupations. Alienation is therefore a major potential organisational issue. It is also potentially very expensive, if it means that you are having to constantly recruit new people.

Wherever you find alienation, begin to build relations with the staff that you think are affected. As you build these relations, find out the causes of alienation and do your best to address them by making the workplace the best possible quality that it can be.

Alienation was a major problem in traditional manufacturing activities. Companies and organisations used to try to compensate by offering high wages. However, good wages made work bearable, but not meaningful. So you need to pay attention to the quality of the working environment and the nature of the job, as well as wages and salaries.

Keeping control

Companies and organisations must have control mechanisms that are suitable for their purposes, whatever the nature of the work or size of the organisation.

You need to be clear about what you're controlling and why. Some things need the tightest of controls – for example, production and service delivery volumes and output. You may also set specific controls on particular activities as follows:

> ✔ Answering all emails within a certain period.
>
> ✔ Answering all customer complaints within a certain period.
>
> ✔ Addressing and remedying all production and service delivery faults within a certain period.

You then set additional controls according to your organisation and the nature of the work you do.

With controls, the key question is, 'Why?' You need to know why you're asking for particular reports, patterns of behaviour and workplace attendance. If you have sound operational reasons, go ahead. If you don't, you need to stop and ask why you're persisting with those particular controls.

You can also use review and evaluation schedules to maintain effective control over your activities. Timetable the schedules into the working hours, and use them in full to evaluate progress and see where problems exist.

Also, make sure that you meet with your staff on a regular basis and that they've the opportunity to raise issues and concerns. Use the performance appraisal processes that you have in place at your organisation to check on progress and ensure that your staff continue to work as you need them to. (For the lowdown on appraisals, head to Chapter 16.)

Use the management information systems that you have – the data and statistics on each aspect of your activities and operations – to see how things are running. Above all, you can see where variances are starting to occur, and when these variances do occur, you can take remedial action. (For more on data, go to Chapter 14.)

Considering location

As an organisational issue, location is vital because you have to:

- ✔ Supervise people who work non-standard hours or spend a long time away from the office.

- ✔ Provide the means to get into work and to get home from work for those who work non-standard hours.

- ✔ Schedule deliveries for times when suppliers can easily reach you. And if you have deliveries to make, you need to be able to send drivers out at times when they'll actually get there and not get snarled up in traffic.

Balancing efficiency and effectiveness

Peter Drucker, the management guru, said, 'Efficiency is doing things right; effectiveness is doing the right thing.' Clearly, both efficiency and effectiveness have their place. Normally, you choose the right thing to do first, and then do it as well as you can. You pay attention to priorities and deadlines, and are mindful of the resources that you'll be using. But you also need to judge whether you have to do the right thing, regardless of cost and resources, or whether you can do something to everyone's satisfaction at a lower cost. You judge each case on its own merits.

Managing non-standard patterns of work

Here are a few examples of the management of non-standard patterns of work:

✔ For night-shift staff working in city centre locations, Tesco extended people's shifts and paid them until 7 a.m. so that they could get home on public transport.

✔ Blue Lantern, the London west-end nightclub, regularly asked its staff to finish at 4 a.m. It contracted a taxi firm so that transport would always be provided for people finishing at this time.

✔ Airline cabin crew working for British Airways are accommodated at Hilton or Holiday Inn hotels when working on long-haul operations.

Each of these examples illustrates the need to commit yourself to supporting the patterns of work that you expect from your people. Each represents an additional expense – a fixed cost – that you need to find from the sales of products and services. To preach perfection, if you were working these hours, what sort of support would *you* need, want and expect? Would you rather work for a company that supported you like this, or one that left you to fend for yourself at all hours of the day or in different parts of the world?

To help maximise and optimise the balance of efficiency and effectiveness, you have at your disposal many IT systems. Companies such as SAS, SAP, Capgemini, Microsoft, Google and Oracle produce systems that are designed to help you manage every aspect of your organisation to maximum efficiency and effectiveness. Each provides:

✔ Business intelligence and market intelligence systems

✔ Financial systems

✔ Risk management systems

✔ Staffing and HR management and information systems

✔ Systems for the evaluation of collective and individual performance

Each also provides systems to help manage logistics, markets, and product and service performance. At the core of these approaches is the capability to store all the information that comes into and goes out of your organisation. You can then call up this information in the formats required, in answer to any question posed.

Each system is capable of development and enhancement as the business grows and diversifies. The systems also come with the promise of support from the companies that install them. That way, in return for a fixed and assured fee, you have a comprehensive body of knowledge at your disposal that you can use as you see fit.

Moving On Up: Growing and Diversifying

As your operations become more and more successful, you start to seek opportunities for growth and diversification. From an operational point of view, you've a choice of two main approaches:

- Seeking new outlets for your existing products and services
- Seeking new proposals for products and services that you can implement from within your existing organisation

You need to look carefully at every opportunity, evaluating whether each one is truly an opportunity or just an empty promise.

If you take this kind of careful approach, you may get a reputation for being dull and unadventurous. People love the excitement of going off into the unknown (especially if they're using someone else's money). If you resist, you can find yourself facing hostility.

To deal with this kind of response, always take a positive view. Say, 'Yes, this looks like a good idea. I'll go away and do some proper work on it,' rather than, 'We don't know a thing about this. We can't possibly do it.' The substance of your response is the same. However, where the latter response is negative, the former response is positive.

One very careful and very successful business leader said the following during a lecture that he gave on national TV:

'We leave as little as possible to chance. We never take unnecessary risks. Every new venture we have gone into has been the result of full and careful evaluation. If we succeed, we work out why we did so well. If we fail, we evaluate and learn the lessons.'

This most risk-averse of people? Richard Branson! If he can take this approach, so can you.

Growing and diversifying effectively means knowing the full capacity of your organisation without investing in new technology, equipment, premises and staff. Look at ways to improve productivity and output from every department, division and function. Evaluate where each section needs to make improvements.

Growing and diversifying always involves costs as well as benefits. Many of the costs are human – asking people to challenge the ways in which they've done things and to seek new and better approaches is always contentious. So you have to commit as much of your resources as necessary to managing whatever growth you are engaged in. You also need to reward people for doing things better, more quickly and in greater volumes – and this normally means increasing pay.

Beware of creating additional administration and control systems. Even when using existing resources, additional systems can decrease the overall cost-effectiveness of what you do. You find yourself having to employ additional support, as well as frontline production and service delivery staff, which means that your cost-effectiveness reduces, even though your business volumes rise.

During the initial phase of its expansion, Walmart grew from 19 stores to 790. During this period, the number of staff at the head office remained the same. When Walmart had grown to 9,000 stores, the head office staff was only three times the amount that it had been when it had 19 stores. This kind of control is the basis for sustainable operational growth.

Chapter 19

Delivering Great Projects

*W*hen you break down business into its components, what it really comes down to is projects. Project work takes place in all kinds of business activities. In this chapter, I explain what project work is – including the benefits and the downsides. Then I walk you through the lifecycle of a project. I cover the importance of deadlines, because any project has deadlines. And I offer tips for becoming a better project manager.

Considering the Nature of Project Work

Projects are one off pieces of work that deliver material and lasting change. Therefore, they have a clear beginning and end. They may be separate and isolated pieces of work, or they may be integrated with other project work that develops or transforms the organisation in its entirety, or in some of its parts.

Here I get you up to speed with what projects are and their typical organisation, and then I take a look at the pros and cons of project work.

Getting to grips with the basics

Project work can take the form of:

✔ **Individual projects:** These projects aren't directly tied to any other projects.

- ✔ **Programmes of projects:** A range of projects or sub-projects contributing to a much larger overall project, or to a much larger overall drive for change. Programmes of projects may also be used to drive changes across the entire organisation.

- ✔ **Portfolios of projects:** Individuals and teams find themselves working on many different initiatives as the core of their workload. Portfolios of projects are managed and directed on a strategic basis to ensure that resources are allocated and deployed to best advantage.

Organisations may also ask individuals and teams to work on projects as part of their own individual and collective development, as well as delivering beneficial changes for the organisation itself.

Employees may be engaged in projects part time or full time, on an individual or team basis:

- ✔ **Part time:** If a person is engaged part time, you can count on conflicting demands on his time, which may lead to the question of who pays for the particular staffing resource. You may also find that individuals who work on projects part time have conflicting demands placed on them by the different bosses for whom they're working.

  With part-time project teams, the complexities of different demands on time are multiplied because team members have their own regular work to handle, so organising suitable times for everyone in the team to collaborate on project activity can be difficult.

- ✔ **Full time:** The problem of supervision is less complex when dealing with full-time employees. However, the drawback is that the individuals concerned are always moving from project to project – they never see how their work turns out when it becomes fully operational.

  When large, complex, major issues arise, organisations create full-time project teams for the duration of the matter at hand. The advantage is that people get to commit themselves full time for the duration of the project and see it through to completion. The disadvantage is that they become semi-detached (or even detached altogether) from their normal departments, work and colleagues.

The largest and most complex of project teams constituted in these ways, and for these purposes, is the *task force*. Normally, when organisations create a task force, the purpose is to work on something that's of enduring pressing concern or to address a crisis.

Project work historically was mainly concerned with building, construction and civil, mechanical and electrical engineering work. Today, all these activities still take place and are delivered as projects. But now you also have space projects, design projects, refurbishment projects, computer and IT projects, publishing projects, strategic planning projects, political projects (driven by governments themselves or driven by their departments, divisions and functions), and vanity and prestige projects (in which organisations seek to deliver the largest, most comprehensive, most distinctive buildings, ships, airplanes, monuments or what have you).

With the advance of technology, much larger activities can take place, which has led to the formation of project-based companies whose speciality is the management of projects. Companies and organisations come together for the purposes of a particular project and create joint and multi-ventures. They establish their own management company for the duration, and then they disband after the project is complete. Project work also now means hiring specialists, consultants and experts in particular fields for the duration of a project or for a part of it.

With large project work, organisations find themselves having to commit far larger bodies of resources for a much longer period of time than they used to. And over long periods of time, circumstances and conditions change, which means that the project may no longer be suitable for its purpose, or it may no longer be cost-effective after completion. For example:

✔ In 1986, the UK government commissioned the 'Trident' nuclear submarine defence system as a key part of its military capability for the Cold War. By the time the project was delivered in 1996, the Cold War was over.

✔ The main reason the Channel Tunnel was completed was that it turned out to be cheaper to finish it than to abandon the project.

Recognising the benefits of project work

Several reasons exist to use project work within an organisation. Project work:

✔ **Changes the focus of the organisation.** After an organisation completes a project successfully, people start to see other possibilities. For example:

• As the result of building a successful out-of-town shopping centre in one place, people now see the possibilities of doing the same thing elsewhere. Designers, builders and engineers shift their focus to what appears to be a major and lucrative area of potential work.

- After setting up an online retail capability for one set of products or services, people think of others. For example, as the result of selling tickets online, all the major airlines now offer car hire, package holidays and hotel rooms – and they developed all these things following the original online ticketing project.

✔ **Is a vital part of staff and organisation development.** You give staff projects to carry out for their own development, as well as to provide change, information and fresh ideas. Employees who do project work begin to recognise their own capabilities and potential. They become expert and knowledgeable in their field. From the organisation's point of view, project work demonstrates the capabilities and potential of their staff, in addition to delivering the results of the project itself.

✔ **Helps to develop teamwork.** People coming together to work on specific issues become comfortable and effective with others. They develop their ability to work as part of a team, playing to their own strengths and those of others and further enhancing their knowledge of the organisation. Working in teams and groups drawn together from across the organisation for specific purposes enables them to take on a variety of different roles.

If you want to understand something quickly, construct a project team or task force. Charge that team or task force with reporting back with as much knowledge and understanding as they can deliver in a particular time period. If you require people to make recommendations for future actions, you've a full structure for a particular proposal in a short period of time, within stated resource constraints. Plus, you've developed individuals and the organisation.

You can't go home again: What projects change

All project work changes things. For example, building and construction projects change the environment and the facilities available to people. IT projects change the working environment and the ways in which organisations operate and conduct business. Civil engineering projects change road, rail and air links and facilities, and so they change the speed and volumes of transport deliveries and travel.

Design projects produce new structures and information.

After a project is completed, you can never go back to how things were if you don't like the finished project. After you've used resources on a project, you can't use them again. And after you've committed yourself to a project, you're committing yourself to doing it in full.

The business case for a project

If you throw resources at business issues, you are aiming to get a quick return. For projects, it is not so simple. You need to recognise the relationship between the resources that you allocate, and the returns that you are seeking. This is the foundation of the business case for a project.

You need to develop and reinforce in people the need to recognise the business case. The *business case* for any project or venture relates to what the organisation can do, and whether the project is worthwhile in commercial terms. So, for example:

✔ If you decide that you can build a 2,000-metre-high building, can you get a return on that investment? If so, how long will it take to get your money back? If not,

do you want to build it as a vanity project, hoping that people recognise how clever you are and so come to you with profitable propositions?

✔ If you double the capacity of your sports arena, are you able to sell twice the number of tickets? Or are you only able to sell twice the number of tickets at half the price (meaning that your revenues stay the same)? If you nevertheless double the number of people coming along, can you sell them anything else?

Organisations have to pay for project work, so you need to be clear on where the returns are going to come from and how long it will take to make them.

Ticking off the trade-offs of project work

All project work involves trade-offs. The key factors are:

✔ Time

✔ Cost

✔ Quality

✔ Safety and security

You're trying to balance these factors to achieve the results you desire. For example, you may have to sacrifice quality in order to complete the project quickly, or, if quality is the top priority, maybe you won't be able to finish the project as soon as you'd like. Similarly, maybe you have to decide between delivering the work on time but over budget (because you've had to commit extra resources to meet the deadline) or delivering it on budget but later than you hoped. Finally, you may not be able to deliver the quality you're striving for within the budget you have to work with – so you go over budget to hit that quality marker, or you lower your expectations in terms of quality in order to stay on budget.

Normally, you can't compromise on safety and security. For example, you can't have a building that's a little bit safe – the building is safe or it isn't. Likewise, you can't have an IT project that's a little bit insecure – the project is secure or it isn't. Safety and security relate to the work you do as well as to the final project. The construction site has to be safe to work on, and the building you construct must be safe for the people using it.

Project finance is a critical area for attention. Unless the work and resources are costed accurately, project finance becomes uncertain. This means that you get 'drift' in which costs rise. So the need to cost everything as accurately as possible in advance is a major area of project expertise. You need to cost everything required for the successful completion of the project. Anything that cannot be costed in advance must be noted and estimated as accurately as possible, using current costs as a guide if possible, or else using the best recent information available.

At each stage of the project, there is a cost implication. If the work is not carried out on time, or fully, or when required, this invariably means that the overall project costs rise.

The Circle of Life: Looking at the Project Lifecycle

Every project has a lifecycle – a beginning, a middle and an end. Think of the project lifecycle as a process. As you design and implement the project, sometimes you need to refer back to the original conception and design. You also look forward as the project unfolds to handing the finished work over to the client. You need to engage regularly with the client to ensure that the project work is in accordance with what the client asked for. If any problems or glitches arise, you address them and iron them out early.

The project lifecycle has three phases:

- Design and conception
- Building and delivery
- Use and value

I cover these phases in the following sections.

Phase 1: Design and conception

The first phase of a project is all about crystallising the idea – and the sooner you can do that, the better. In this phase, companies may produce models, mock-ups and computer-aided images to illustrate the idea. Then they show these ideas to interested parties, project experts and those who hold the purse strings.

Non-verbal communication is much stronger than simply using words to tell people things. If you've models and images to show, the message is much more powerful than just a verbal description.

Phase 2: Building and delivery

Getting the green light to go ahead with a project is hard. And life doesn't get any easier when it comes to building and delivering the project. This phase has a lot to do with timelines and milestones – you have to ensure that everyone involved delivers the project on schedule.

In between project milestones, you must keep an eye on the project's progress. You're looking in particular for issues that have cropped up that may keep you from meeting the deadline, may put you over budget or may cause the quality to suffer.

This phase may involve tough decisions:

✔ Should we put in additional resources (and increase the costs)?

✔ Should we miss the deadline? Can we make up the time down the road?

✔ Should we rethink our goals when it comes to quality, making a few compromises that may be noticeable to us but not to the end users?

Going for gold: Olympic parks

Cities around the world compete vigorously for the chance to host the Olympic Games. Design and conception have been critical features in the awarding of every Olympic Games since 1984. The winning and losing bids alike have produced excellent designs and presentations. They've used every means at their disposal, including videos, computer-aided design and computer-generated images, site visits and celebrity endorsements. They've delivered full presentations of the Olympic projects in their context and environment. They've given a sense of the overall ambience they envisage for the finished facilities. They've generated images of smiling, happy people as they make their way to the Olympic events. And as a result, the winning cities have generated work worth a tremendous amount of money — billions of pounds (or dollars).

The lesson: in today's competitive environment, with companies and organisations competing ever more ferociously for work, any advantage that you can give yourself at the design and conception stage only delivers additional value to your organisation.

Working with the client

For all but the smallest projects, you need a way to interact with your client. The relationship between yourself and the people you're working for has to stay strong throughout the duration of the project. You need to ensure that you have:

✔ A series of regular formal meetings to check on the project's progress officially

✔ Continuous informal contact between representatives of the project and the client

✔ A way for people to raise concerns and discuss problems as soon as they become apparent

Before the project gets started, you need to make sure that you're on the same page when it comes to time, cost and quality, as well as safety and security, and you create a written statement of the formalities you have completed at the handover stage.

For large or long-term projects, you have to formally constitute client liaison because, over the duration, individuals from your organisation and your client's organisation are likely to move or change jobs. New people come into the picture, and they have to be able to pick up the brief and know what's going on immediately.

For small or short-term projects, you don't have to be quite so formal. Still, even if you're only doing a three-week project for your boss, you should meet at least once or twice. At the least, you need to meet just before you deliver the work, if only to make sure that you haven't forgotten something.

Phase 3: Use and value

Ideally, everyone involved (and especially the client) approved the use and value of the project in the design phase. However, the real use and value only become apparent when you complete the work and hand it over.

You need to formalise the completion and handover. For large projects, everything must meet contractual terms. At handover, the client and those who delivered the work note each point formally and sign it off. Then the project team or manager writes a short statement agreeing to the handover and close-out of the project. The client takes delivery of the project and puts the finished work to the uses for which it was produced.

After the handover and closeout, your relationship with the client may end. However, the project typically continues to ensure that the project team hammers out any operational glitches as soon as they become apparent. For large projects especially, clients usually retain the project team for several months at least, until it has fully tested and evaluated the finished work for its intended use and it becomes clear that everything is working as planned.

Mi casa es su casa?

Failure to take care of small details can lead to catastrophic failures, as seen in southern Spain. Over the past 20 years, thousands of new homes have been built along the Mediterranean coast. The project management at each site and phase has, on the face of it, been first class throughout. Presentations to prospective home-owners were strong enough to attract large numbers of buyers from the UK, as well as from Germany and the Netherlands. The result was the regeneration and development of what had been a quiet area along the southern Spanish Mediterranean coast.

Everyone agreed that the houses were built to a really high standard. The buyers believed the houses were top quality, cost-effective and affordable. Everyone was happy!

But not for long. When the Spanish authorities came to register the new homeowners, they found that many of the houses had been built without planning permission; the project managers had made various assumptions that they could get away with not seeking proper planning permission. But they couldn't get away with it: the Spanish regional authorities in Alicante, Valencia and Malaga ordered the demolition of any house for which planning permission had not been explicitly and formally granted. Without planning permission, houses weren't covered by insurance. People whose homes were demolished lost everything.

Across the country, all the Spanish regional authorities looked to see whether they too had houses without planning permission. The result: many more properties were demolished.

This situation left the banks that had provided mortgages and other finance with a large port-folio of properties that were now worthless. As a result, people lost confidence in the property market. House values across the country fell by up to three-quarters in some areas. For the banks, the debts became unserviceable. In May 2012, La Caixa and Bankia, two of Spain's larg-est retail banks, announced that they could not meet their obligations and demanded up to €20 billion to bail them out.

The lesson is that if you get any part of project work wrong, or fail to complete a critical task, then you cause untold trouble for the future. In any project work, you must attend to all of the details if you are to succeed.

Time after Time: Setting and Meeting Deadlines

In project work, time is of the essence. Getting milestones and deadlines in place is key. In this section, I fill you in on two key issues related to time:

- ✔ The critical path of a project
- ✔ The absolutes of project work

Critical paths

The *critical path* of a project shows:

✔ The longest amount of time you may need to carry out a project

✔ The least amount of time in which you can carry out the work

Figure 19-1 is a network diagram showing a critical path.

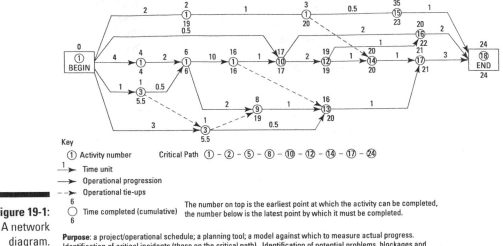

Key

① Activity number

①→ Time unit

→ Operational progression

--→ Operational tie-ups

6
○ Time completed (cumulative)
6

The number on top is the earliest point at which the activity can be completed, the number below is the latest point by which it must be completed.

Critical Path ① – ② – ⑤ – ⑧ – ⑩ – ⑫ – ⑭ – ⑰ – ㉔

Figure 19-1:
A network
diagram.

Purpose: a project/operational schedule; a planning tool; a model against which to measure actual progress. Identification of critical incidents (those on the critical path). Identification of potential problems, blockages and hold-ups.

After you've worked out the longest and shortest possible time frames, you can structure sub-schedules and activities. In this way, you know when to order resources, staff, technology, expertise and everything else that you need to deliver the project on time.

It is also important to identify critical incidents within the process. Here are some ways in which those involved in projects normally classify critical incidents:

✔ If the project team has to carry out events in a particular order, make sure that this sequence is clear in advance.

✔ If you have to order technology or expertise for a particular date or time, include this fact within your network.

✔ Note where holdups will occur if individuals don't carry out a particular activity on time.

When you're looking at time networks and the critical paths, be sure to factor in those things that you can't control, whatever the size, scope and scale of the project. Especially for larger and longer-term projects, you need to be aware of the following:

✔ **What happens if a supplier, contractor or consultant goes bankrupt or is otherwise unavailable when the time comes:** If you've scheduled such work from them many months, or even years, into the future, you need to have a contingency plan. If you're depending on the work in order to meet constraints and project demands and you don't get the work done, you hold up everything else.

✔ **What happens if the client requests modifications:** If the client asks for modifications, you have to factor these in. If the needs or changes are time-critical, failure to do these when requested delays delivery of the project.

✔ **What happens if you have to hold things up:** If you have to change the critical path, you need to let everyone know. You may have to negotiate changes in schedules and deliveries with contractors, consultants and experts. And they may not be readily available when you need or want them.

When arriving at your critical path, make sure that you've factored in all these elements. Identify the earliest and latest that you can start each element of the project. And be clear on the trouble that you'll cause yourself and the whole project if you have to change the schedule – whether for reasons outside your control or not.

Some absolutes

In addition to the critical path, other time absolutes exist in project work. Here are a few examples:

✔ If something takes 20 days to achieve, you can't speed up the process simply by throwing money and other resources at it.

According to an old Russian proverb (aren't proverbs always old?), 'You can't make a baby in one month by working nine times as hard.' Some activities have time absolutes attached to them. Be sure that you know what they are.

✔ If someone has told you that he's available to deliver his expertise or contribution only at a particular time, you have to work around this.

✔ If you need something by a particular date (for example, the opening of the Olympics, Christmas, a visit by the Queen), this date is your absolute deadline. Start at this point and work backward from it, fitting everything in accordingly.

> ✔ If, as the result of your deadline, you've a clear trade-off between finishing the job but with reduced quality or completing only part of the job but to the required quality, you've a clear choice to make.

In practice, most things are negotiable. If there are absolutes, then make these clear to everyone at the outset. However, if you're involved in project work, avoid giving the impression to the client that everything around you is chaotic. This reinforces the need to have the best possible client relationship (refer to the 'Working with the client' sidebar, earlier in this chapter).

Managing Projects Like a Pro

Project work is hard enough to complete on time, and to cost, quality, and security and safety constraints. However, the following sections can help you manage like a pro.

Following top management tips

Incorporate this guidance into your project management expertise and practice and you won't come a cropper:

> ✔ **Decide what the project specification includes, and what it doesn't.** When somebody asks you to do something along the way, or asks for additional resources, you've a clear basis on which to give your answer. If the scope of the project includes what the person's requesting, you say yes. Otherwise, the answer is no.
>
> If you agree to changes without reference to the project specs, the project easily starts to drift and you lose or dilute the overall purpose.
>
> ✔ **Make sure that you draw up the project plan in full detail before you start work.** Keep the plan up to date, and include any changes. Give everyone a copy of the project plan so they know where their contribution fits in and why that contribution is important.
>
> ✔ **Always keep at the front of your mind the business case for the project, and the value that the project is supposed to deliver when completed.** You need to do this when delivering project work internally, in which case you've a defined statement of value to which to work. It also applies, of course, when delivering projects for clients, who state their own business case for you to work to.

Get agreement for any changes as early as possible in the project lifecycle. If you agree changes at the conception and design stages, little harm is done or cost incurred. But if changes become necessary late into the work itself, they're expensive and time-consuming, and you can bet that they're going to push the overall costs up and disrupt the final phases of the work. They can even lead to delays on the completion and handover.

 Project management is becoming recognised in the UK, and in many other places as well, as an expertise and discipline in its own right. Getting professional and expert training and development in project management stands you in excellent stead for the future. In the UK (as well as in North America), the Association for Project Management (APM; www.apm.org.uk) runs a professional qualification for those wanting to develop their skills, knowledge, behaviour and expertise in the field. This qualification is widely recognised, and it lays the foundation for managerial effectiveness.

 Project work, and the management of projects, requires a high degree of energy, enthusiasm and commitment, as well as expertise. If you can develop this expertise, as well as the energy and enthusiasm, not only are you going to be an expert project worker and manager, but you'll also become highly sought after!

There is also the PRINCE2 project methodology. PRINCE stands for 'projects in controlled environments' and PRINCE2 is the second version of the programme-led approach that takes you through all of the techniques and expertise that you need to provide the basis for excellent project work. And you could check out *PRINCE2 For Dummies* by Nick Graham (Wiley), available from all good bookshops!

Designing and structuring project organisation

In addition to being a pro at project management techniques, you need to have properly organised structures in order to deliver successful and effective project work. Here are the elements that you need:

- ✔ **Work-based schedules:** Schedules that state clearly what various members of the project team must do at particular times.

- ✔ **People-based schedules:** A variation of the work-based schedule, showing who needs to be in particular places, at particular times.

- ✔ **Estimating expertise:** A view as to the effectiveness and accuracy of the costs and benefits of the particular project.

✓ **Quality management and supervision:** Making yourself as expert as possible in every aspect of the project and then seeing for yourself whether the project team is delivering it to quality, as well as on time and to cost.

You also need to develop your own monitoring, review and evaluation expertise at all phases of the project. Look especially at the extent to which you met your cost and time constraints. If you did so, you can reflect on the reasons why, and the information and data that you took into account. If you didn't, identify the points at which you (and the project itself) started to go wrong. Use all this data to inform your planning for future projects. This process also helps you develop your expertise in the time and cost areas for the future.

Structure also entails fully effective administrative support. For larger projects, this support means creating a dedicated project office. The project office:

✓ Indicates where and when problems are likely to arise

✓ Keeps a tight rein on costs and expenditure, and maintains ledgers and accounts

✓ Keeps the project plan and work-based schedules up-to-date

✓ Keeps you informed of specific dates and milestones

✓ Makes sure that everybody works to their schedules

✓ Orders technology, expertise and raw materials so that they arrive at the project when required

Finally, the question of project leadership. If you're put in charge of a project, you sometimes need to defer to the expertise of others, even though you remain in overall authority and are accountable for the project's success or failure. So you need to have as much confidence as possible in the expertise that you bring in. You also need to know when to defer to those with expertise, when to override them and why.

Chapter 20

Using Technology to Your Best Advantage

*I*n this day and age, technology is essential to every organisation. A key part of business is identifying what technology can do for you and how to use it successfully. In this chapter, I fill you in on these subjects. I also show you some misuses and abuses of technology, and explain why they occur. I tell you how technology affects competition, and product and service delivery. Finally, by its nature, technology is always evolving, so I close out the chapter by considering the question of obsolescence and replacement.

Seeing What Technology Is and What It Can Do for You

All parts of an organisation use technology. Technology is integrated into production, service, administrative and support functions. And, as such, it represents a major business overhead. You need to plan your use of technology and have in place a strategic approach to its implementation, usage, depreciation, write-off, obsolescence and replacement.

In order to decide what you need from technology, you need to know

- Who your customers are and what they expect from you in terms of quantity, quality and reliability

- What your competitors are providing that you aren't, and what you're providing that your competitors aren't

- The supply side of your business

- Where investment in technology and the expertise needed to maximise its potential will make a difference

Clearly, this process varies among organisations. However, any business should evaluate each of the following areas when it comes to technology:

- Advertising and marketing

- Communications among staff, departments, divisions and functions

- Customer, supplier and distribution management

- Information management

- Manufacturing (if you're in production) or service delivery management (if you're in services)

- Project work and project management

- Service delivery and support, as well as managing customer relations

Think about where you can improve or tighten your operations and activities, and the contribution that technology makes in support of this goal.

 The key driver to implementing technology is this question: Will introducing new technology enable you to do the work faster, to a higher value and quality, more accurately and with fewer errors than what you have already? If the answer is yes, then you can begin to plan. If the answer is no, look elsewhere.

In the following sections, I talk about what technology does for you and how to use technology.

Recognising the value of technology

Measuring and assessing the value of *anything* is hard, and doing so for technology is no different. Consider the value of technology to:

- **Business development,** through gaining access to social media and engaging in digital and viral marketing

- **Customers,** in terms of reducing complaints and increasing product and service quality

REAL WORLD EXAMPLE

Barcode breakdown

Some years ago, P&O Ferries tried to replace its ticketing processes with a barcode. This barcode would be printed out and stuck on car windscreens. P&O introduced technology that could read a barcode every 15 seconds.

Blinded by the dazzle of 'every 15 seconds', P&O introduced the technology without piloting or testing it. It quickly became apparent that 'every 15 seconds' was possible only in perfect or laboratory conditions. The technology couldn't read a barcode if it was creased, if the weather was bad or if the car was more than 5 yards from the scanner. In practice, when handling car ferry operations, all these situations occurred. Plus, customers found that getting the barcode printout off the car windscreen after it had been fixed in place required a serious scrubbing and washing effort.

Finally, it turned out that 'every 15 seconds' was far from accurate. In perfect conditions, the barcode system could process four cars every minute. However, in *actual* conditions, taking into account the fact that people were driving up to the scanner and then waiting for it to activate, it took 30 to 90 seconds to process each car. When this fact was related to the practical need of processing up to 1,500 cars per hour, it quickly became clear that it was the wrong technology, in the wrong place, at the wrong time. It was delivering a particular service less effectively, more slowly and with a greater number of faults than what had been in place with the previous ticketing system.

The bottom line: technology can easily dazzle people, but after you get over the 'cool factor', bring your feet back down to Earth and measure the effectiveness of the technology just as you would any other tool. Otherwise, you may end up spending a lot of time and money on something that doesn't do any good.

✔ **Staff,** in terms of making their working lives more productive, interesting and challenging, as well as in terms of creating opportunities for them for the future

✔ **The business,** in terms of increasing productivity and reducing errors and rejects

✔ **The supply side,** improving the accuracy of orders of raw materials, commodities and information

Think of value in terms of return on investment (ROI). If you make improvements to quality, accuracy, speed and service, you need to see increases in profit, turnover and productivity. Spending £1 million on technology is no use if you only generate an additional £50,000 of business.

Throwing customer service out the window

If you're like me, you've spent a lot of time trying to speak to people at your bank on the telephone. And you've experienced the frustrations of:

✔ Listening to syrupy recorded voices telling you to press different buttons for particular services

✔ Listening to (supposedly) soothing music while you wait to be connected

✔ Finally getting through to a live person, only to hear her tell you that she's the wrong person to deal with your query before she gives you another number to call

This approach is technology driven. It's not about excellent and improved customer service. However, because all the banks do this,

they've established a new industry norm for customer service. Here, banks have used technology to develop and establish a standardised approach. This approach is acceptable to customers and cost-effective to the banks. In this case, what is being delivered is of medium value rather than top quality.

Crucially for the banks (and for any other company or industry that uses this form of customer service technology), they know exactly what it costs to run these services. The cost is more or less fixed, and they can plan for it. And because this method is an industry norm, customers have to put up with it.

So, businesses can use technology to establish particular standards – and these standards don't have to be high.

So when you are evaluating technology, relate the improvements that it brings in terms of:

✔ What you can afford

✔ The size of your markets

✔ The additional value that you're delivering to your customers as well as to the ROI you need to see. Calculating ROI on technology is often very difficult in practice, because you cannot always relate each improvement in performance directly to the investment in new technology. So you need to take the elements above of affordability, markets and value into account also.

Be sure to measure value from the perspective of the users too. If you invest in technology, your people have to be willing to learn and use it. Making technology part of your company behaviour and culture isn't straightforward. If you don't consult with your staff, you may encounter a lot of resistance from people who don't want to give up their old and comfortable ways. You may also encounter resistance from people whose career paths change as a result.

To get support from your employees, make sure that they're involved. Here are a few ways to draw them in:

- ✔ Ask your employees what technology they need to do their jobs better.

- ✔ Show employees what technology is available and how it can make their lives easier, and more productive and rewarding.

- ✔ Provide incentives for using the technology, and ensure that people are rewarded for progress and advancement.

- ✔ Make the whole process of adopting new technology as participative and rewarding as you can.

Using technology

You use technology to secure and enhance your competitive position, and produce better quality and volumes of products and services than you could without technology.

Whatever technology you use, you need to plan for it and evaluate it. Technology planning usually covers a period of time into the future, as well as meeting present demands. You need to structure your planning to train (and, if necessary, retrain), all members of staff in what you implement.

In practice, many companies and organisations purchase technology and IT systems without looking to the future, and without considering what they already have. Here are some key points to remember:

- ✔ **Don't buy technology just because that technology is fashionable.** It has to make sense for your business and your activities.

- ✔ **Plan for the right period of time.** Some business environments are pretty stable and predictable, so it makes sense to plan three to five years into the future. But if your environment is more volatile, that time-frame may be reduced to as little as six months.

- ✔ **Make the planning process a team effort.** Get everyone involved.

- ✔ **Get feedback from your customers.** Make sure that the systems are as user-friendly as possible for them.

- ✔ **Balance the costs of upgrading your present systems against going into new systems.** Be clear about the additional benefits that any upgrade is going to deliver, relative to what you have now.

Nothing is perfect. When you look at technology for what it can do, also ask yourself what it *can't* do, where the flaws are, and what else you need or want it to do. That way, you arrive at an informed view and you won't be disappointed when the technology arrives.

Following are some other key concerns in the use of technology.

Working practices

Working practices have to relate to operational demands. For example, you have to keep plastic extrusion technology working continuously. Cleaning and restarting it if it stops costs many thousands of pounds, so you have to have someone on duty all the time. Another example: chemical production requires expert staff on hand all the time in cases of accidents, shutdowns and errors in the computer programs that determine and implement the chemical mixes. In both cases, businesses have to make commitments in terms of staffing and expertise. These commitments are part of the overall investment and costs of the technology.

In your own use of technology, consider the outlay on equipment and the other costs associated with its usage. Be sure to include the costs of employees, service, upgrades and replacements. Include the costs of buying and using portable or mobile technology.

The bill can quickly come to many thousands of pounds. If you multiply this amount by the number of people you employ, you get an idea of the critical need to make the use of technology as productive as possible.

Safety

You have to ensure the safety of everyone using technology.

For industrial production technology, ensuring safety is straightforward – industrial designers include safety processes and procedures at the point of commissioning and implementation. Companies then provides any specialist training, clothing or equipment required and put specific procedures in place for what to do in an emergency.

But screen and computer usage have to be safe also. Safety (and health) issues are less clear and obvious in these cases. Here are the issues that you need to be aware of:

✔ Alienation and isolation (from spending your whole working day with a computer rather than with other people)

✔ Back problems (from sitting in one position for too long)

✔ Headaches, especially migraines

✔ Repetitive strain injuries from keyboard usage

✔ The effects on people's eyesight

These matters aren't easy to identify or quantify, but you have to try.

The wider effects of technology in the workplace

If technology has transformed the ways in which companies and organisations do business, it has also transformed working lives. Instead of having people come into work, you can give them technology and equipment, and they can work anywhere, any time.

If you're in productive activities, many of your employees have become machine minders rather than craftspeople or technicians. Where once productive activities were carried out on an individual basis, now all that's necessary is to set up a machine – then you can produce as many or as few of the items as you need. You simply reset the machine for its next productive activity. The set-up requires its own skills and expertise, of course, and staff need training. But today the skills and expertise are in setting the machine, instead of producing the item.

If you're in web-based activities, you're likely to offer your employees (or, indeed, require them to work) non-standard shift patterns and hours. You need to do so because websites have to be updated around the clock.

If you're in technology-based maintenance activities, you're likely to have to work non-standard hours. Technology, equipment and websites need to be maintained and repaired when they break down or crash, and they can break down or crash at any time.

The demands that you're placing on your staff are evolving along with technological developments and advances, technology changes, locations and hours of work. In many cases, technology also changes the working environment and working relations. Here's why:

- ✔ People don't have the same hours as their co-workers.

- ✔ People don't have the same numbers of co-workers, so the human and social aspects of work change.

- ✔ People don't have the same face-to-face relations because many of their interactions are now by phone or email.

- ✔ Even if people do turn up to work, they're likely to be working on widely varying schedules –and others too have irregular patterns of attendance.

On an individual basis, you're often empowering people, giving them more control over their working lives and developing them as individuals.

However, see this point in context: you're also not giving them any collective identity or sense of belonging to the organisation. They no longer have the physical and human contact with the people with whom they'd be working if you still used traditional patterns of work. And you may find yourself the subject of resentment if they think that you're impinging on the non-working parts of their lives.

So changes and developments in technology in turn change and affect every aspect of organisational life and structure, and these changes and developments affect every aspect of the lives of the people who work for you. And while some of these changes appear to be good and beneficial, others need very careful consideration to ensure that they are indeed positive.

WARNING! Give people regular and substantial breaks away from screens. (In the UK, employers are required to give people at least a 15-minute break every two hours.) And if these issues become a serious cause for concern in your company and its work, seek professional occupational health advice about how to manage the human side while at the same time getting the work done.

Security

For industrial and production technology, you need to be prepared for shutdown, malfunction or emergency. You need:

- Shutdown mechanisms
- Early warning systems
- Staff to be on hand to make sure that the particular shutdown or emergency is quickly contained
- Procedures that tell people what to do

For information systems, security of data is a major issue. Here are the systems and procedures you must have in place:

- Backups in case your data stores and banks malfunction or crash
- Clear definition of access to particular information and data
- Firewall technology to prevent people breaking into and corrupting your systems and data
- Protections to ensure that you don't accidentally release confidential information into the public domain
- Standards that ensure that your people don't accidentally leave their laptops and smartphones lying around

Security of financial transactions must be absolute. Anyone who buys or sells online must commit to all the systems necessary to ensure that individual transactions, including financial and personal data, are fully secure. Any personal and financial data that you store – whether your customers' or your employees' – must also remain secure. Anything bought or sold online must meet the same constraints as the retail or wholesale equivalent – customers must get what they ordered, and they must pay the price that they agreed to and the transaction must be secure. If anything goes wrong, companies must provide redress.

If your organisation gains the reputation of not being fully secure, you'll quickly lose business. Those who succeed in online transactions do so only because their security is known and believed to be absolute. Security has to be an absolute priority and commitment as part of your technology investment.

Security and confidence

A little while ago, a senior civil servant at the Ministry of Defence was on his way home from work. He was tired and had fallen asleep. As the train approached his station, he woke with a start, picked up his bag and rushed to jump off. He had left his laptop on the train. The laptop was full of sensitive, restricted information that could have been of immense value to hostile powers.

The laptop was never found. The security authorities assessed in full the potential damage to Britain's security. Although it was found to be potentially serious, the assessment ultimately concluded that a professional enemy security service would have found nothing on the laptop that it couldn't have worked out for

itself. What was much *more* serious was the loss of confidence. Britain's allies would now start to wonder just how secure the data that they had provided was. The Ministry of Defence wondered whether it should change its procedures and working practices.

All this drama occurred because of something that most people have done. This story indicates just how easily a security breach occurs (whatever line of business you're in). It also indicates that technology changes personal responsibilities, patterns of behaviour, obligations and accountability. Technology doesn't make life easier – it just changes the complexities.

Focusing on Information Technology

Everyone has information technology (IT) of one sort or another. Even the smallest independent operator uses IT in ordering supplies, keeping accounts up to date and managing stock levels. At the other end of the spectrum, the largest and most diverse organisations in the world use IT as one of the major cornerstones of their existence. They have IT systems to keep in touch with each other, to manage on a daily basis and to inform strategic and operational decisions.

IT won't solve your business problems. Who uses the IT, why and how they use it is critical to its value. So make sure that what you have is user-friendly, as well as secure, comprehensive and fit for your purposes.

You're looking for IT to:

- ✔ Build and develop loyal relationships with customers
- ✔ Link with strategic partners to speed up processes such as product development and manufacturing

✔ Link everyone in the company with everyone else, as well as with necessary sources of information within and outside the company

✔ Provide immediate information on pricing, products and services to suppliers and customers

✔ Provide speedy responses to customer and supplier complaints, as well as product and service problems

When you've the capability to link everyone in your business to central sources of information, and then you let your customers and suppliers tap into certain areas of that information, you gain enormous power.

Information is valuable. And if you provide the effective means for managing and using that information to your advantage, you develop your competitive position still further.

Identify the capacity that you need in your IT systems. Some organisations install new systems, or upgrade what they already have, to cope with today's business volumes 'plus a bit more'. But this approach is no longer good enough. You need projections and forecasts that state what would happen if website traffic and IT usage were to double, treble or more. You need to determine the largest conceivable upload and download volumes that you may have to handle, then get quotes for different systems and capacities, instead of just going with something that looks comfortable or familiar.

When evaluating information technology, keep in mind the following key points:

✔ **Recognise that you aren't an expert.** By all means, make sure that you get to know as much as possible in all technology and IT matters with which you have direct contact. But know that IT is an expertise in its own right. If you had a legal issue, you'd call a lawyer, so why not call an IT expert if you've an IT issue? Doing so frees up your time to be doing what you do best, and saves money and stress in the long run.

✔ **Be clear about what you want out of the system.** The new system has to integrate with what you already have, and process, store and retrieve the information that you already have, as well as new material.

✔ **Involve as many people as possible who are going to use the technology in its commissioning and implementation.** That way, you'll get early and first-hand knowledge and experience of the things that are important to them.

Look before you leap

One top and famous university struggled for over ten years with its IT systems before it realised that it needed a truly strategic approach based on capacity, demand and potential growth. Here are some of the problems it had faced in the past:

✔ Teaching and lecture theatre technology, and teaching and learning support systems crashed regularly.

✔ Financial and HR information was only available at certain times of the day because of other demands on the systems at peak times.

✔ Suppliers' invoices were lost within the system.

✔ Student information was lost or corrupted. Notoriously, one department found itself going back to a cohort of final-year students and asking them what marks they'd achieved throughout their periods of study because part of the system had wiped out the results.

✔ A number of offers of places on courses made to potential students were lost.

✔ Email systems were upgraded three times in four years to accommodate increases in traffic.

✔ The university authorities told everyone who worked at the university not to use the student information and support systems during peak periods because they would corrupt and crash. This resulted in other peaks occurring – with the same corruptions and crashes.

✔ Teaching and learning support systems regularly failed to save student work and other data.

This last item finally caused the university to admit that it had no real idea what technology or IT capability or capacity it needed or wanted. Accordingly, the university's top management took two days out with external experts and consultants to thrash out the problems and difficulties. For the first time, the university's top management was forced to define what it needed and wanted in terms of IT capacity. Only then was a fully comprehensive strategic approach devised.

✔ **Ask 'Why?'** Asking questions is key, especially when you're being asked to make a substantial investment in technology replacements and upgrades. You aren't rejecting the idea – you simply want to know why this idea is the best solution. Bring a business view to technology issues and problems. However wonderful a system is, it only has value if it does the job that you need.

✔ **Be clear about what your ROI is and where it will come from.** See the nearby sidebar 'Measuring ROI'.

Measuring ROI

When it comes to IT systems, you can't measure ROI exactly. However, you can make a start by looking at it from the point of view of the damage to ROI if the systems aren't adequate, secure or easy to use. Consider the following:

✔ Corrupted documents that are illegible or have to be substantially rewritten after users open them

✔ Emails that delete themselves when the recipients open them

✔ Loss of clarity and integrity of financial and numerical data, meaning that anything involving numbers and statistics gets called into question

✔ Percentage of orders lost as the result of system malfunction

✔ Retrieved data that differs from the data that was stored

If you project these issues using example percentages (for example, what's the cost to the business of losing 1 per cent, 10 per cent or 20 per cent of orders), you begin to see what you're investing in. And if the average value of each order is £100, and you take 20 orders a day, then the ROI, even when calculated in this nebulous way, quickly becomes tangible.

Don't be be blinded by science or the brilliance of information technologists, nor feel pressurised into accepting something just because an expert in the field says that you should do so. Say 'no' to technology improvements and upgrades until you've seen the business case for them. You don't want to be in the position of having something that's intrinsically wonderful but not effective or productive in your environment.

Bringing Technology to Bear on Your Products and Services

Production and service technology exists to ensure that you work more quickly, more cost-effectively, with fewer faults and errors, and to higher standards and quality than would otherwise be possible. This concept needs to be your guide at all times when considering both the technology itself and upgrades and replacements.

You have to accept additional factors and costs, including the following, when you're considering production and service technology:

✔ Maintenance schedules

✔ Projections of likely useful life

> ✔ Replacement and upgrade costs
>
> ✔ Staff training
>
> ✔ Website hosting costs

When you're satisfied that your systems will deliver all this, you've the basis for progress. Otherwise, you need to reconsider what's on offer and look elsewhere.

Keeping time with a Swiss watch

In the 1960s, the Swiss watch industry, which had existed for hundreds of years, began to collapse. The watches produced in Switzerland were expensive, produced by individual craftsmen and of varying quality. When digital technology came along, it was adopted by Far Eastern manufacturers. These manufacturers quickly found that they could produce watches that were cheap and much more accurate than the Swiss equivalent.

Nicolas Hayek was asked to evaluate the Swiss watch industry and to recommend to the government whether the industry should be closed down altogether. A manufacturing expert, Hayek had made a name for himself by evaluating the technology that the Swiss army used. Turning his attention to the watch industry, he asserted that it could be saved as long as it:

✔ Invested in production technology

✔ Developed a mass brand

The Swiss government agreed, and Hayek went ahead.

The mass brand became Swatch. Hayek found that Swatch could produce watches as cheaply and to the same quality as anything made in the Far East through investment in the latest production technology. Accordingly, watch manufacturing shifted away from craftsmen to machines. Machines now produced the components to the highest possible standards. These components were then used to manufacture and deliver the mass brand in large enough quantities to ensure the enduring viability and profitability of the Swiss watch industry.

Hayek adopted the same approach as the top brands of the Swiss watch industry. To the brand values of watches carrying the Tissot and Longines names, Hayek added the crucial qualities of accuracy and reliability. The result was the resurrection and development of these brands to standards of accuracy that were better than anywhere else in the world.

Delivering the results at the end of another record year, Hayek stated: 'We now produce watches more cost-effectively than anywhere else in the world. We do this using Swiss labour, on Swiss wages, and using Swiss technology, on Swiss premises. As you know, land values in Switzerland are the highest in the world. However, because we took time to know and understand the technology, and planned strategically for the development of the industry, we now have something that can compete with anyone and anything from anywhere in the world, on quality, value and cost-effectiveness.'

As new products and services delivered by technology come on-stream, make sure that you evaluate them from the customers' point of view. If you're producing physical products, integrate your productive effort with market and customer research and responses. Evaluate the responses and look for places where you can improve product quality and delivery. In doing so, you make products more attractive. And you see what customers actually think (good and bad), rather than what you *think* they think!

If you're delivering a web-based service, you must have staff to monitor and update every aspect of the web provision on a minute-by-minute basis, 24 hours a day. For example:

- ✔ News websites update their content every time something occurs. If they didn't, the websites would quickly lose the sponsors' advertisements on which they depend for revenues.

- ✔ Travel websites need up-to-the-minute travel information. Giving people information that's days, or even hours, out of date isn't acceptable.

- ✔ Retail websites need to include new product and service ranges as soon as they become available. Customer frustration and anger builds when, as soon as they try to buy something, they get a message like: 'This product is no longer available; however, people who bought this, also bought . . .' or 'This product is currently out of stock. Please try later.'

- ✔ Business-to-business sites need to ensure that the product and service volumes that are available are completely correct. Failure to do so causes potential customers to cast around elsewhere for sites that do deliver what they promise.

However good value (or cheap) your product or service is, the fundamentals of quality and reliability must still be there. Ryanair's promise of cheap flights only holds value as long as the service is reliable and punctual. Amazon's prices only hold value if deliveries are made in the 24- to 48-hour period that it promises. If you run web-based activities such as these, you have to deliver everything that you promise or imply. And you can only deliver all your promises if your site is fully up to date.

Keeping Up with the Competition in the Technology Age

Technology has value only if it enhances the volume and quality of everything you do and increases your profitability and ROI.

In addition to production, administration and information management, you need to use technology to its best advantage in each of the following areas in order to enhance all aspects of your competitiveness:

✔ **Marketing:** You can enhance your marketing efforts with technology to ensure that your overall presentation is as excellent as possible. Use technology in the production of posters, leaflets, direct mail, sales literature, and product and service descriptions. You can also use technology to evaluate the data that you hold about your customers and clients so that you can target them to best possible effect with your products and services.

Use technology-driven media so that you come out on the first pages of search engine results, and so that you're presented as often and as effectively as possible on Facebook and Twitter. Create your own Facebook, LinkedIn and MySpace pages so that people can quickly and easily find you. Where possible, use Twitter to further your marketing and public relations effort. (For more on marketing, head to Chapter 10.)

✔ **Human Resources (HR):** HR activities use technology to sort out potential applicants that come in from recruitment websites whenever vacancies are announced. You have to tread a fine line. On the one hand, you want to attract a wide field of good-quality candidates quickly and effectively. On the other hand, you don't want to be swamped with résumés. You can use technology to manage the triggers that attract applicants online.

As you evaluate your recruitment effort, make a note of the best sources that you have for getting the staff that you need and want. In the future, make sure that you continue to attract from the most effective sources, and stop using the websites that otherwise swamp your recruitment effort. (Check out Chapter 16 for more on recruiting employees.)

The ways in which you use staff data further enhance your competitiveness from an HR point of view when you:

- Measure rates and frequency of staff turnover by occupation, location and length of service.

- Measure absence and sickness by occupation, location and length of service.

- Evaluate where your disciplinary and dismissal issues come from.

- Identify the main sources of grievances and disputes, and their content.

- Identify where and why accidents and injuries occur.

Your use of data is crucial to your development of the overall staff effort. Cut out general perceptions and preconceptions. If you use data effectively, your interventions in the HR field are informed with real evidence (please flip to Chapter 17 for more on the data used by HR).

Keeping Current with Technology

As you probably know all too well, technology has a finite useful life. You have to be prepared to replace it and upgrade it. Your technology may be rendered obsolete by someone else's invention that makes what you do uncompetitive or not cost-effective. When this happens, you have to find cost savings from elsewhere within the business or replace the technology.

This applies to all of the technology that you are using. For example:

- ✔ Production systems become obsolete, cumbersome or uncompetitive if they have to be rejigged to accommodate new designs or materials

- ✔ Information storage systems fill up invariably much more quickly than all but the most expert and enlightened managers envisage

- ✔ Website capacity needs to be capable of handling all volumes of traffic no matter how light or – crucially – heavy

- ✔ Internal intranets and email systems are constantly being upgraded as companies and organisations continually find that what they thought was over capacity is now very quickly transformed into under capacity

- ✔ Security systems are in constant need of upgrade as those who would seek to breach them are always devising new ways of breaking in.

In many cases, you need to be prepared to see the costs incurred in installing and implementing technology as 'sunk costs' rather than a capital investment that you can depreciate.

Moore's Law states that the capacity of technology doubles every 18 months. This statement doesn't mean that your technology will become obsolete in 18 months. But it does indicate the speed of technological development and the advances being made. In many cases, your technology will remain adequate for a long time into the future. But you may have to upgrade your technology sooner than you'd like – and if you put it off, you could end up losing business.

Part VII
The Part of Tens

Enjoy an additional Part of Tens chapter online at www.dummies.com/extras/businessstudies.

In this part . . .

✔ Listen, participate and volunteer! Find out how to gain as much as you possibly can from your business school experience.

✔ Further your business knowledge and develop your understanding of the business world by learning about networking, internships and volunteering.

Chapter 21

Ten Tips for Succeeding at Business School

. . . .

In This Chapter

▶ Getting involved in enriching activities

▶ Developing your enquiring mind

▶ Gaining knowledge from speakers and conferences

▶ Ticking all the books off your reading list

. . . .

So you're off to business school, or at a school, college of higher education or university. It's an exciting time. But keep in mind that you are one of many others who have the same ambitions and aspirations as yourself. So what can you do to make sure that you stand out from the rest and gain as much as you possibly can from your time at business school? Well, in this chapter, I give you ten quick-grab pointers. Take them to heart and you'll look back in years to come and know that you did your utmost to succeed.

Contribute

Everyone who works at your business school expects you to contribute. Whether you're on an undergraduate, postgraduate or executive programme, take an active interest in everything that's going on around you. Make sure also that your contribution is valuable and worthwhile.

How exactly do you contribute? Well, you're no doubt happy to do the things you're already comfortable with. If, for example, you're brilliant at organising 'out of course' events, go for it! However, don't shy away from contributing to things that you've no particular experience at or interest in – in doing so you gain experience and knowledge, which may just pique your interest.

Join the staff–student consultative committees and other bodies that enable you to have a say in what's going on and that reinforce your active engagement.

Ask Questions

At business school you attend lectures, seminars and other classes, and those running them always ask, 'Any questions?' Take advantage!

After you leave business school, you're going to be asked to justify and defend your point of view. You can get no better grounding for doing so than getting into the habit of asking questions of school, college and university lecturers and tutors, and then debating the answers with them. Asking questions develops your debating, analytical and evaluative skills.

Of course, asking questions in front of a large, knowledgeable and enthusiastic audience isn't always easy. Don't let a lack of confidence stop you! To get the best out of your course at business school, you need to push yourself out of your own comfort zone to do things that don't necessarily sit easily with you. And often the questions you ask are burning in the minds of others around you. Be the one brave enough to speak up!

Here are some top questioning tips to help you hone your technique:

- Be prepared. While the class is underway, think of questions and then think of ways in which to ask them.

- Especially if the material is contentious, make sure that you ask for alternative points of view to those being put forward.

- Think of ways to ask follow-up questions: ask for examples that support a general point; ask for further examples if the answer given was an example.

- Even if you have understood everything that has been given in the answer, ask the person to restate their answer.

- Never be afraid to say: 'I don't understand this point, so please can you explain it?' Your classmates will always be grateful for this – they too often won't have understood but were too afraid to speak up!

Look to staff members with questions too. When you come to know which members of staff have particular expertise, find the opportunity to discuss their subject with them as a key part of building your knowledge.

Go to Classes That Aren't on Your Course (In Addition to Those That Are!)

At business school you follow a course of study that's more or less prescribed. That doesn't prevent you from going to other classes and building on your fountain of knowledge and understanding. And the classes you attend may become a focus for further study and interest in the future. As a further benefit, the more that you sit in on other classes, the more you encourage others to do so also, so you're contributing to the further development of your classmates, and to the business school overall. Win-win!

In some cases you can just drop in on a class and sit and listen; in other cases, you need to ask the permission of the person running the particular event. But don't worry; they'll allow you to sit in. It's unheard of for anyone to forbid eager students from sitting in on classes!

Listen to Guest Speakers

Every business school worth its salt puts on regular events at which they invite guest speakers to present. These speakers come from every walk of industry, commerce and public service and from all kinds of occupations and companies, and they give up their time for the benefit of the generations that follow them. Go along to events, listen to the speakers and meet them where possible. Find out how the speakers got where they have and discover the mistakes that they made (a critical lesson: we all make mistakes and their value lies in the lessons learned). Then apply the knowledge you gain to your own situation.

Some guest speakers are from areas that don't interest you or that you don't know much about. Don't let that put you off attending their events, because in doing so you build knowledge and understanding that informs your career choices and future areas of activity and interest.

Attend Conferences

All business schools put on their own conferences, and most send their students to events elsewhere also. Take full advantage.

At conferences you meet students, faculty and people from industry, commerce and public services whom you would not otherwise have access to. You get to know them and the things that they do. You get a different perspective and find out things that you did not know before. And you get fresh exposure to the familiar stuff.

Be prepared to contribute (see the previous section 'Contribute'). When you go to conferences and other events, the organisers and speakers there expect audiences to have a view and to participate in the proceedings. So think of information you want to pick up – and then make sure that you do so (asking questions is an ideal way; see the section 'Ask Questions' earlier in this chapter). Then, when you return to your studies, you can relate everything that you've picked up at the conference to what you're studying, and so gain a much wider perspective.

Make the Most of Group Work

All business schools ask students to do a fair volume of group work. Whatever the subject or purpose, the groups are structured so as to give everyone the best possible chance to make their full and required contribution, and to deliver a piece of work at the end that everybody's proud of.

At all times when doing group work, you must make a full and active contribution, and take whatever steps are necessary to ensure that the rest of the members of the group are fully engaged. From time to time, this means that you're going to have to take the lead in group activities and even become the group leader for the particular assignment.

When you're leader, make sure that you know and understand everything that's going on and everyone is involved. You need to gain a handle quickly on the levels of motivation of the other group members. You don't want your own future compromised by the fact that you've had to work with unengaged and unmotivated people. So if your team members don't have the same level of commitment as yourself, then take the following steps to ensure that they get engaged quickly:

✔ Ask them why they are not engaged; listen to the answer and then respond to it. If they have problems elsewhere then make sure that the whole group knows and supports them through this. If they are slacking or freeriding, then make it clear that this will not do, and that you will get help from the tutor to sort it out if they don't now engage.

✔ Find out which bit of the work they will make a big contribution to, and agree the division of work with all of the group members.

✔ Never be afraid to go to the course tutor with problems of engagement: you don't have to carry passengers and you shouldn't.

Working with people who aren't pulling their weight isn't easy (and many would say that it's not fair!). However, if you're placed in an uncomfortable or difficult position, you can always ask for support from your faculty members or the course tutor.

Join Societies

All universities and colleges have a huge range of societies you can join. I recommend that you become involved with as many of these as possible.

Of course, some societies directly relate to your course. So from that point of view, you can become involved with societies related to business, economics, entrepreneurship, finance and banking, and so on. But also get involved with societies that are nothing to do with your course. You need to get away from the work from time to time (everyone does!). You also need to make sure that you have the same active interest in leisure pursuits that you do with your studies.

All universities and colleges also listen to proposals for the establishment of new societies. So if you have an idea for setting up something that does not presently exist, speak to the relevant authorities, gain support and away you go! Most colleges and universities have start-up funding available, to enable you to at least get your idea off the ground. And if you want support from department or faculty members, then just ask. In every department or faculty, somebody is willing to put their ideas, time and other resources into a particular proposal, and to make any contacts necessary elsewhere in the university or college.

Read

Many students these days concentrate only on getting the grades, but to gain the absolute maximum from your time at business school, this isn't enough. You need to research, read around everything and find out as much as you possibly can about whatever the subject matter is. Use the libraries, computer suites and research facilities to their maximum potential.

Each course you take at business school has a reading list. Believe it or not, the school doesn't put these lists on course outlines for fun, or to pad them out! The material on the lists is essential or highly desirable reading so that you gain the knowledge and understanding that you need for the future. So read as much as you possibly can from the lists, and make sure that you acquire and absorb the knowledge you need.

Also form your own reading lists and habits. Get into the habit, above all, of looking once a day at:

- ✔ A newspaper or journal (whether printed or online)
- ✔ A book or article directly to do with your course
- ✔ A book or article that's nothing to do with your course

None of this reading need take long; however, it's all essential. In particular, reading about issues that have nothing to do with your course means that you constantly broaden your perspective and outlook on the world; you build a much greater fund of general knowledge than would otherwise be the case. Also, through reading you develop a much broader range of interests. You get into the habit of finding out about new things, which can stimulate interest in a particular subject.

Volunteer

Schools, colleges and universities are always looking for volunteers. You can volunteer for activities that relate to your course of study, and activities in other areas. Here are the benefits of volunteering:

- ✔ **Action:** You get involved in *doing* things rather than studying things.
- ✔ **Contribution:** Volunteering is one way of putting your developing knowledge, understanding and expertise to work, and is a great contribution, both to the university or college and to the world at large.
- ✔ **Experience:** You broaden your all-round experience. Whether helping to put on a conference, working with the deprived or helping to settle new students into the university or college, you're building your skills, knowledge and understanding of how people behave and how things work.
- ✔ **People:** You get to work with people you don't otherwise know. And when you're doing volunteer work with people that you do know, you get a fresh perspective on their character, and you begin to sort out those who are prepared to work hard from those who are not!

So make sure that when volunteers are called for, you're one of the first to say 'Yes!'

Enjoy!

Last and most important: make sure that you enjoy your time at business school! Take the opportunity to make friends, build networks and get involved with as much as you possibly can, so your time as a student is rich, rewarding and fulfilling. Going to business school (or for that matter going to study anything at school, university or college) isn't an opportunity afforded to everyone, so make the most out of every opportunity and experience that comes your way.

Chapter 22

Ten Ways to Put Your Knowledge to Work Outside the Classroom

. . . .

In This Chapter

▶ Gaining experience with internships, volunteering and casual jobs

▶ Digging deep to find out about businesses

▶ Building effective networks

▶ Getting mentors on board

. . . .

The only way to develop the knowledge and understanding that you gain at business school is to put it to use outside the classroom. You need to push yourself in every direction, constantly looking for experiences and *making* opportunities arise by being proactive. No experience is wasted: you continually relate what you discover at business school to the world of work, and vice versa.

In this chapter, you find ten key areas to focus on outside of the classroom, ensuring growth of your business knowledge. From internships and work experience to networking and mastering your CV, you find out about the best ways to develop your understanding of the business world.

Taking Internships

Major companies and organisations offer *internships* – periods of work arranged, agreed and structured for undergraduates, postgraduates and those on executive programmes. Internships:

✔ Allow you to get to know the companies and organisations, and the work that they do

✔ Allow the companies and organisations to get to know you, and what you're like

✔ Give you an insight into the sort of work that you'd actually be asked to do should you join them

If you get the opportunity, you should take an internship. With the jobs market as it is, every chance to shine in front of an employer, and every opportunity to build your CV with work experience, is vital. Even if the internship is only a short one, you should take it if offered.

Companies and organisations expect interns to be effective in what they're asked to do while at work, whatever the length or nature of the internship.

Internships last one to four months, or a year. Taking short internships gives you a good, broad range of knowledge and understanding. But keep in mind that you won't gain as wide an experience of the company or organisation as you would get over a year. Also, you may have a great time for a month, but yet fail to understand in full the commitment required to work for a more extended period of time.

Get as much internship experience as you possibly can. All companies and organisations look at business school graduates in terms of what they've done as well as their grades; and the more you've done, the more your CV and experience stand out from the rest.

Because times are hard, you may not get the internship of your choice. Picture the scenario: you've tried and tried to get an internship in a finance company – and you've failed. Suddenly, along comes an opportunity to work for a high-fashion retailer. What do you do? All things being equal, you take the opportunity. You're adding to your CV/resume all of the time. You're building up the body of your experience; and you may find that you enjoy high-fashion retail and want to make a career in this area after all.

Working Outside of Your Studies

Make sure that you get other work experience beyond that which your course can give you. The benefits of wide experience in the world of work are that you get to understand:

- The nuts and bolts of doing frontline work
- Customer reactions – different customers react in different ways according to the levels of service that you provide
- What it takes to get effective and profitable business delivered, and how customers and clients react and respond to excellent service

Work experience stands you in good stead for when you go out to work in your chosen career. Many companies and organisations insist that their graduates start work on the frontline of the business. So, for example:

> ✔ A marketing management trainee at Unilever may go to corner shops to sell chocolate products.
>
> ✔ A banking trainee may work as a cashier for a period of six months.
>
> ✔ A technology consulting trainee may spend three months writing up a project to evaluate all the work that the particular client does.

A great deal of casual work is enjoyable and fulfilling. You have to work to other people's standards, deliver excellent service and work with people you wouldn't otherwise necessarily come across. And if you approach everything with a sunny and positive attitude, you spread this attitude to others – sunny and positive attitudes are always infectious!

Volunteering

As well as volunteering as part of your college or university activities, volunteer in the community so you can put your knowledge to work.

Countless organisations in every community ask for volunteers – indeed, many depend on volunteers for their very existence. Find out what opportunities are available, make arrangements to go and meet with the organisations, and then choose activities that best suit your skills, interests and available free time.

Maintain high standards in your volunteering as you would in a job. Be punctual, be polite and be committed to the work during your volunteering period.

Visiting Companies and Organisations

All business schools arrange visits to companies and organisations (and visits from companies and organisations and their staff). Whenever opportunities to visit companies and organisations come up, take them.

Try to make sure that you get to visit those companies and organisations with which you want to become familiar. If a visit isn't provided as a part of your business school activities, then seek out those at the school who can put you in touch with the companies in which you're interested.

While you're visiting companies and organisations, observe the ways in which staff conduct themselves. Look also at the furnishings, technology and other equipment that they use. Get a feel if you can for the ambience and culture, and the ways in which staff behave and conduct themselves while at work. Find out what particular jobs actually involve. In doing so, you form your perceptions about an organisation, which is then reinforced by your meetings and interaction with the staff and their demeanour and approach to you.

Considering Customer Service

Get plenty of first-hand experience of customer service, and also observe interactions between customers and staff. When you go to businesses – shops, travel agents, railways, the post office – analyse how staff manage customers. Note what's good and decide to incorporate it into your own customer service approach, and identify issues so you never repeat the mistakes you see.

Observe the levels of customer service at places that are perceived to have a top-quality approach. In the UK, go to places like John Lewis and Marks & Spencer. Compare and contrast the customer service in organisations that pride themselves on this aspect of their business with those that have poor customer service. Work out how the weaker organisations can improve, and how the good organisations can ensure that standards remain high.

Networking

All your business school, internship, casual work, volunteering and visiting experience provides the basis for one of the most essential facilities of your life – your network. You build up a fund of personal and professional contacts to whom you can turn when you're looking for jobs and opportunities. You also use your network:

✔ When you need problems solved

✔ When you need emergency products and services at short notice

✔ In times of crisis

You need people to come and do excellent work for you, whether as staff, business partners or as experts in their field. If you take full advantage of everything a business school has to offer, and the work opportunities afforded alongside, you quickly build up the foundations of an excellent network. With the proliferation of social and professional networking websites such as Facebook (www.facebook.com) and LinkedIn (www.linkedin.com), you have the opportunity to keep fully up-to-date with your network and to develop it online. And even with contacts you've only developed online but have never actually met, as soon as the need arises you have the names of people you can turn to. And of course, they have your name too!

Evaluating Your Own Behaviour

Apply what you're discovering in business school about what makes a good employee/employer to yourself. Ask yourself, are you:

- ✔ Cheery and positive?
- ✔ Committed?
- ✔ Honest and transparent?
- ✔ Approachable?
- ✔ Even in temperament?
- ✔ Willing to help others out? (If you help others, you're much more likely to gain help from them. Everyone needs help and support from time to time; and if you show yourself to be supportive of others, you're more likely to get support in return when you need it.)
- ✔ Respectful of others at all times? (Showing politeness and respect means that you too will be treated in these ways – which enhances all working relationships.)

The more 'yes' answers you can give to these questions, the more people are going to enjoy working with you and turn to you for help and assistance; and ultimately, the more people will involve you in ground-breaking projects.

Taking positive and committed attitudes rubs off on other people. You consistently form mutually beneficial working relationships that enhance every part of your work and working life.

Reading

Your business school requires you to read textbooks, journals and online resources. But also read:

- ✔ The quality press, especially (in the UK, for example) *The Telegraph*, *The Guardian*, or *The Independent*.
- ✔ The specialist business press, especially *The Wall Street Journal*, *Financial Times*, and Bloomberg publications.
- ✔ Professional and specialist journals: these journals cover all aspects of business, and relate what you study to what goes on in the real world.

✔ Company and organisation literature. Make sure that you know about the companies, organisations and business sectors with which you're going to be involved. Show those you work with that you're well informed. Go to interviews and selection centres with as much company knowledge as possible. Know about organisations for which you volunteer. And even in casual work, know about the company employing you.

Everyone is fired up by their own business! Richard Reed, who founded Innocent Smoothies, is completely passionate about the quality of ingredients that go into his drinks. And Julian Metcalfe, who founded Pret A Manger, is completely passionate about the quality of sandwiches. Their passion draws them into every aspect of their industry, not just their own business, and includes, for example, finding out about the content and quality of ingredients, and then going out to see for themselves. So this kind of reading, and the knowledge that comes from it, is essential whatever sector you're going to go into.

Learning from Mentors

A *mentor* is someone to whom you turn for advice, guidance, information and evaluation of your work. During the course of your time at business school, build up your own group of people you can turn to when you need this kind of support and understanding.

You can find mentors among the staff, tutors and alumni at your business school, and you can find others in the world of work. Identify the people in whom you have confidence, and then choose your mentors on the basis of:

✔ Their knowledge and expertise

✔ Their personality, which needs to be patient and positive in developing you

✔ Their receptiveness to you, and confidence in you

✔ The extent to which you have confidence and faith in the person

✔ Mutual personal liking and respect

You need to identify the people in whom you have confidence and then begin to build the relationship. When you approach a potential mentor, make sure that she knows that a mentor is what you're seeking. She then knows clearly what you expect from her, and you can then go on and develop the relationship. She can then choose – or not – to mentor you.

If she agrees, you work out a pattern of meetings and contacts whereby you achieve certain things over periods of time; and you work out also what the purpose of each contact or meeting is (for example, to review progress, or to get involved in a particular project or venture). She too has her own needs from the relationship, and you must be sure to agree to these. If she has specific tasks for you to accomplish, you must do them.

Many business schools have organised mentoring programmes that match business students with alumni in similar areas of expertise and with a specific programme and time-frame. This is an ideal opportunity that students should take advantage of if available, but is still subject to the compatibility of the match.

Not everyone that you ask will agree to mentor you, and not everyone who agrees will necessarily make a good mentor. If you find that the relationship isn't working, then meet with the mentor and agree on a different approach, or else agree to end the relationship.

So make clear to anyone whom you do approach:

- ✔ Why you're approaching her
- ✔ What you would like her to do for you
- ✔ What you're going to do in return – for example, if you ask the mentor to make contacts on your behalf, you must follow them up

When you have the agreement, you then need to build the relationship so that from time to time you can:

- ✔ Approach the mentor as a sounding board with ideas
- ✔ Get help when you have problems
- ✔ Ask for guidance when opportunities come your way
- ✔ Get input when you lose out on opportunities

You base a mentoring relationship on trust. If you ask for guidance, you can debate what the mentor suggests, of course, but when the two of you determine the course of action, you must follow this decision. If circumstances change and the course of action needs to change also, then if possible debate this situation with the mentor before you implement what now needs to happen.

If for any reason things don't work out and you lose confidence in your mentor, make sure that you close the relationship on a basis of trust and respect. And always thank anyone for their time and interest in developing your career.

Creating a Winning Curriculum Vitae

Everything that you do at business school and all the experience that you gain alongside goes into one thing – your *curriculum vitae* (CV), the document that recruiters analyse to determine whether you're a suitable fit for a position. The more experience you have, the better your CV.

Here are some top tips for CVs:

✔ Keep your CV fully up-to-date and no more than two pages long.

✔ Where required, tailor your CV to the positions you're applying for. Use the knowledge that you've gained from your studies, and from your contacts with companies, to ensure that what is being asked for is well to the fore on your CV. For example, if the job is asking for IT expertise, then make sure that you emphasise this requirement.

✔ If the company asks for the CV to be presented in a particular format or template, then try to do so. Within the template, use your knowledge to ensure that you emphasise the points that they're looking for.

✔ If the company asks for a covering letter with the CV, then make sure that you emphasise what you can do for them as well as what they can do for you. Again, use your knowledge from your studies and research to ensure that you do know as much as possible about the company when applying.

Your CV won't get you a job (except in rare circumstances), but it can get you interviews and opportunities to take assessments and tests at which you can wow recruiters with your positive attitude and how you apply your knowledge and experience.

Index

• *C* •

About the Author

Richard Pettinger has taught at University College London since 1989, where he is Principle Teaching Fellow (Reader) in management education. He teaches on the foundation courses, organisational change, strategic management and consultancy courses. He has also taught the management of change, human resource management and leadership to a wide range of undergraduate, postgraduate, professional and international students. Richard is working to develop the strength of provision in the Department of Management, Science and Innovation, building an undergraduate and graduate programme in information management for business, presently ranked very highly in the UK league tables.

Since 2005, Richard has been Visiting Professor at the Jagiellonian Business School, Krakow, teaching strategic management and developing a common UCL/Jagiellonian syllabus in strategic management and organisational change. He is also presently working at Singapore Polytechnic, and with the University of Maribor, Slovenia.

Richard is the author of over 40 business and management books and textbooks, including *Management For Dummies* and *Weekend MBA For Dummies*.

Author's Acknowledgements

I acknowledge three pioneering business leaders and managers who have had great influence on the ways in which things have turned out: John Taylor, who sets very high standards all round; Jack Cadogan at the Manpower Services Commission, who let me do things my way; and Graham Winch, who started me off at UCL. I have had wonderful support and enthusiasm all the way through from Ram Ahronov, Peter Antonioni, Roger Cartwright, Kelvin Cheatle, Frances Kelly, Paul Griseri, Jacek Klich – great colleagues all round. Thanks for the great work of Erica Peters and Mike Baker, and everyone at Wiley in making this project into something that we can all be proud of. Finally, I would like to dedicate this book to my wife Rebecca, without whom nothing is possible.

Publisher's Acknowledgements

We're proud of this book; please send us your comments at `http://dummies.custhelp.com`. For other comments, please contact our Customer Care Department within the U.S. at 877-762-2974, outside the U.S. at (001) 317-572-3993, or fax 317-572-4002.

Some of the people who helped bring this book to market include the following:

Project Editor: Jo Jones

Commissioning Editor: Mike Baker

Assistant Editor: Ben Kemble

Development Editors: Elizabeth Kuball and Charlie Wilson

Technical Reviewers: Peter Antonioni and Lynn McGregor

Production Manager: Daniel Mersey

Publisher: Miles Kendall

Cover Photo: Beth Brooks

Project Coordinator: Kristie Rees

Take Dummies with you everywhere you go!

Whether you're excited about e-books, want more from the web, must have your mobile apps, or swept up in social media, Dummies makes everything easier .

| Visit Us | Like Us | Follow Us | Watch Us |
| Join Us | Pin Us | Circle Us | Shop Us |

FOR DUMMIES®

A Wiley Brand

BUSINESS

978-1-118-73077-5

978-1-118-44349-1

978-1-119-97527-4

MUSIC

978-1-119-94276-4

978-0-470-97799-6

978-0-470-49644-2

DIGITAL PHOTOGRAPHY

978-1-118-09203-3

978-0-470-76878-5

978-1-118-00472-2

Algebra I For Dummies
978-0-470-55964-2

Anatomy & Physiology For Dummies, 2nd Edition
978-0-470-92326-9

Asperger's Syndrome For Dummies
978-0-470-66087-4

Basic Maths For Dummies
978-1-119-97452-9

Body Language For Dummies, 2nd Edition
978-1-119-95351-7

Bookkeeping For Dummies, 3rd Edition
978-1-118-34689-1

British Sign Language For Dummies
978-0-470-69477-0

Cricket for Dummies, 2nd Edition
978-1-118-48032-8

Currency Trading For Dummies, 2nd Edition
978-1-118-01851-4

Cycling For Dummies
978-1-118-36435-2

Diabetes For Dummies, 3rd Edition
978-0-470-97711-8

eBay For Dummies, 3rd Edition
978-1-119-94122-4

Electronics For Dummies All-in-One For Dummies
978-1-118-58973-1

English Grammar For Dummies
978-0-470-05752-0

French For Dummies, 2nd Edition
978-1-118-00464-7

Guitar For Dummies, 3rd Edition
978-1-118-11554-1

IBS For Dummies
978-0-470-51737-6

Keeping Chickens For Dummies
978-1-119-99417-6

Knitting For Dummies, 3rd Edition
978-1-118-66151-2

FOR DUMMIES

A Wiley Brand

SELF-HELP

978-0-470-66541-1

978-1-119-99264-6

978-0-470-66086-7

LANGUAGES

978-0-470-68815-1

978-1-119-97959-3

978-0-470-69477-0

HISTORY

978-0-470-68792-5

978-0-470-74783-4

978-0-470-97819-1

Laptops For Dummies 5th Edition
978-1-118-11533-6

Management For Dummies, 2nd Edition
978-0-470-97769-9

Nutrition For Dummies, 2nd Edition
978-0-470-97276-2

Office 2013 For Dummies
978-1-118-49715-9

Organic Gardening For Dummies
978-1-119-97706-3

Origami Kit For Dummies
978-0-470-75857-1

Overcoming Depression For Dummies
978-0-470-69430-5

Physics I For Dummies
978-0-470-90324-7

Project Management For Dummies
978-0-470-71119-4

Psychology Statistics For Dummies
978-1-119-95287-9

Renting Out Your Property For Dummies, 3rd Edition
978-1-119-97640-0

Rugby Union For Dummies, 3rd Edition
978-1-119-99092-5

Stargazing For Dummies
978-1-118-41156-8

Teaching English as a Foreign Language For Dummies
978-0-470-74576-2

Time Management For Dummies
978-0-470-77765-7

Training Your Brain For Dummies
978-0-470-97449-0

Voice and Speaking Skills For Dummies
978-1-119-94512-3

Wedding Planning For Dummies
978-1-118-69951-5

WordPress For Dummies, 5th Edition
978-1-118-38318-6

Printed and bound by CPI Group (UK) Ltd, Croydon, CR0 4YY